MARRIAGES
of
McMINN COUNTY,
TENNESSEE

1821-1864

MARRIAGES

of

McMINN COUNTY, TENNESSEE

1821-1864

Compiled by
EDYTHE RUCKER WHITLEY

With an Index by
Deborah G. Sherr & Richard W. Lewis

CLEARFIELD

Library of Congress Catalog Card Number 83-81459

Reprinted for Clearfield Company by
Genealogical Publishing Company
Baltimore, Maryland, 2014

ISBN 978-0-8063-1040-4

Introduction

cMINN COUNTY, Tennessee was formed on November 5, 1819, carved out of lands ceded to the United States by the Cherokee Indians. Along with McMinn County, Monroe and Bradley counties embraced the largest and best portions of the land thus ceded. The county seat at Athens was laid off in 1821/22 and by 1823 the county courts were formally established.

The marriage records of McMinn County are somewhat disorganized, but those in this compilation are all that I know anything about for the early period of the county's existence. Many of the earliest records, I am certain, have been lost, for it was not until the middle of the twenties that they were recorded in a book for preservation. Those recorded in books marked "C", "D", and "E", along with some loose bonds for the period 1821-1838, form the basis of this present work.

Once again I should like to call the reader's attention to the dates in these records. The first date given in each entry is the date of issue of either the marriage bond or license. The date following (in parentheses) is the date the marriage was performed. If no date of marriage is given, then the single date provided refers merely to the date of issue of the marriage bond and does not *prove* that a marriage actually took place.

Edythe Rucker Whitley
Nashville, Tennessee

McMINN COUNTY, TENNESSEE

Marriages, 1821-1864

Loose Bonds, 1821-1838

Rubin Johnson to Nancy A. Bryan, Nov. 8, 1821.
    Andrew Cassada, BM. (Nov. 8, 1821)
Joseph McGendey to Nancy Brown, Mar. 20, 1821.
Bark Foreman to Rachel Torbalt, Mar. 29, 1821.
    (Mar. 29, 1821)
Nathaniel Crittenden to Saprina Beckett, Dec. 17, 1823.
    By Jesse Dodson, M.G., John Gee, BM.
Banner Shields to Nancy Bailey, Nov. 29, 1823.
    Elijah Dodson, BM. (Nov. 29, 1823)
Joseph M. Dake to Margarette Desham, Aug. 17, 1824.
    By Henry Price, J.P. (Aug. 17, 1824)
James Thompson to Nancy Reed, May 4, 1824.
    By Henry Bradford, J.P. (May 4, 1824)
James Grigsby to Lidy Hedrick, June 30, 1824.
    Merady Hix, BM. (June 30, 1824)
John Crossland to Elizabeth Adams, Nov. 10, 1825.
    By James McKamy, J.P. (Nov. 10, 1825)
Coonrod Farner to Edy Cearl, Sep. 9, 1825.
    By Jas. McKamy, J.P. (Sep. 9, 1825)
Daniel Yount to Betsey Shepheard, Dec. 21, 1825.
    By James McKamy, J.P. (Dec. 21, 1825)
James Walker to Charlotte Craven Dean, Oct. 12, 1824.
    By Robert McClary, J.P., Robert W. McClary, BM.
    (Oct. 12, 1824)
Willis Smith to Polly Tabor, Sep. 28, 1825.
    By W. Porter, J.P. (Oct. 1, 1825)
Benjamin Erwin to Catharine Erwin, Dec. 20, 1825.
    By Abner Lawson, M.G. (Dec. 20, 1825)
James H. King to Douisan Center, July 4, 1825.
    By Irby Holt, P.G. (July 5, 1825)
Jesse Farmer to Martha Henderson, Aug. 23, 1825.
    By Geo. Bowman, L.P. of M.E.C. (Aug. 23, 1825)
Moses Barnes to Rebecca Benton, Jan. 1, 1825.
    Abraham Barnes, BM. (Jan. 1, 1825)
Samuel Turk to Elizabeth Dixon, Oct. 9, 1826.
    By Joseph Torbett, J.P. (Oct. 12, 1826)
Abraham Stout to Ann Brookshire, July 5, 1826.
    By Thos. W. Norwood, M.G. (July 6, 1826)
Jacob Shapman to Marthee Burk, Oct. 12, 1826.
    By John Miller, J.P. (Oct. 12, 1826)

1

James R. Sexton to Betsey Batson, Aug. 7, 1826.
  Joel Brock, BM.
Ephraim Pierce to Lucinda Hambrick, July 27, 1826.
  Robert Ritchardson, William H. Newman, BM. (July 27, 1826)
Nimrod Moore to Cassa Davis, Aug. 26, 1826.
  Joseph Dunn, BM. Aug. 26, 1826)
Ashael Bradack to Nancy Seay, Dec. 26, 1827.
  William T. Gresham, BM. (Dec. 26, 1827)
Abraham Golden to Patsey Branham, Aug. 1, 1827.
  John Spencer, BM. (Aug. 1, 1827)
Severe Bailey to Nancy Officer, Aug. 15, 1827.
  James Officer, BM. (Aug. 15, 1827)
Robert W. Porter to Menada Cates, July 29, 1827.
  Henry Amarine, BM. (July 29, 1827)
Wade H. Atkins to Elizabeth Melvin, June 29, 1827.
  By John Miller, J.P. (July 1, 1827)
Alexander Wakefield to Nancy Orr, Apr. 11, 1827.
  By Thos. W. Norwood. (Apr. 12, 1827)
John Edwards to Elizabeth Evans, June (or July) 19, 1827.
  (June or July 19, 1827)
John Wilson to Lucinda Lawson, Dec. 5, 1827.
  By Daniel Newman, J.P. (Dec. 6, 1827)
Elijah Casteel to Patience Taber, Mar. 24, 1827.
  By Merrimon(?). (Mar. 24, 1827)
Irvan Donahoo to Nancy Napier, Apr. 29, 1828.
  (Apr. 29, 1828)
John Thomasson to Louize Casst, July 14, 1828.
  Daniel McCoy, BM. (July 14, 1828)
Woodson Seay to Keziah Larrew, Aug. 20, 1828.
  By John S. Wilson, J.P. (Aug. 20, 1828)
James W. Wilson to Catharine Shamble, Aug. 1, 1828.
  C. G. Murrell, BM. (Aug. 1, 1828)
Joseph Smith to Elizabeth Roberts, Aug. 21, 1828.
  James Williams, BM. (Aug. 21, 1828)
John Blanton to Matilda Armstrong, Mar. 1, 1828.
  Isham Amorine, BM.
Joseph McVay to Nancy Edwards, May 11, 1828.
  Abraham Gonce, BM.
Absolem C. Hayes to Marthy Colwell, June 28, 1828.
  John S. Heath, BM. (June 28, 1828)
R. P. Caldwell to Elizabeth Dodson, Feb. 16, 1828.
  Jesse Dodson, BM.
Joseph Morton to Elizabeth Long, Apr. 4, 1828.
  James Lonley, BM. (Mar. 4, 1828)
Asbury M. Coffey to Mary G. Bradford, July 22, 1828.
  Jonathan Allen, BM. (July 22, 1828)
David Stephen (or Stephens) to Sarah Clemmons, Dec. 25,
  1828. Aby Coats, BM. (Dec. 25, 1828)
James Smith to Nancy Fields, Aug. 30, 1828.
  Hiram Cooper, BM. (Aug. 30, 1828)
Cary A. Armstrong to Sarah Farner, Dec. 30, 1828.
  D. Cantrell, Esq. (Jan. 2, 1829)
Thomas Humphrey to Lucinda Tinsley, Feb. 18, 1828.
  (Feb. 18, 1828)

2

William S. Baker to Adella Bailey, Sep. 1, 1828.
William Shamblin, BM. (Sep. 1, 1828)
Charles Cate to Narcessa McMillan, Dec. 1, 1828.
John H. Porter, BM.
Thomas Campbell to Dolly Snow, Nov. 6, 1828.
Izerael E. Crowell to Sarah Tate, Nov. 22, 1828.
By John S. Wilson, J.P. (Nov. 22, 1828)
Joseph H. Brown to Huldy Logan, Jan. 9, 1828.
Sidna Bolden, BM. (Jan. 9, 1828)
Robert Dugan to Louisa Aerington, Apr. 30, 1828.
James Allison, BM. (Apr. 30, 1828)
Robert Monroe to Mary Fields, May 13, 1828.
Robert Dugan, BM. (May 13, 1828)
Albia Coats to Polly Senter, May 23, 1828.
Robert Scott, BM. (May 23, 1828)
Daniel Hull to Elizabeth E. Smedley, Dec. 30, 1829.
By John Courtney. (Dec. 30, 1829)
William Lorison to Emelia Billingsley, Aug. 11, 1829.
Joseph Billingsley, BM. (Aug. 11, 1829)
Elijah Gillingwaters to Polly Weavers, Dec. 10, 1829.
By Henry Bradford, J. W. McMillin, BM. (Dec. 10, 1829)
Richard Kelly to Mary Jackson, Dec. 2, 1829.
By Cantrell, J.P. (Dec. 3, 1829)
James Duglass to Elizabeth Firestone, Oct. 8, 1829.
David Firestone, BM. (Oct. 8, 1829)
John A. Thompson to Joana Pierce, Sep. 5, 1829.
James B. Thompson, BM. (Sep. 5, 1829)
James S. Cromwell to Margaret Shields, Mar. 4, 1829.
John B. Cromwell, BM. (Mar. 4, 1829)
Fletcher Edwards to Betsey Black, Feb. 4, 1829.
Frederick Crysock, BM. (Feb. 4, 1829)
Peter Clark to Crate Humphrey, Feb. 18, 1829.
Edmond Casteel, BM. (Feb. 18, 1829)
David Cowan to Matilda Templeton, Aug. 13, 1829.
David Barden, BM. (Aug. 13, 1829)
George W. Bellew to Mary Ann Caywood, Oct. 15, 1829.
Thomas C. Ripley, BM. (Oct. 15, 1829)
William Keelin to Malinda Green, Sep. 9, 1829.
William McDonald, BM. (Sep. 9, 1829)
Benjamin Cox to Jane Hawkins, Nov. 16, 1827.
By _____ Couch, J.P. (Nov. 18, 1827)
Robert Murphy to Rebecca Jane Shields, Dec. 7, 1829.
Edward Ramsy, BM. (Dec. 7, 1829)
Bennet Arnold to Dorcas Wiseman, Oct. 27, 1829.
James M. Howell, BM. (Oct. 27, 1829)
John Erwin to Malinda Atkinson, July 29, 1829.
By John Courtney. (July 30, 1829)
Samuel Latimore to Nancy Starr, Dec. 29, 1829.
By John Belding, M.G., Wm. S. Cowan, BM. (Dec. 29, 1829)
Levil Langford to Sarah Randolph, Mar. 21, 1829.
George Weathers, BM. (Mar. 21, 1829)
Hugh Smith to Elizabeth J. Fyffe, Dec. 15, 1829.
By Robt. Tate, M.G. (Dec. 15, 1829)
George Breeden to Mary Lowry, Dec. 18, 1829.
Coonrod Stanner, BM. (Dec. 18, 1829)

Richd. Kelly to Mary Jackson, Dec. 2, 1829.
    Wm. Kelly, BM. (Dec. 2, 1829)
Alexander Wiles to Rebecka McKeean, Dec. 18, 1829.
    Alfred Thomasson, BM. (Dec. 18, 1829)
Fletcher Edwards to Betsy Black, Feb. 4, 1829.
    By J. W. McMillin, J.P. (Feb. 9, 1829)
John Camp to Polly Parkison, Feb. 16, 1829.
    By J. W. McMillin, J.P. (Feb. 18, 1829)
Saml. Morgan to Margaret Vanzant, Dec. 20, 1829.
    Ezekiel Vanzant, BM. (Dec. 20, 1829)
Edwin Ditmore to Rhoda Riggs, Dec. 8, 1829.
    John Lane, Sherwood W. Pearson, BM. (Dec. 8, 1829)
John Stead to Sarrah Harkrider, Dec. 29, 1829.
    Elias Presnell, BM. (Dec. 29, 1829)
Edmond Chambers to Elizabeth Taylor, Apr. 20, 1829.
    Wm. Caves, BM. (Apr. 20, 1829)
Boling Smith to Mildred Rogers, Apr. 25, 1829.
    Humphrey Reynolds, BM. (Apr. 25, 1829)
William Griffin to Ann L. Davis, Apr. 20, 1829.
    R. P. Bowman, BM. (Apr. 20, 1829)
Levi Lemmons to Arsley Hicks, May 4, 1829.
    By James Senter, J.P., Saml Edmissons, BM. (May 4, 1829)
Prior Lea to Minerva Heard, May 4, 1829.
    Wm. B. A. Ramsey, BM. (May 4, 1829)
James Romack to Polly McDonnell, May 14, 1829.
    By Benj. Isbell, J.P., Robert John, BM. (May 14, 1829)
Jefferson Dodson to Sarah Smith, July 23, 1829.
    John Dodson, BM. (July 23, 1829)
John F. Clark to Drucilla Amos, June 26, 1829.
    By Obediah Belding, Elihu S. Barclay, BM. (June 29, 1829)
Sipe Howell to Catharine Crow, June 18, 1829.
    Sipy T. Sewells, Thomas Guthrie, BM. (June 18, 1829)
Christian Peters to Nancy Pearce, Nov. 28, 1829.
    By Robert Dotson, J.P., Thomas G. Willett, BM. (Nov. 28,
    1829)
George Ubanks to Eliza Burch, Nov. 28, 1829.
    John Morris, BM. (Nov. 28, 1829)
Joseph Herdin to Eliza Christian, Nov. 26, 1829.
    James Christian, BM.
John Tate to Eliza Jane Wear, July 30, 1829.
    (July 30, 1829)
Saml. Barnett to Culton _____, Nov. 23, 1829.
    By Fielding Pope, M.G. (Oct. 23, 1829)
William Kitchen to Lilly Urserry, Oct. 22, 1829.
    By J. Evans, J.P. (Oct. 23, 1829)
John Jacks to Mary Ditmore, Apr. 7, 1829.
    Joseph Rabourn, BM.
John Hoyl to Mary Love, Feb. 12, 1829.
    Augustine P. Fort, BM. (Feb. 12, 1829)
John McRoy to Sarah Arnel, Mar. 24, 1829.
    Curtes McRoy, BM. (Mar. 24, 1829)
Abraham B. Neal to Rebecca Pickins, Feb. 11, 1829.
    Reece Pickins, BM. (Feb. 11, 1829)
Moses Casey to Elizabeth Coe, May 19, 1829.
    By Wm. Dotson, J.P. (May 27, 1829)

4

McMINN COUNTY MARRIAGES

Lawson W. Rogers to Marena L. Jordan, June 16, 1829.
William Hogan, BM. (June 16, 1829)
George King to Rebecca Slaughter, July 2, 1829.
John Slaughter, BM. (July 2, 1829)
Ephraim Reinhardt to Juliet Duke, May 8, 1829.
By D. Cantrell, Esq. (May 14, 1829)
David P. Loyd to Eliza Pitner, Feb. 12, 1829.
Jeptha Sivels(?), BM. (Feb. 12, 1829)
John Sutton to Nancy McCall, Mar. 2, 1829.
Benjamin S. Crow, BM. (Mar. 2, 1829)
George Wade to Ann Reid, Nov. 19, 1829.
By J. Ivans, J.P. (Nov. 19, 1829)
Fielding Pope to Theresa C. Meigs, Mar. 24, 1829.
By R. McAlpin, Solomon Bogart, BM. (Mar. 24, 1829)
Allen Burks to Tenesse Roberts, July 4, 1829.
Edmund Roberts, BM. (July 4, 1829)
Asa Smith to Rhoda Casada, Feb. 4, 1829.
By Jesse Dodson. (Feb. 5, 1829)
Frederick S. Williams to Mary Barnet, Mar. 11, 1829.
Saml. A. Ewing, BM. (Mar. 11, 1829)
John A. Lewis to Patsy Bullard, Dec. 25, 1829.
(Dec. 25, 1829)
Jacob W. Slaughter to Elizabeth King, June 24, 1829.
(June 24, 1829)
Jeremiah Pack to Jane Bailey, Feb. 12, 1829.
Andrew Pack, BM. (Feb. 12, 1829)
Peter Fite to Mary Barnet, Mar. 11, 1829.
By J. W. Norwood, (Mar. 15, 1829)
John Adams to Sely Galloway, Nov. 13, 1829.
Daniel Kelly, BM. (Nov. 13, 1829)
James Deputy to Peggy Hardin, Feb. 26, 1829.
Saml. Wheeler, BM. (Feb. 26, 1829)
Thomas L. Richardson to Francis Cate, Dec. 7, 1829.
Wesley Kenman, BM. (Dec. 7, 1829)
James H. Witt to Parthaney Kirksey, Jan. 26, 1830.
Rutherford Witt, BM. (Jan. 26, 1830)
William B. Green to Haney Owins, Dec. 21, 1829.
Russell H. Smith, BM. (Dec. 21, 1829)
James Gresham to Milly Rucker, Nov. 3, 1829.
Jesse Gresham, BM. (Nov. 3, 1829)
Major Lea to Roady Ireland, July 27, 1829.
By D. Cantrell, Esq. (July 26, 1829(?)
George Cobb to Susan Amos, Aug. 12, 1829.
William C. L. Adams, BM. (Aug. 12, 1829)
John Dodson to Elizabeth Fields, Aug. 28, 1829.
James Smith, BM. (Aug. 28, 1829)
Moses Casey to Elizabeth Coe (no date given).
James Ellison, BM.
Thompson Sanders to Nancy Fox, Apr. 5, 1830.
By Jas. M. Cartney, J.P. (Apr. 8, 1830)
Thomas Stanfield to Malinda Rush, Apr. 6, 1832.
Syrus Rush, BM.
I. S. McConnell to M. M. McClatchey, Feb. 28, 1832.
Hamilton L. Alexander, BM.

William Gibson to Jane Thompson, Apr. 12, 1834.
  Hutson Johnson, BM. (Mar. 12, 1834(?)
Hugh Lusk to Joannah Matheys, Feb. 11, 1835.
  John D. Lowery, BM. (Feb. 11, 1835)
Thomas N. Napier to Mary Shelton, Jan. 14, 1835.
  Robt. K. Hamilton, BM.
Samuel Shelton to Mary Wessengton(?), Dec. 12, 1836.
  By Jonathan Thomas, J.P. (Dec. 15, 1836)
James Rutherford to Polly Ann Dicks, ____, 1837.
Nathaniel Barnett to Martha Patty, Aug. 3, 1837.
  By R. Gregory. (Sep. 18, 1837)
John Seybert to Martha Stephenson, Mar. 6, 1837.
  By A. B. Neal, J.P. (Mar. 11, 1837)
Adam Burger to Mary Hawkins, Sep. 22, 1837.
  By Robert Randolph, M.B. (Sep. 24, 1837)
Daniel M. Helvey to Syphey Roberts, Apr. 5, 1838.
  By Henry Price, M.G. (Apr. 5, 1838)

Book "C" 1838-1848

William Logan to Malinda Cantrell, Feb. 19, 1838.
By Samuel Carlock, J.P. (Feb. 20, 1838)
William T. Burk to Adaline Amanda Carter, Feb. 14, 1838.
By Wm. Shamblin, J.P. (Feb. 15, 1838)
Banister Colin to Polly Armstrong, Feb. 19, 1838.
By Saml Lowan, J.P. (Feb. 19, 1838)
Michael Zargles to Malinda Mansell, Feb. 6, 1838.
By Robert Mansell, M.G. (Feb. 8, 1838)
Jackson Johnson to Lorency McDonald, Jan. 26, 1838.
(no returns)
Patrick Armstrong to Martha Owens, Jan. 25, 1838.
(no returns)
James Dyer to Florantha Vaughn, Jan. 18, 1838.
By Wm. Dotson, J.P. (June 4, 1838)
Wilson Vaughn to Katherine McDougald, Jan. 3, 1838.
(no returns)
John Hunnycut to Katherine Hackler, Jan. 6, 1838.
(no returns)
Andrew ONeal to Anna Caroline Delay, Jan. 24, 1838.
(no returns)
Elzay Triplet to Maiden Chapman, Jan. 24, 1838.
By Wilson Chapman, M.G. (Jan. 24, 1838)
Jothan Gregory to Mira Badford, Feb. 5, 1838.
(no returns)
Isaac Mizes to Nancy Cunningham, Jan. 30, 1838.
(no returns)
Samuel Edmondson to Rachel Madon, Feb. 23, 1838.
By Wm. Shamblen, J.P. (Feb. 29, 1838)
James Buckner to Susanah Stephenson, Feb. 25, 1838.
By Robert Gregory, M.G. (Feb. 25, 1838)
James Rucker to Elizabeth Gregory, Feb. 26, 1838.
By Laskin Taylor, J.P. (Feb. 27, 1838)
Telmon Dennis to Martha Amos, Feb. 28, 1838.
(no returns)
Abraham Roland to Nancy Clark, Mar. 1, 1838.
By M. John Camp, J.P. (Mar. 4, 1838)
William John to Rebecca Detherage, Mar. 21, 1835(?)
By Russel Lam, J.P. (Mar. 21, 1835(?)
James F. Hill to Elizabeth Mayfield, Mar. 22, 1838.
(no returns)
Vincent G. Ditmore to Mary Mannery, Mar. 24, 1838.
By Jas. Barnett, J.P. (Mar. 24, 1838)
Daniel M. Helvy to Teplecy Roberts, Apr. 5, 1838.
By Henry Price, M.G. (Apr. 5, 1838)
Pleasant M. Farris to Lucinda Hill, Apr. 5, 1838.
(no returns)
John S. Martin to Lucy Greenwood, Mar. 17, 1838.
By J. A. Barnett, J.P. (Apr. 18, 1838)
Sampson Stephen to Elizabeth Foster, Apr. 19, 1838.
(no returns)

Josiah Childres to Anna Shelton, Apr. 21, 1838.
By R. J. Moore, J.P. (June 5, 1838)
Timothy Pack to Lidia Burger, May 5, 1838.
By Jas. C. Carlock, J.P. (May 6, 1838)
Henry J. Brock to Sarah Cloud, May 11, 1838.
By Barney Casteel, Elder in the C. Church. (May 21, 1838)
Lawrence R. Brock to Polly Clam, May 24, 1838.
By Barney Casteel, Elder. (May 29, 1838)
John W. Tennell to Martha Briant, May 26, 1838.
By Jacob McDaniel, M.G. (May 28, 1838)
Allen Hayley to Elizabeth Rice, May 29, 1838.
By Benjamin Isbell, J.P. (May 29, 1838)
John Owens to Elizabeth A. Rutherford, June 5, 1838.
By David Cantrell, J.P. (June 5, 1838)
Robert L. Johnson to Nancy Yearwood, June 12, 1838.
By James Sewel, M.G. (June 12, 1838)
James M. Armstrong to Belinda Baker, June 13, 1838.
By Ralph Ledford, M.G. (June 14, 1838)
Nathaniel Fannon to Mary Emaline Chamley, June 24, 1838.
By A. Slover, M.G. (June 24, 1838)
Zachariah Atkin to Mary Ann Anderson, June 30, 1838.
By Larkin Tailor, J.P. (July 1, 1838)
William F. Brown to Manda M. Rentfro, July. 5, 1838.
By John Lots, M.G.
George W. Gaut to Nancy W. Dorsey, July 11, 1838.
By Robert Frazier, M.G. (July 19, 1838)
Beverly Greenwood to Biddy Bolding, July 12, 1838.
By R. J. Moore, J.P. (Oct. 3, 1838)
Joshua Carney to Patience Lewis, July 14, 1838.
By C. Sanders, M.G. (July 11, 1838)
James B. McCartney to Elizabeth L. Mechail, July 14, 1838.
By J. Murphy, M.G. (July 19, 1838)
William Hitchcock to Eliza Sewel, July 15, 1838.
By Karkin Taylor, J.P. (July 15, 1838)
John L. Long to Eliza Cox, July 17, 1838.
By John Courtney, M.G. (July 17, 1838)
William Collins to Mary E. Ady, July 31, 1838.
By A. Slover, M.G. (July 31, 1838)
Clement Woods to Rebecca Harmon, Aug. 2, 1838.
By Wm. Dotson, J.P. (Aug. 2, 1838)
Jonathan Johnes to Celia Browder, Aug. 6, 1838.
By A. Slover, M.G. (Aug. 10, 1838)
John Marshall to Jane Branham, Aug. 15, 1838.
(no returns)
Walter M. McGill to Isabella Anderson, Aug. 16, 1838.
By Abel Pearson, M.G. (Aug. 16, 1838)
Elias H. Kinner to Elizabeth Grisham, Aug. 18, 1838.
By Charles W. Rice, J.P. (Aug. 19, 1838)
Jonathan Romine to Lucinda Goode, Aug. 20, 1838.
By Elizah Hunt, J.P. (Aug. 21, 1838)
Jesse Tunnel to Rebecca Davis, Aug. 18, 1838.
By A. Slover, M.G. (Aug. 19, 1838)
Samuel Malone to Malinda Cavet, Aug. 22, 1838.
By A. Barb, J.P.

Demmon Dorsey to Elizabeth Newman, Aug. 22, 1838.
By L. Monson, M.G. (Aug. 23, 1838)
James R. Brown to Thunay Barnett, Aug. 27, 1838.
By Thos. L. Hoyl, J.P. (Aug. 27, 1838)
James Perry to Polly Hart, (no date given).
(no returns)
Samuel Sampson to Nancy Rudd, Aug. 29, 1838.
By John U. Gaugley, J.P. (Aug. 29, 1838)
Nathan Kelly to Mary Triplett, Aug. 29, 1838.
By L. Morrison, M.G. (Aug. 30, 1838)
Thomas Newton to Eliza Morris, Aug. 30, 1838.
By John Walker, M.G. (Sep. 6, 1838)
Joseph Walker to Anna Stephenson, Sep. 2, 1838.
(no returns)
Edmun D. Robert to Susanah Mansell, Sep. 6, 1838.
By Robt. Randolph, M.G. (Sep. 7, 1838)
William Carr to Nancy Gorden, Sep. 7, 1838.
By R. E. Leadford, M.G. (Sep. 9, 1838)
Jonathan D. Smith to Margaret Esmon, Sep. 13, 1838.
By David F. Jamerson, M.G. (Sep. 13, 1838)
Washington Patterson to Mary Ann Collier, Sep. 13, 1838.
By A. Barb, J.P. (Sep. 13, 1838)
Allen Boon to Anna Hardy, Sep. 15, 1838.
By D. Cantrell, J.P. (Sep. 16, 1838)
Gilbert Randolph to Marinda Miers, Sep. 15, 1838.
By Robt. Randolph, M.G. (Sep. 16, 1838)
G. W. Lemon to Jane Price, Sep. 15, 1838.
By Wm. Shamblin, J.P. (Sep. 23, 1838)
Thomas Metcalf to Martha Smith, Sep. 15, 1838.
(no returns)
David Brown to Polly Swanford, Sep. 18, 1838.
By Wm. M. Karney, J.P. (Sep. 23, 1838)
Mathias R. Bellows to Sarah Jane Clemontson, Sep. 18, 1838.
By L. R. Morrison, V.C.M. (Sep. 18, 1838)
Christopher Slager to Jane Buttram, Sep. 19, 1838.
By Wm. Jones, M.G. (Sep. 19, 1838)
William Malone to Matilda Woods, Nov. 20, 1838.
(no returns)
James Bryant to Sarah Ann Gulleage, Nov. 25, 1839(?)
John S. Franklin to Pamelia Buttram, Sep. 17, 1838.
By Henry Price, M.G. (Sep. 17, 1838)
Roberts Lemons to Peggy Conner, Sep. 20, 1838.
By Wm. Shambler, J.P. (Oct. 4, 1838)
Wilson Dugan to Casander Long, Oct. 30, 1838.
By J. C. Carlock, J.P. (Oct. 30, 1838)
Philip Owens to Susan Bedford, Sep. 27, 1838.
By Larkin Taylor, J.P. (Feb. 4, 1839)
James H. Mouldin to Elizabeth Owens, Sep. 27, 1838.
By Thomas L. Hoge, J.P. (Sep. 28, 1838)
John Carter to Pamelia Haymes, Sep. 25, 1838.
By Jacob McDaniel, M.G. (Sep. 27, 1838)
John Patrick to Margaret Mires, Oct. 5, 1838.
(no returns)
John Wiginton to Elizabeth Lawson, Oct. 1, 1838.
By Wm. Jones, M.G. (Oct. 1, 1838)

Asael Poe to Ann Hellum, Oct. 10, 1838.
    By A. B. Niel, J.P. (Oct. 18, 1838)
William C. Townsend to Katherine Roland, Oct. 13, 1838.
    By I. Wampey, M.G. (Oct. 18, 1838)
Nathan Lawson to Delila Green, Oct. 13, 1838.
    By Jonathan Thomas, J.P. (Oct. 13, 1838)
William S. Fagan to Eliza Sattefield, Oct. 16, 1838.
    By Thos. L. Hoge, J.P. (Oct. 16, 1838)
William T. McCallie to Elizabeth D. Parryman, Oct. 16,
    1838. By Wm. McNarey, J.P. (Oct. 25, 1838)
Coleman W. Chapman to Ann Ferguson, Oct. 20, 1838.
    (no returns)
A. Woodward to Mary L. Sullins, Oct. 22, 1838.
    (no returns)
William Ray to Polly Jenny Dobbs, Oct. 25, 1838.
    By Jonathan Thomas, J.P. (Oct. 25, 1838)
John R. Wooten to Ann Walker, Oct. 27, 1838.
    By John Heniger, M.G. (Oct. 30, 1838)
Mortimer Spradlin to Louvicy Lawson, Oct. 29, 1838.
    By Jonathan Thomas, J.P. (Oct. 29, 1838)
Nathanl McNabb to Susan C. McInturff, Nov. 5, 1839.
    By A. Kinser, J.P. (Nov. 12, 1839)
Charles Harris to Isbell Snoddy, Nov. 5, 1838.
    By Lewis Brewer, M.G. (Nov. 5, 1838)
David W. Beaver to Anna Thomas, Nov. 8, 1838.
    By George W. Mayo, J.P. (Nov. 8, 1838)
Jeremiah Farris to Elizabeth Addison, Nov. 10, 1838.
    (no returns)
James Martin to Patsy Herald, Nov. 12, 1838.
    By David F. Jamerson, J.P. (Nov. 12, 1838)
John E. Haynes to Lucinda A. Zeyler, Nov. 13, 1838.
    By A. Slover, M.G. (Nov. 16, 1838)
John McNenny to Mary Long, Nov. 15, 1838.
    (no returns)
Esom Franklin to Susan Collier, Nov. 16, 1838.
    (no returns)
Isaac Cannon to Rupey Kibble, Nov. 17, 1838.
    By L. L. Ball, J.P. (Nov. 18, 1838)
Patton Lane to Susan Haynie, Nov. 19, 1838.
    By Wilson Chapman, M.G. (Nov. 19, 1838)
William S. Hambright to Sarah B. Moose, Nov. 23, 1838.
    (no returns)
Henry B. David to Nancy Pickens, Nov. 20, 1838.
    By Obediah Belding, M.G. (Nov. 20, 1838)
William G. James to Annalize Townsley, Dec. 4, 1838.
    By Wm. Shambler, J.P. (Dec. 4, 1838)
Hessol P. Haynie to Mary Davis, Dec. 10, 1838.
    By L. Brewer, M.G. (Dec. 10, 1838)
Arthur Nelson to Synthy Robison, Dec. 14, 1838.
    By Thos. L. Hoge, J.P. (Dec. 15, 1838)
William Killingsworth to Jane Ellison, Dec. 18, 1838.
    By Wm. Shamblin, J.P. (Dec. 20, 1838)
Sandford Prince to Joana Thomas, Dec. 18, 1838.
    By A. C. Robeson, J.P. (Dec. 27, 1838)

McMINN COUNTY MARRIAGES

James H. Lowry to Margaret Emaline Kirkpatrick, Dec. 19,
1838. By Abel Pearson, M.G. (Dec. 20, 1838)
John Dillard to Rebecca Hellums, Dec. 22, 1838.
By John Courtney, M.G. (Dec. 25, 1838)
Benj. T. Zeigler to Susan Mansell, Dec. 26, 1838.
(no returns)
John Holland to Martha Hayes, Dec. 24, 1838.
(no returns)
Washington Jackson to Long Bowsen, Dec. 31, 1838.
(no returns)
Philip Ellis to Louisa Harden, Jan. 7, 1839.
By Andrew Crawford, J.P. (Jan. 8, 1839)
George Dotson to Nancy Bond, Jan. 2, 1839.
By A. Barb, J.P. (Jan. 3, 1839)
John Mysy to Emily Hayes, Jan. 11, 1839.
By John Fasnur, M.G. (Jan. 17, 1839)
Laisens ONeal to Hayney Owens, Jan. 2, 1839.
(no returns)
Terry Kelly to Debby Emmerson, Jan. 4, 1839.
By Jas. Barnett, J.P. (Jan. 4, 1839)
Richard T. Good to Martha Dorsey, Jan. 4, 1839.
By A. Slover, M.G. (Jan. 6, 1839)
Thomas Snodgrass to Caroline Moore, Jan. 3, 1839.
(no returns)
James Swawford to Jane Randell, Jan. 1, 1839.
By John Wellas, J.P. (Jan. 1, 1839)
Madison Payne to Margaret Tally, Jan. 2, 1839.
By Andrew Crawford, J.P. (Jan. 3, 1839)
Daniel McDonald to Charlotte R. Campbell, Jan. 2, 1839.
By Robert Gregory, Minister of the Baptist Church.
(Jan. 2, 1839)
George W. Queener to Rachel Lattemore, Jan. 1, 1839.
By J. C. Carlock, J.P. (Jan. 3, 1839)
William Armstrong to Elizabeth White, Jan. 2, 1839.
By David Cantrell, J.P. (Jan. 3, 1839)
Mecayah Dorsey to Emaline Pertileo, Jan. 14, 1839.
By A. Slover, M.G. (Jan. 14, 1839)
John Sevier Lee to Emaline Henderson, Jan. 16, 1839.
By Robert Gregory, Minister of the Baptist Church.
(Jan. 17, 1839)
William Worley to Sarah Shook, Jan. 16, 1839.
By G. N. Mayo, J.P. (Jan. 17, 1839)
William Underwood to Peggy Salina Mires, Jan. 17, 1839.
(no returns)
Buttean Holman to Luvicy Triplett, Jan. 19, 1839.
By A. Slover, M.G. (Jan. 19, 1839)
Absalem C. Hayes to Matilda Eaten, Jan. 21, 1839.
By A. C. Robeson, J.P. (Jan. 24, 1839)
Merit R. Wears to Sarah Jane Pearce, Jan. 23, 1839.
(no returns)
Andrew I. Brown to Elizabeth Sanders, Jan. 26, 1839.
(no returns)
Nat. D. Smith to Eliza Goode, Jan. 29, 1839.
(no returns)

John L. Kline to Serena J. Holt, Jan. 30, 1839.
(no returns)
John B. Mansell to Mary S. Newman, Feb. 14, 1839.
(no returns)
Robert Sharp to Nancy Ann Brown, Feb. 28, 1839.
(no returns)
William P. Turk to Nancy G. McMinn, Mar. 6, 1839.
(no returns)
Samuel Walker to Eliza White Cotter, Mar. 13, 1839.
By Jas. Bellingsly, J.P. (Mar. 13, 1839)
John Anderson to Sarah Matthews, Feb. 6, 1839.
By Geo. W. Mayo, J.P. (Feb. 7, 1839)
Calloway Baker to Delila Peters, Mar. 30, 1839.
By John McGaughey, J.P. (Mar. 30, 1839)
James M. Dawson to Susanah Knox, Apr. 4, 1839.
Joseph Tucker to Mary Fox, Apr. 5, 1839.
By John McGaughey, J.P. (Apr. 5, 1839)
Allen Maller to Elizabeth Snodgrass, Apr. 11, 1839.
(no returns)
Matthew Turnley to Nancy M. Isbell, May 27, 1839.
By Wm. C. C. C. George, M.G. (May 27, 1839)
James R. Ash to Margaret Rebecca Martin, May 28, 1839.
By T. B. Love, J.P. (May 28, 1839)
Hiram Madareies (or Madaries) to Elizabeth Boon, May 30,
1839. By D. Cantrell, J.P. (May 30, 1839)
Lewis Burnett to Charity Swanford, May 31, 1839.
(no returns)
Chas. Moore to Mary Cantrell, June 4, 1839.
(no returns)
Washington Breadwell to Phany Callahan, June 14, 1839.
(no returns)
Samuel A. Peters to Phebe S. Peters, June 13, 1839.
(no returns)
Isaac Low to Elizabeth H. Long, June 13, 1839.
By D. Cantrell, J.P. (June 13, 1839)
Jacob Low to Sarah Akin, June 15, 1839.
By John McGaughey, J.P. (June 15, 1839)
William C. McLin to Nancy A. Lasiter, June 19, 1839.
By A. Barb, J.P. (June 20, 1839)
C. R. Blackwell to Anna Cregg, June 19, 1839.
By Thomas Hoge, J.P. (June 19, 1839)
Alfred G. Weaver to Elizabeth Harris, June 19, 1839.
By Hamilton Bradford, J.P. (June 20, 1839)
M. Wall to Eliza Baker, June 19, 1839.
(no returns)
Joseph Hicks to Lewcy Ann Franklin, June 25, 1839.
By Robt. Frazier, M.G. (June 26, 1839)
Elisha Miller to Elizabeth McCully, Dec. 4, 1839.
(no returns)
G. W. Culpepper to Sarah Forgg, Dec. 4, 1839.
By E. Newton, M.G. (Dec. 5, 1839)
William Southard to Katherine Trout, Dec. 7, 1839.
By Russell Lane, J.P. (Dec. 12, 1839)
William Graves to Margaret A. Hood, Dec. 12, 1839.
(no returns)

McMINN COUNTY MARRIAGES

John W. Smith to Nancy M. Nailo, Dec. 12, 1839.
(no returns)
John O. Torbet to Evilin C. Trim, Dec. 18, 1839.
(no returns)
John G. Miller to Martha Wilson, Dec. 20, 1839.
By A. Barb, J.P. (Dec. 24, 1839)
Robert P. Julian to Rosanna Bond, Dec. 21, 1839.
By A. Barb, J.P. (Dec. 24, 1839)
William Edwards to Charlotte Young, Dec. 24, 1839.
(no returns)
William Johns to Jane Armstrong, Dec. 31, 1839.
(no returns)
John Gyerris to Elizabeth Butler, Jan. 3, 1840.
By Moses A. Cass, J.P. (Jan. 3, 1840)
John Miller to Eliza Carter, Jan. 8, 1840.
(no returns)
Adam Shiphugh to Louisa Cash, Feb. 1, 1840.
(no returns)
Mark Mulvany to Eliza Davis, Feb. 3, 1840.
By Jonathan, J.P. (Feb. 6, 1840)
M. Walls to Eliza Baker, June 19, 1839.
By C. M. Rice, J.P. (June 19, 1839)
Thomas Crawford to Amanda Hegdon, June 27, 1839.
By Hamilton Bradford, J.P. (July 7, 1839)
Sherrod Barksdale to Eliza Owens, July 1, 1839.
By T. L. Hoyl, J.P. (July 4, 1839)
Lorenzo D. Frazier to Hannah Briant, July 2, 1839.
By A. Barb, J.P. (July 9, 1839)
William Glaze to Pamelia Rudd, July 4, 1839.
By D. Cantrell, J.P. (July 4, 1839)
Daniel Kirk to Eliza Edwards, July 6, 1839.
(no returns)
Jonathan Hanks to Mary Kipps, July 9, 1839.
By John McCartney, J.P. (July 11, 1839)
William W. Haymes to Mary C. Robison, July 13, 1839.
By I. M. Kelly, M.G. (July 18, 1839)
William Weatherly to Rachel McAlister, July 15, 1839.
By Wm. J. Wetcher, M.G. (July 18, 1839)
William V. Willis to Lucinda Newton, July 16, 1839.
By Edward Newton, M.G. (July 18, 1839)
Charles Martin to Malinda Shelton, July 18, 1839.
(no returns)
Henry King to Elizabeth Haymes, July 23, 1839.
By C. W. Rice, J.P. (July 23, 1839)
Edward D. Cannon to Madux(?) _____, July 23, 1839.
By N. C. Cook, J.P. (July 25, 1839)
George W. Fennell to Rachel Orr, July 27, 1839.
(no returns)
Charles Cate to Mary P. Baker, Aug. 8, 1839.
By J. M. Kelly, M.G. (Aug. 8, 1839)
Joseph Scott to Sarah Ann Samson, Aug. 8, 1839.
By L. R. Morrison, V.D.M. (Aug. 8, 1839)
Levan A. Ward to Charity Salle, Aug. 8, 1839.
By A. Sloan, M.G. (Aug. 8, 1839)

Samuel Matheny to Esther Lacy, Aug. 10, 1839.
(no returns)
David Pennington to Matilda Brigham, Aug. 16, 1839.
(no returns)
William Casteel to Elizabeth Elliot, Aug. 16, 1839.
(no returns)
James Pain to Amanda Mulkey, Aug. 22, 1839.
By M. T. Hoyl, J.P. (Aug. 23, 1839)
Isaiah Rudd to Martha Owen, Aug. 27, 1839.
(no returns)
John Detmore to Amanda Bolding, Sep. 2, 1839.
By CSSNDEKS(?), M.G. (Sep. 12, 1839)
John C. Armstrong to Nancy Weare, Sep. 10, 1839.
By Ralph E. Tedford, M.G. (Sep. 12, 1839)
William Lee to Emaline Reynolds, Sep. 11, 1839.
By Robert Gregory, M.G. Baptist. (Sep. 12, 1839)
Thomas Jones to Matilda Keeton, Sep. 12, 1839.
By Wm. Jones, M.G. (Sep. 12, 1839)
Christian Peters to Olevia Benton, Sep. 12, 1839.
By John McGaughey, J.P. (Sep. 12, 1839)
Elijah Benton to Sarah Pearce, Sep. 14, 1839.
(no returns)
John W. Malone to Sarah Casteel, Sep. 16, 1839.
(no returns)
William Devault to Louisa Pearson, Sep. 21, 1839.
(no returns)
Hezekiah Randolph to Eliza Detmore, Sep. 21, 1839.
By R. I. Moore, J.P. (Sep. 22, 1839)
H. D. Middleton to Mary Wilson, Sep. 23, 1839.
By A. Barb, J.P. (Sep. 26, 1839)
John C. Gaut to Sarah A. McReynolds, Sep. 26, 1839.
By L. R. Morrison, V.G.M. (Sep. 26, 1839)
McKarry Penneon to Nancy Frazier, Sep. 26, 1839.
By John McGaughey, J.P. (Sep. 26, 1839)
Thomas Parsons to Nancy Waters, Oct. 1, 1839.
By C. H. Price, J.P. (Oct. 2, 1839)
Isaac N. Ervin to Phebe R. Trim, Sep. 5, 1839.
(no returns)
John Grisham to Nancy Bebibim, Oct. 15, 1839.
By Jonathan Thomas, J.P. (Oct. 15, 1839)
Samuel Julian to Mary B. Smith, Oct. 7, 1839.
By A. Bach, J.P. (Oct. 7, 1839)
Marion Grisham to Ruby Isham, Oct. 7, 1839.
By Jonathan Thomas, J.P. (Oct. 7, 1839)
John C. Johnson to Anna McCollum, Oct. 8, 1839.
By C. W. Rice, J.P. (Oct. 10, 1839)
Warren Trew to Martha Pickens, Oct. 23, 1839.
By M. C. Hawk, M.G. (Oct. 26, 1839)
Drew Leaper, to _____, Oct. 25, 1839.
John Frost to Emeline C. Trim, Dec. 18, 1839.
By J. Courtney, M.G. (Dec. 18, 1839)
Henry Steed to Tebetha Noel, Oct. 30, 1839.
By Floyd McGouegal. (Oct. 31, 1839)
Nathaniel McNabb to Sarena Caroline McInturff, Nov. 5,
1839. By A. Kinser, J.P. (Nov. 12, 1839)

McMINN COUNTY MARRIAGES

John Mason to Margaret Hughes, Oct. 8, 1839.
By Joseph Minge, J.P. (Oct. 10, 1839)
William Grant to Margaret Hood, Dec. 10, 1839.
By L. R. Morrison, V.D.M. (Dec. 11, 1839)
Elijah Benton to Sarah Pearce, Sep. 15, 1839.
By J. McGaughey, J.P. (Sep. 15, 1839)
John Bookout to Celia Massingell, Feb. 8, 1830(?)
By J. C. Carlock, J.P. (Feb. 8, 1830(?)
William Harrid to Amanda Butler, Feb. 10, 1840.
By Jonathan Thomas, J.P. (Feb. 10, 1840)
Thomas Jones to Matilda Keaton, Sep. 12, 1839.
By Wm. Jones, M.G. (Sep. 13, 1839)
A. I. Baker to Mary Henderson, Jan. 1, 1840.
By A. H. Harris, M.G. (Jan. 3, 1840)
Thomas Lattimore to Elizabeth Queener, Jan. 1, 1840.
By J. C. Carlock, J.P. (Jan. 2, 1840)
Thomas W. Gordan to Elizabeth Mansell, Feb. 12, 1840.
(no returns)
Edmund Dotson to Susanah Casey, Feb. 13, 1840.
(no returns)
Robert G. Peters to Elizabeth Bond, Jan. 22, 1842(?)
By John McGaughey, J.P. (Jan. 23, 1840)
James M. Stubbs to Rachel Smith, Feb. 15, 1840.
(no returns)
James Bryant to Sarah Ann Gulliage, Nov. 25, 1839.
(no returns)
Adam Shipleigh to Louisa Cash, Feb. 1, 1840.
By Madison C. Hawk, M.G.M.E. Church (Feb. 3, 1840)
William Graves to Margaret A. Hood, Dec. 11, 1839.
(no returns)
Jackson Prince to Mahala Cross, Dec. 25, 1839.
(no returns)
Alfred Dotson to Elizabeth Patty, Dec. 31, 1839.
By Robert Gregory, M.G. Baptist. (Jan. 2, 1840)
William John to Jane Armstrong, Dec. 31, 1839.
By D. Cantrell, J.P. (Dec. 31, 1839)
James Benton to Matilda Wood, Nov. 20, 1839.
By Robert Gregory, M.G. Baptist. (Nov. 21, 1839)
William Rutherford to Elizabeth Slacnere, Jan. 6, 1840.
(no returns)
John Queener to Elizabeth Butler, Dec. 3, 1839.
(no returns)
John W. Kirksey to Tabitha Boling, Dec. 2, 1839.
By C. Sanders, M.G. (Jan. 2, 1840)
R. D. Jones to Martha King, Jan. 2, 1830(?)
(no returns)
T. Peak to A. Pusmon, Jan. 23, 1840.
(no returns)
S. K. Crawford to Susanah Hackler, JAn. 24, 1840.
By J. W. Weltree, M.G. (Jan. 24, 1840)
Henry Glase to Martha Arnurn, Jan. 20, 1840.
By Russel Lane, J.P. (Jan. 21, 1840)
David Lovel to Katherine Lowers, Feb. 20, 1840.
(no returns)

McMINN COUNTY MARRIAGES

William Edwards to Charlotte Young, Dec. 24, 1840(?).
  By Ezekiah Wards, M.G. (Dec. 25, 1839)
David G. Orr to Susan Johnson, Feb. 20, 1840.
  (no returns)
Elijah Smith to Eliza Colier, Feb. 20, 1840.
  By D. Cantrell, J.P. (Feb. 28, 1839(?)
William Tortner to Anna Huckaby, Feb. 21, 1840.
  By William Dotson, J.P. (Feb. 26, 1840)
Henry Goforth to Nancy Smart, Feb. 26, 1840.
  By L. L. Ball, J.P. (Feb. 27, 1840)
William Shields to Elizabeth Lee, Feb. 27, 1840.
  By Hamilton Bradford, J. Pell Mac Ely(?) (Feb. 27, 1840)
Chas Moore to Mary Cantrell, June 6, 1839.
  By John Walker, M.G. (June 6, 1839)
Henry Moore to Ann Fyke, Jan. 5, 1840.
  (no returns)
Lorenzo Dow Gillian to Cealy Ann Dyer, Feb. 29, 1840.
  (no returns)
John Crisp to Polly Bond, Mar. 18, 1840.
  By A. W. Cunningham, J.P. (Mar. 19, 1840)
Berry Dodd to Sarah Rutherford, Mar. 19, 1840.
  By H. C. Cooke, J.P. (Mar. 19, 1840)
James ONail to Nancy Parsons, Mar. 2, 1840.
  By A. Kinser, J.P. (Mar. 2, 1840)
Elisha White to Usly Cloud, Mar. 2, 1840.
  By Moses A. Case, J.P. (Mar. 2, 1840)
James Barksdale to Katherine Webb, Apr. 1, 1840.
  By H. C. Cook, J.P. (Apr. 1, 1840)
J. D. Shelton to Elizabeth A. Brown, Mar. 16, 1840.
  (no returns)
A. B. Ellis to Matilda Lawson, Mar. 25, 1840.
  By Jonathan Thomas, J.P. (Mar. 25, 1840)
John Cusp to Polly Bond, Mar. 18, 1840.
  (no returns)
Gilmore Randolph to Mary Brookshire, Mar. 24, 1840.
  By Reece Jones, J.P. (Mar. 26, 1840)
Wm. Howard to Partina Center, Jan. 28, 1840.
  By H. C. Cook, J.P. (Jan. 28, 1840)
Daniel Sane to Emily E. Dickard, Apr. 10, 1840.
  (no returns)
Hugh Kile to Mary Dixon, Apr. 11, 1840.
  By M. W. Cunningham, J.P. (Apr. 11, 1840)
David H. Gorman to Ruth Long, Apr. 13, 1840.
  By A. F. Gerald, M.G. (Apr. 14, 1840)
Rufus Green to Nancy Cofer, Apr. 15, 1840.
  By Elijah Hurst, J.P. (Apr. 15, 1840)
James Anderson to Mary West, Apr. 18, 1840.
  By David F. Jamerson, J.P. (Apr. 25, 1840)
George Monroe to Eliza Pearson, Apr. 25, 1840.
  By David F. Jamerson, J.P. (Apr. 25, 1840)
Bloomfield Logan to Mary Ann Cantrell, Apr. 30, 1840.
  By C. Sanders, M.G. (Apr. 30, 1840)
John H. Lumpkin to Mary Jane Crutchfield, May 5, 1840.
  By L. R. Morrison, V.C.M. (May 5, 1840)

McMINN COUNTY MARRIAGES

Allen Keeton to Elizabeth Love, May 6, 1840.
(no returns)
Wesley Casada to Elizabeth Gaston, May 6, 1840.
By H. Ingram, M.G. (May 7, 1840)
James C. Wright to Mary Beavers, May 19, 1840.
By John Tate, M.G. (May 19, 1840)
Eli Smith to Elizabeth Vale, June 1, 1840.
By John Tate, M.G. (June 1, 1840)
Renne Maesay to Rebecca Long, June 1, 1840.
By Jesse Locke, M.G. (June 2, 1840)
Joel K. Brown to Hester Ann Brown, June 5, 1840.
By John Tate, M.G. (June 5, 1840)
Benjamin C. Sherrle to Lucinda Lawson, Juen 2, 1840.
By Jonathan Thomas, J.P. (June 18, 1840)
James Parkison to Mary Ann Clemonson, July 7, 1840.
By John Tate, M.G. (July 7, 1840)
Hugh Studdard to Ailey Milton, July 13, 1840.
By Uriel Johnson, J.P. (July 28, 1840)
John Lovel to Polly Stephens, July 24, 1840.
By Moses A. Cass, J.P. (July 30, 1840)
William K. Waugh to Katherine Colvill, July 30, 1840.
(no returns)
William Powers to Anne Housley, Aug. 31, 1840.
(no returns)
Charles P. Copeland to Elizabeth Ann Thompson, Aug. 5,
1840. By Bynum Jarnagin, J.P. (Aug. 6, 1840)
Daniel McDaniel to Emiline Redfearn, Aug. 5, 1840.
By Richard A. McAdoo, J.P. (Aug. 6, 1840)
Madison W. McCluskey to Mary E. Campbell, Aug. 10, 1840.
By A. Slover, M.G. (Aug. 10, 1840)
Solomon M. Smallen to Sarah Pugh, Aug. 17, 1840.
By A. C. Robeson, J.P. (Sep. 1, 1840)
Charles A. Pickens to Malinda Smith, Aug. 19, 1840.
By T. B. Love, J.P. (Aug. 19, 1840)
William Hays to Margaret Battles, Aug. 21, 1840.
By Ezekiel Ward, M.G. (Aug. 22, 1840)
James D. Dennis to Malinda Green, Aug. 26, 1840.
By Richard A. McAdoo, J.P. (Aug. 27, 1840)
John Rusner to Sarah A. McCartney, Aug. 24, 1840.
By Ralph E. Tedford, M.G. (Aug. 24, 1840)
William Dixon to Nancy Cannon, Aug. 26, 1840.
(no returns)
Jesse White to Jemima Elliot, Sep. 3, 1840.
By Moses A. Cass, J.P. (Sep. 3, 1840)
Andrew Harris to Sarah Crouch, Sep. 12, 1840.
By T. B. Love, J.P. (Sep. 17, 1840)
Henry Nelson to Jane Bailey, Sep. 17, 1840.
By T. L. Hoyl, J.P. (Sep. 17, 1840)
John Ferguson to Susan J. Patty, Sep. 28, 1840.
By Robert Gregory, M.G. Baptist. (Sep. 29, 1840)
William H. Crockett to Mary Thornton, Oct. 6, 1840.
By John Scruggs, M.G. (Oct. 8, 1840)
Camel Atkinson to Dorcus Newberry, Oct. 7, 1840.
(no returns)

Obed C. Patty to Eliza S. Millard, Oct. 14, 1840.
By Robert Gregory, M.G. Baptist. (Oct. 15, 1840)
Allen Dotson to Martha Arnwine, Oct. 15, 1840.
By John Foster, J.P. (Oct. 15, 1840)
Isaiah Tetters to Mary Gallant, Oct. 19, 1840.
By George Monroe, M.G. (Oct. 22, 1840)
Thomas P. Moore to Margaret Lipscomb, Oct. 21, 1840.
(no returns)
Joseph Maddox to Leticia Green, Oct. 21, 1840)
By Floyd McGougal. (Oct. 22, 1840)
George W. Cooke to Sarah J. Gilbreath, Oct. 21, 1840.
By Wilson Chapman. (Oct. 22, 1840)
James McCamis to E. J. Cooper, Oct. 22, 1840.
L. R. Morrison, V.D.M. (Oct. 22, 1840)
Wm. Z. Thompson to Margaret Holmes, Oct. 23, 1840.
By Robt. McAdoo, J.P. (Oct. 23, 1840)
Jeremiah Lawson to Dicy Ellis, Oct. 26, 1840.
(no returns)
James U. Coleman to Elizabeth J. Walker, Oct. 29, 1840.
(no returns)
Absolom D. Kigby to Elizabeth Trimul, Nov. 3, 1840.
(no returns)
John Mizer to Susannah Lewis, Nov. 5, 1840.
By C. W. Rice, J.P. (Nov. 5, 1840)
Jackson Triplett to Rhoda Varnell, Nov. 16, 1840.
By T. B. Love, J.P. (Nov. 19, 1840)
Joseph L. Levan to Hulda Mayfield, Nov. 19, 1840.
By John Tate, M.G. (Nov. 19, 1840)
John K. Boyd to L. Barb, Nov. 21, 1840.
By Jonathan Thomas, J.P. (Nov. 26, 1840)
Caswell Golden to Orinda Harmon, Nov. 21, 1840.
By David F. Jameson, J.P. (Nov. 22, 1840)
William Smart to Lucinda Graves, Nov. 26, 1840.
(Dec. 3, 1840)
John H. Naves to Katherine Huse, Dec. 3, 1840.
(no returns)
James H. Cardwell to Hazy Mitchell, Dec. 8, 1840.
By H. Ingram. (Dec. 8, 1840)
P. W. Breeds to Algaline Barker, Dec. 9, 1840.
By T. B. Love, J.P. (Dec. 10, 1840)
James Dugger to Lucinda Lorgin, Dec. 9, 1840.
(no returns)
Benjamin C. Davis to Rachel Davis, Dec. 10, 1840.
(no returns)
Elijah F. Gerald to Nancy McCally, Dec. 14, 1840.
By A. F. Gerrel, M.G. (Dec. 14, 1840)
Andrew M. Hankins to Eliza Wade, Dec. 14, 1840.
By C. W. Rice, J.P. (Dec. 15, 1840)
Jackson G. Dake to Anne Riddle, Dec. 22, 1840.
By George Yost, M.G. Methodist Protestant. (Dec. 22, 1840)
Hiram Loughmiller to Evaline Carroll, Dec. 22, 1840.
(no returns)
John R. Garland to Sarah A. Churn, Dec. 23, 1840.
By L. R. Morrison, V.D.M. (Dec. 25, 1840)

Merrit B. Stroud to Rebecca Proffet, Dec. 24, 1840.
By F. McGougal. (Dec. 24, 1840)
Alfred Hanks to Sarah Smith, Dec. 25, 1840.
By John Jenkins, J.P. (Dec. 25, 1840)
Robert Wright to Vera Shile, Jan. 1, 1841.
By Josephine Minzs, J.P. (Jan. 5, 1841)
James A. Barkes to Elizabeth Love, Jan. 6, 1841.
By Lewis Brewer, M.G. (Jan. 7, 1841)
Robert Elder to Mary Witt, Jan. 8, 1841.
By Ezekiel Ward, M.G. (Jan. 14, 1841)
Jackson Shelton to Rachel Casady, Jan. 16, 1841.
By David L. Jameson, J.P. (Jan. 17, 1841)
Wm. P. Copeland to Eveline Card, Jan. 19, 1841.
By Bynum Jarnagin, J.P. (Jan. 19, 1841)
William Malone to Elizabeth Casteel, Jan. 8, 1841.
By John W. Barnett, J.P. (Jan. 19, 1841)
Robert P. Sharp to Calesta Casada, Jan. 19, 1841.
(no returns)
John M. Courtney to Katherine Neal, Jan. 20, 1841.
By G. E. Mountcastle. (Jan. 21, 1841)
Hamilton Jarnagin to Nancy Emerson, Jan. 20, 1841.
By A. C. Robeson, J.P. (Jan. 21, 1841)
George Trotter to Nancy Howard, Jan. 26, 1841.
By T. B. Love, J.P. (Jan. 26, 1841)
Thomas Crabtree to Easter Green, Jan. 27, 1841.
By John Jenkins, J.P. (July 5, 1841)
John W. Davis to Nancy A. Young, Jan. 27, 1841.
By Richard A. McAdoo, J.P. (Jan. 27, 1841)
Matthew S. Kirk to Louesa Philips, Feb. 2, 1841.
By R. A. McAdoo, J.P. (Feb. 2, 1841)
James M. Gallaher to Elmira Sparks, Feb. 2, 1841.
By Uriel Johnson, Esq. (Feb. 2, 1841)
Elisha Cox to Isabella Dickson, Feb. 3, 1841.
By Byrum Jarnagin, J.P. (Feb. 4, 1841)
James C. Queener to Eliza Trew, Feb. 3, 1841.
By T. B. Love, J.P. (Feb. 11, 1841)
Henry Brown to Reuhanna Shoemaker, Feb. 4, 1841.
By H. M. Dodson, J.P. (Feb. 4, 1841)
Hugh Tweening to Letice W. Smith, Feb. 7, 1841.
By T. B. Love, J.P. (Feb. 7, 1841)
Joseph Smith to Delila Orr, Feb. 10, 1841.
By James Smith, J.P. (Feb. 11, 1841)
Spencer Beavers to Mary Cobbs, Feb. 11, 1841.
By J. McGaughy, J.P. (Feb. 11, 1841)
David Cantrell to Sarah Derrick, Feb. 11, 1841.
By Bynum Jarnagin, J.P. (Feb. 11, 1841)
George W. Million to Nancy Robeson, Feb. 13, 1841.
By Jonathan Thomas, J.P. (Feb. 14, 1841)
Norris Humphrey to Angeline Ellis, Feb. 13, 1841.
By Jonathan Thomas, J.P. (Feb. 14, 1841)
Spartan Allen to Rachel Stephenson, Feb. 18, 1841.
By John Tate, M.G. (Feb. 18, 1841)
David Rose to Sarah Ann Newland, Feb. 18, 1841.
By John Rogers, J.P. (Mar. 1, 1841)

Zechiaria Swinboro to Jucilla Davis, Mar. 1, 1841.
  By John Rogers, J.P. (Mar. 1, 1841)
John Wood to Martha Wilson, Mar. 4, 1841.
  By John Rogers, J.P. (Mar. 5, 1841)
Woodson Weatherby to Elizabeth Hank, Mar. 4, 1841.
  (no returns)
John Spear to Eliza C. Mansfield, Mar. 9, 1841.
  By John Tate, M.G. (Mar. 9, 1841)
John Hinkle to Lydia E. Miller, Feb. 20, 1841.
  By T. B. Love, J.P. (Feb. 21, 1841)
Eli Hudgins to Elizabeth Hale, Mar. 16, 1841.
  (no returns)
Joseph Couch to Mary Ware, Mar. 17, 1841.
  (no returns)
Samuel Stewart to Mary Hammontree, Mar. 14, 1841.
  By John Rogers, J.P. (Mar. 14, 1841)
Reece Harkrider to Mahala Horton, Mar. 23, 1841.
  By Richard A. McAdoo, J.P. (Mar. 23, 1841)
Lamber Bunch to Sarah Willis, Mar. 27, 1841.
  By Richard A. McAdoo, J.P. (Mar. 30, 1841)
William Newton to Jane L. Smith, Mar. 27, 1841.
  By Henry N. Dodson, M.G. (Mar. 27, 1841)
William Ashly to Elizabeth Cook, Apr. 6, 1841.
  By C. Sander, M.G. (Apr. 6, 1841)
Chandler Liming to Mary A. Higgins, Apr. 6, 1841.
  By Uriel Johnson, J.P. (Apr. 6, 1841)
Jacob K. Errickson to Martha Mansil, Apr. 14, 1841.
  By Wm. Stewart, M.G. (Apr. 15, 1841)
Walter B. Mansel to Mary Roberts, Apr. 14, 1841.
  By Wm. Stewart, M.G. (Apr. 15, 1841)
John Gallaher to Jane Richards, Apr. 14, 1841.
  By Uriel Johnson, J.P. (Apr. 14, 1841)
Henry Arnold to Mary Hously, Apr. 17, 1841.
  (no returns)
John L. Bridges to Hellen E. Blackwell, Apr. 20, 1841.
  (no returns)
Isaac G. Wright to Dorcas C. Smith, Apr. 22, 1841.
  By Jonathan Thomas, J.P. (Apr. 30, 1841)
William W. Rector to Elizabeth McPherson, Mar. 20, 1841.
  (no returns)
S. K. Ruder to Mary M. Bridges, Apr. 7, 1841.
  By L. R. Morrison, V.D.M. (Apr. 9, 1841)
G. P. L. Coffman to Elizabeth A. Wear, Apr. 10, 1841.
  By Robert Mansell, M.G. (Apr. 13, 1841)
William W. Rector to E. A. Wear, Mar. 4, 1841.
  By Joseph Mansell, J.P. (Mar. 4, 1841)
David Rose to Sarah Ann Newland, Feb. 27, 1841.
  By John W. Barnet, J.P. (Feb. 28, 1841)
Isaac Tenny to Angeline Blackwell, May 3, 1841.
  By T. B. Love, J.P. (May 4, 1841)
Henry Williams to Jane Edens, May 15, 1841.
  By M. C. Hawk, M.G. (May 20, 1841)
Wm. H. Jack to Jane Cook, May 16, 1841.
  By M. A. Cass, J.P. (May 18, 1841)

McMINN COUNTY MARRIAGES

George W. Gallahon to Mary Ann Smith, May 19, 1841.
By J. Thomas, J.P. (May 20, 1841)
Alexander H. Keith to Sarah Ford, May 20, 1841.
By R. W. Patty, M.M.E.C. (May 20, 1841)
James H. Rhea to Lucinda Cash, May 25, 1841.
By John Jenkins, J.P. (May 26, 1841)
Elijah Rudd to Eliza Garland, May 25, 1841.
(no returns)
James A. Small to Martha J. Rollings, June 1, 1841.
By Thos. H. Small, M.G.C.P.C. (June 3, 1841)
Landon C. Peters to Margaret Smith, June 9, 1841.
By T. B. Love, J.P. (June 10, 1841)
James F. E. Kinnian to Elizabeth A. Killingsworth,
June 12, 1841. By C. W. Rice, J.P. (June 27, 1841)
Sam'l John to Rebeckah Frazier, June 23, 1841.
By A. C. Robeson, J.P. (June 24, 1841)
C. R. Hoyl to S. M. Cooke, July 7, 1841.
By Wilson Chapman, M.G. (July 8, 1841)
Fourris Fellaynor to Nancy M. Cantrell, July 20, 1841.
By Rev. Joseph Peeler. (July 27, 1841)
Thomas Williams to Maranda Randolph, July 26, 1841.
By Rus Jones, M.G. (July 27, 1841)
Alexander Culton to Sarah F. Newman, July 27, 1841.
By John Scruggs, M.G. (July 27, 1841)
James Shell (or Schell) to Lucinda White, July 27, 1841.
By J. H. Benton, J.P. (July 27, 1841)
James R. Barnet to Sarah A. Thornton, July 28, 1841.
By John Scruggs, M.G. (july 29, 1841)
William Novel to Marinda Hartly, Aug. 5, 1841.
By James Sewell, M.G. (Aug. 5, 1841)
William B. Dearmon to Mary Cook, Aug. 10, 1841.
By Moses A. Cass, J.P. McMinn Co. (Aug. 10, 1841)
Madison Johnson to Nancy Presly, Aug. 13, 1841.
By Tandy L. Rice, J.P. (Aug. 13, 1841)
David Powers to Tabitha Hously, Aug. 14, 1841.
By Russell Lane, J.P. (Aug. 15, 1841)
A. B. Brown to Mary Newland, Aug. 16, 1841.
By Robert Frazier, M.G. (Jan. 19, 1842)
Samuel C. Riddle to Sarah C. Dake, Aug. 17, 1841.
(no returns)
John Colville to Martha Jarnagin, Aug. 20, 1841.
By L. R. Morrison, V.D.M. (Aug. 20, 1841)
James Baker to Louisa Bayless, Aug. 21, 1841.
(no returns)
James Underwood to Polly West, Aug. 23, 1841.
By T. S. Rice, J.P. (Aug. 27, 1841)
Gideon Combs to Elizabeth Hammer, Aug. 24, 1841.
By L. R. Morrison, V.D.M. (Aug. 24, 1841)
Cornelius P. Vandyke to Rachel Thompson, Aug. 25, 1841.
(no returns)
John N. Delzell to Nancy J. Lowry, Aug. 31, 1841.
By L. R. Morrison, V.D.M. (Aug. 31, 1841)
James W. Rogers to Elizabeth Barksdale, Sep. 1, 1841.
(no returns)

Isaac H. McNabb to Jane M. Wear, Sep. 11, 1841.
  By R. A. McAdoo, J.P. (Sep. 16, 1841)
Jesse Melton to Nancy Erskin, Sep. 16, 1841.
  By Hiram Ingram, M.G. (Sep. 17, 1841)
John Haley to Mary Thompson, Sep. 18, 1841.
  By C. Taliaferro, M.G. (Sep. 19, 1841)
Thomas Riggins to Matheirsa Pugh, Sep. 18, 1841.
  By A. H. Benton, J.P. (Sep. 18, 1841)
Pleasant Bryant to Polly Rucker, Sep. 18, 1841.
  (no returns)
H. Wm. Aldehoff to Ellen M. McCallie, Sep. 20, 1841.
  By M. C. Hawk, M.G.M.E. Church. (Sep. 21, 1841)
John B. Harris to Sarah Gregg, Sep. 22, 1841.
  By T. L. Hoyl, J.P. (Sep. 23, 1841)
James M. Jones to Matilda Luttrell, Sep. 22, 1841.
  By M. W. Cunningham, J.P. (Sep. 23, 1841)
Robert E. Cochran to Sarah W. Dodson, Sep. 27, 1841.
  By Robert Gregory, M.G. Baptist. (Oct. 5, 1841)
Arby H. Smith to Kiziah L. Barker, Sep. 30, 1841.
  By T. B. Love, J.P. (Oct. 7, 1841)
John Myers to Mary J. Snoddy, Oct. 5, 1841.
  By John Rogers, J.P. (Oct. 6, 1841)
John Smith to Elizabeth Heck, Oct. 6, 1841.
  (no returns)
Joseph Willhite to Elizabeth Walker, Oct. 9, 1841.
  By L. L. Ball, J.P. (Mar. 12, 1842)
John W. Marshall to Nancy Smith, Oct. 18, 1841.
  By James Sewell, M.G. (Oct. 22, 1841)
Alfred Carroll to Viney Buttram, Oct. 18, 1841.
  By William Dotson, J.P. (Oct. 19, 1841)
Charles Thompson to Lucinda Shelton, Oct. 26, 1841.
  By Richard A. McAdoo, J.P. (Oct. 26, 1841)
John A. McNutt to Sarah Stone, Oct. 27, 1841.
  By R. W. Patty, M.G.E.C. (Oct. 28, 1841)
Robert Gallahan to Josiah Pierce, Nov. 15, 1841.
  By Edward Newton, M.G. (Nov. 18, 1841)
Sterling Shelton to Charlotte A. Gregory, Nov. 13, 1841.
  By Jonathan Thomas, J.P. (Nov. 14, 1841)
W. F. Lenoir to Elizabeth C. Goddard, Nov. 16, 1841.
  By James Sewell, M.G. (Nov. 20, 1841)
Abraham Walker to Mahala Kinchelow, Nov. 17, 1841.
  By L. L. Ball, J.P. (Nov. 17, 1841)
Washington Weatherby to Emily J. Brannock, Nov. 23, 1841.
  (no returns)
Martin Gold to Rebecca Fox, Nov. 23, 1841.
  By M. C. Hawk, M.G.M.E.C. (Nov. 25, 1841)
F. L. Yokum to F. S. Henderson, Nov. 27, 1841.
  By James Sewell, M.G. (Nov. 31, 1841)
John Miller to Pamela Dobbs, Dec. 1, 1841.
  By Joseph Minze, J.P. (Dec. 2, 1841)
W. H. Rothwell to Venila Arnwine, Dec. 4, 1841.
  By Jonathan Thomas, J.P. (Dec. 9, 1841)
Churchwell Hale to Catharine Roberts, Dec. 9, 1841.
  By Jonathan Thomas, J.P. (Dec. 9, 1841)

Isham W. Farmer to Mary Bedford, Dec. 9, 1841.
  By R. A. McAdoo, J.P. (Dec. 9, 1841)
Buford Peak to Malinda Breck, Dec. 11, 1841.
  By L. L. Ball, J.P. (Dec. 17, 1841)
J. W. Howard to Mary Payne, Dec. 15, 1841.
  (no returns)
John Gregory to Parrilee Atkinson, Dec. 18, 1841.
  By L. L. Ball, J.P. (Dec. 21, 1841)
Bogan Cash to Elizabeth A. King, Dec. 21, 1841.
  By William Dotson, J.P. (Dec. 21, 1841)
Oliver P. Foster to Malinda C. Gibson, Dec. 21, 1841.
  By T. B. Love, J.P. (Dec. 23, 1841)
N. H. Cansler to Hannah Reynolds, Dec. 28, 1841.
  By John Scruggs, M.G. (Dec. 30, 1841)
Thomas Shelton to Elizabeth Wright, Dec. 28, 1841.
  By R. A. McAdoo, J.P. (Jan. 6, 1842)
John Newman to Catherine St. John, Dec. 28, 1841.
  By Robert Gregory, M.G. Baptist. (Dec. 30, 1841)
John H. Read to Elijah Pugh, Dec. 29, 1841.
  (no returns)
Manuel Parkison to Julia Dougherty, Jan. 6, 1842.
  By John Jenkins, J.P. (Jan. 6, 1842)
Stephen Paris (or Pharis) to Mrs. Hudah Ball, (Jan. 10,
  1842. (no returns)
John Drake to Rachel Baldwin, Jan. 20, 1842.
  By A. C. Robeson, J.P. (Jan. 20, 1842)
Asahel Carlock to Mary Douglass, Jan. 26, 1842.
  (no returns)
Jesse A. Ware to Margaret Long, Jan. 20, 1842.
  (no returns)
James A. Newton to Scynthia C. Allison, Jan. 23, 1842.
  By William L. Forest, M.G. (Jan. 27, 1842)
John S. Goodwin to Jane Hannah, Jan. 25, 1842.
  By John W. Barnette, J.P. (Jan. 25, 1842)
Caleb Vinson to Margaret Vinson, Jan. 25, 1842.
  By Jonathan Thomas, J.P. (Jan. 29, 1842)
Patrick Annshougal to Martha Vinson, Jan. 31, 1842.
  By J. H. Benton, J.P. (Jan. 31, 1842)
Edward H. Carnay to Matilda Worley, Feb. 3, 1842.
  By Robert Frazier, M.G. (Feb. 3, 1842)
Dudley Fields to Elizabeth Carroll, Feb. 7, 1842.
  By Jonathan Thomas, J.P. (Feb. 10, 1842)
Herrod Rudd to Margaret Reatherford, Feb. 16, 1842.
  (no returns)
Jacob Cain to Fany Ogle, July 21, 1842.
  (no returns)
James Stanfield to Caroline Roberts, Feb. 21, 1842.
  By M. C. Hawk, M.G.M.E. Church. (Feb. 24, 1842)
Wm. Brown to Lucinda Cooper, Feb. 22, 1842.
  By Robert Gregory, M. Baptist. (Feb. 22, 1842)
Michael Bowerman to Mary A. Smith, Feb. 22, 1842.
  By John Jenkins, J.P. (Feb. 22, 1842)
Johnson Woods to Rebecca Fowler, Feb. 23, 1842.
  By John Jenkins, J.P. (Feb. 23, 1842)

23

McMINN COUNTY MARRIAGES

Peter Carter to Jarusha Dobbs, Mar. 2, 1842.
  By Joseph Minzer, J.P. (Mar. 3, 1842)
W. H. Slover to Sarah J. Jarnagin, Feb. 7, 1842.
  By M. C. Hawk, M.G.M.E. Church. (Feb. 8, 1842)
Silas Emery to Margaret Julian, Feb. 8, 1842.
  (no returns)
Elias Wilkinson to Easter Dearmon, Mar. 2, 1842.
  By M. A. Cass, J.P. (Mar. 2, 1842)
Joseph Cole to Glaphrey Heard, Feb. 28, 1842.
  By T. S. Rice, J.P. (Mar. 1, 1842)
John Southard to Elizabeth Southard, Mar. 7, 1842.
  By T. S. Rice, J.P. (Mar. 8, 1842)
Stephenson Poe to Hannah Bishop, Mar. 9, 1842.
  By John Jenkins, J.P. (Mar. 10, 1842)
Stephen Wallin (or Walling) to Sarah Bishop, Mar. 10,
  1842. By Robert Frazier, M.G. (Mar. 10, 1842)
William Sehorn to Ann E. Coleman, Mar. 17, 1842.
  (no returns)
Isaac Benson to Jane Collier, Mar. 22, 1842.
William Duke to Nancy Killingsworth, Mar. 23, 1842.
  By C. W. Rice, J.P. (Mar. 24, 1842)
Burton Lewis to Elizabeth Logan, Mar. 24, 1842.
  By E. P. Bloom, J.P. (Mar. 24, 1842)
William Wyatt to Mary Pike, Mar. 28, 1842.
  By J. H. Benton, J.P. (Mar. 28, 1842)
George O. Patty to Laura S. Newman, Mar. 29, 1842.
  By Robert Gregory, M. Baptist. (Mar. 29, 1842)
Daniel Pearce to Barbara Barrett, Apr. 14, 1842.
  (no returns)
Hiram Day to Rhoda Shulton, Apr. 20, 1842.
  (no returns)
Lawson H. Wilkerson to Frances Calhoun, Apr. 19, 1842.
  (no returns)
Frederick Green to Jane Romerus, Feb. 9, 1842.
  By M. W. Cunningham, J.P. (Feb. 10, 1842)
Benjamin F. Henderson to Ursula Culton, Apr. 26, 1842.
  By J. H. Benton, J.P. (Apr. 26, 1842)
Matthew Cagle to Kaziah J. Morgan, Apr. 26, 1842.
  By Thos. Camp, J.P. (Apr. 28, 1842)
John Ranins to E. E. Rogers, May 6, 1842.
  (no returns)
George Barksdale to Martha Green, May 10, 1842.
  By A. Carlock, J.P. (May 10, 1842)
Hathorn Hood to Rhuey Marshall, May 11, 1842.
  By R. A. McAdoo, J.P. (May 15, 1842)
W. J. McClatchey to M. L. Rowles, May 11, 1842.
  By Henry Price, M.G. (May 12, 1842)
Henry Williams to Elizabeth Nichols, May 12, 1842.
  By M. C. Hawk, M.M.E. Church. (May 15, 1842)
Benjamin Tucker to Eliza Erskin, May 21, 1842.
  By Tapley Gregory, J.P. (May 23, 1842)
Robert Miller to Letty McGuire, May 21, 1842.
  By R. A. McAdoo, J.P. (May 22, 1842)
Jacob Overholser to Malinda Whaley, June 11, 1842.
  (no returns)

McMINN COUNTY MARRIAGES

James M. Casada to Minerva Nelson, June 13, 1842.
   By R. W. Patty, M.M.E. Church. (June 21, 1842)
Benjamin Wells to Fathamany Prather, June 16, 1842.
   By Robert Frazier, M.G. (June 16, 1842)
William D. Durham to Ann Faulkner, June 23, 1842.
   (no returns)
Sterling C. Beavers to Ann Eliza Beavers, July 12, 1842.
   By Hiram Ingram, M.G. (July 12, 1842)
John C. Casad to Nancy J. McAmis, July 21, 1842.
   By R. W. Patty, M.M.E. Church. (July 21, 1842)
James Braden to Susan Derrick, July 25, 1842.
   By E. P. Bloom, J.P. (July 26, 1842)
James Hall to Elizabeth J. Johnston, July 26, 1842.
   By Nathan Harrison, M.M.E. Church. (July 26, 1842)
John E. Monger to Elizabeth Bond, July 28, 1842.
   By Samuel Wilson, J.P. (July 28, 1842)
James Hays to Lucinda Russel, Aug. 2, 1842.
   By Elisha Hays, J.P. (Aug. 4, 1842)
John T. Forgy to Jane Weaks, Aug. 4, 1842.
   By Elisha Hays, J.P. (Aug. 4, 1842)
Joseph Robeson to Nancy C. Mayfield, Aug. 6, 1842.
   By Robert Frazier, M.G. (Aug. 7, 1842)
Joshua B. Jones to Evaline T. Jamerson, Aug. 10, 1842.
   By J. Sewell, M.G. (Aug. 10, 1842)
Henry Wassom to Mary Garreson, Aug. 11, 1842.
   By G. W. Wallis, J.P. (Aug. 12, 1842)
James Pangles to Lydia McKeehan (or McDeehan?), Aug. 13,
   1842. (no returns)
John McGinley to Mary Ann Matthews, Aug. 18, 1843.
   (no returns)
Samuel Gentry to Charlotte Dougherty, Aug. 18, 1842.
   By Green L. Reynolds, J.P. (Aug. 22, 1842)
Jabez Weddows to Mary Ann Ford, Aug. 18, 1842.
   By L. R. Morrison, V.D.M. (Aug. 18, 1842)
Lewis Ramsey to Susannah Newman, Aug. 23, 1842.
   By R. A. McAdoo, J.P. (Aug. 23, 1842)
Wesley Walker to Elvira Crisp, Aug. 25, 1842.
   By Dickerson Morris. (Aug. 25, 1842)
William W. McLester to Amelia Metcalf, Aug. 31, 1842.
   By Robert Snead, M.G. (Sep. 1, 1842)
Richard T. Engledow to Elizabeth Sehorn, Aug. 31, 1842.
   By J. Cunningham, J.P. (Aug. 31, 1842)
Thomas Caldwell to Mary Ann Logan, Sep. 1, 1842.
   (no returns)
Pleasant N. Lee to Susan Lee, Sep. 14, 1842.
   By Robert Gregory, M. Baptist. (Sep. 15, 1842)
William T. McCallie to Mrs. Mary Forgy, Sep. 16, 1842.
   By Joel Culpepper, J.P. (Sep. __, 1842)
Daniel Parkeson to Rebecca K. Dodson, Sep. 14, 1842.
   By W. F. Forrest, M.G. (Sep. 16, 1842)
Franklin Wilson to Sarah B. Marcum, Sep. 20, 1842.
   By M. D. Anderson, J.P. (Sep. 20, 1842)
Elijah Graham to Lewann Browder, Sep. 20, 1842.
   By J. H. Benton, J.P. (Sep. 20, 1842)

McMINN COUNTY MARRIAGES

Charles F. Coleman to Sarah Worsay, Sep. 27, 1842.
    By Jonathan Thomas, J.P. (Sep. 28, 1842)
William H. Howard to Nancy L. Steed, Sep. 27, 1842.
    By Justus Steed, J.P. (Sep. 27, 1842)
Williamson Brickson to Elizabeth Mansell, Sep. 30, 1842.
    (no returns)
James W. Owen to Amelia Kirkpatrick, Oct. 3, 1842.
    By L. R. Morrison, V.D.M. (Oct. 4, 1842)
Gabriel Cantrell to Alzira McMinn, Oct. 4, 1842.
    By Green L. Raynolds, J.P. (Oct. 4, 1842)
Stephen Balley to Ann Everton, Oct. 8, 1842.
    By A. Carlock, J.P. (Nov. 3, 1842)
James S. Russell to Maldonetty Cate, Oct. 10, 1842.
    By Wilson Chapman, M.G. (Oct. 20, 1842)
Ezekiel Beam to Jane Loyd, Oct. 11, 1842.
    By M. D. Anderson, J.P. (Oct. 11, 1842)
John J. Payne to Lucinda Parris, Oct. 11, 1842.
    By Hiram Ingram, M.G. (Oct. 12, 1842)
William Southard to Rebecca R. M. John, Oct. 13, 1842.
    By Justus Steed, J.P. (Oct. 13, 1842)
William J. Rice to Martha Lusk, Oct. 13, 1842.
    By W. H. Ballew, J.P. (Oct. 13, 1842)
Bennet Waters to Minerva Bannock, Oct. 13, 1842.
    By C. W. Rice, J.P. (Oct. 13, 1842)
Colvin Williams to Elizabeth Sherrell, Oct. 13, 1842.
    By John Gaston, M.G. (Oct. 13, 1842)
Eli Dixon to Mary Couch, Oct. 14, 1842.
    By Robert Gregory, M.G. Baptist. (Oct. 15, 1842)
James McMinn to Matilda Buck, Oct. 18, 1842.
    By M. C. Hawk, M.G.M.E. Church, (Oct. 20, 1842)
Jesse B. Dodson to Sarah Newton, Oct. 22, 1842.
    By N. Harrison, M.G. (Oct. 20, 1842(?)
David Bradford to Sarah Dougherty, Oct. 25, 1842.
    By John Jenkins, J.P. (Oct. 25, 1842)
Jacob Green to Susannah Crisp, Oct. 26, 1842.
    By J. H. Benton, J.P. (Oct. 26, 1842)
Andrew A. Kinser to Pheoby Kinchelo, Oct. 26, 1842.
    By L. L. Ball, J.P. (Nov. 2, 1842)
Henry Camron to Margaret A. Stephens, May 10, 1842.
    By L. L. Ball, J.P. (May 14, 1842)
William S. Roberts to Katherine Walker, Nov. 2, 1842.
    By L. L. Ball, J.P. (Nov. 3, 1842)
William Calahan to Martha Browder, Nov. 3, 1842.
    (no returns)
Alfred Barksdale to Winny Yancy, Nov. 4, 1842.
    By A. Carlock, J.P. (Nov. 4, 1842)
James Pennington to Jane Vincent, Nov. 8, 1842.
    By John Jenkins, J.P. (Nov. 8, 1842)
John McGenty to Nancy Gentry, Nov. 9, 1842.
    By C. Sanders, M.G. (Nov. 9, 1842)
Thos. W. Cunningham to Dicy Wilson, Nov. 17, 1842.
    By W. F. Forest, M.G. (Nov. 17, 1842)
William Manary to Zany Sower, Nov. 17, 1842.
    By M. A. Cass, J.P. (Nov. 17, 1842)

McMINN COUNTY MARRIAGES

Parmer Branham to Susannah Howard, Nov. 22, 1842.
  By J. H. Benton, J.P. (Nov. 22, 1842)
George W. Moore to Marg Goss, Dec. 1, 1842.
  By G. W. Wallace. (Dec. 1, 1842)
Jacob Wimberly to Elizabeth Gray, Dec. 1, 1842.
  By C. Sanders, M.G. (Dec. 1, 1842)
Benjamin Roberts to Ann Helvy, Dec. 6, 1842.
  By Tapley Gregory, J.P. (Dec. 11, 1842)
William W. Anderson to Laura P. Smith, Nov. 13, 1842.
  By L. R. Morrison, V.D.M. (Nov. 13, 1842)
Joseph Malone to Mary Miller, Dec. 16, 1842.
  By Samuel Wilson, J.P. (Dec. 16, 1842)
Elizabeth McCallister to Ruth Bishop, Dec. 19, 1842.
  By Thomas Camp, J.P. (Dec. 19, 1842)
John Wacacy to Nancy Chapman, Dec. 26, 1842.
  By Wilson Chapman, M.G. (Dec. 26, 1842)
Walter Rothwell to Charlotte Lawson, Dec. 21, 1842.
John M. Ellis to Hannah Maples, Dec. 21, 1842.
  (no returns)
William Eaton to Jane Robeson, Dec. 27, 1842.
  By Moses Swanney, J.P. (Dec. 28, 1842)
William H. Freeman to Mildred A. Thornton, Dec. 28, 1842.
  By Wilson Chapman, M.G. (Dec. 28, 1842)
Galloway Carmel to Mary Thompson, Jan. 2, 1843.
  By R. A. McAdoo, J.P. (Jan. 3, 1843)
Joseph Wolff to Dorcas Trimm, Jan. 3, 1843.
  By Neil Buttram, P. of G. (Jan. 11, 1843)
Erwin S. Minzes to Saphronia Buttram, Jan. 3, 1843.
  By Neil Buttram, P. of G. (Jan. 8, 1843)
David Pearce to Mary Triplett, Jan. 7, 1843.
  By W. F. Forest, M.G. (Jan. 8, 1843)
Prior H. Walker to Mary Ann Cate, Jan. 12, 1843.
  By A. Slover, M.G. (Jan. 12, 1843)
William Carter to Elizabeth Creevs, Jan. 12, 1843.
  By W. H. Ballew, J.P. (Jan. 12, 1843)
Benjamin F. Welcker to Sarah E. Reagan, Jan. 17, 1843.
  By J. Sewell, M.G. (Jan. 17, 1843)
Pleasant M. Rivers to Ruhanny Fisher, Jan. 21, 1843.
  By John Jenkins, J.P. (Jan. 22, 1843)
Edwin S. Joy to Sarah E. Fitzgerald, Jan. 26, 1843.
  By Robert Snead, M.G. (Jan. 26, 1843)
William Stone to Elizabeth Cofer, Jan. 26, 1843.
  By M. D. Anderson, J.P. (Jan. 26, 1843)
David D. Ballew to Celia D. Sparks, Feb. 4, 1843.
  By E. P. Bloom, J.P. (Feb. 9, 1843)
John M. Trew to Mary Ann Trew, Feb. 6, 1843.
  By Samuel Snoddy, J.P. (Feb. 8, 1843)
James S. Liner to Lucy V. Ahl, Feb. 7, 1843.
  By Joel Culpepper, J.P. (Feb. 8, 1843)
Absolom H. Doan to Sarah L. Brown, Feb. 7, 1843.
  (no returns)
Jabez Fitzgerald to Caroline Kirkpatrick, Feb. 8, 1843.
  By Abel Pearson, M.G. (Feb. 8, 1843)
Rufus Green to Amy Bledsoe, Feb. 8, 1843.
  By R. A. McAdoo, J.P. (Feb. 8, 1843)

McMINN COUNTY MARRIAGES

Nicholas Aerheart to Clarinda Eden, Feb. 8, 1843.
 By A. Harem, M.G. (Feb. 9, 1843)
Robert Walker to Julian Philips, Feb. 10, 1843.
 By H. S. Godsey, M.G. (Feb. 12, 1843)
George W. Crittenden to Lucinda Caldwell, Feb. 11, 1843.
 By M. D. Anderson, J.P. (Feb. 12, 1843)
John Elliott to Sarah Carney, Feb. 11, 1843.
 (no returns)
Levi Long to Mary Wilson, Feb. 13, 1843.
 (no returns)
Marcellus M. Dodson to Susan Hardy, Feb. 16, 1843.
 By L. R. Morrison, V.D.M. (Feb. 16, 1843)
Henry Emerson to Minerva Pearce, Feb. 18, 1845.
 By Edward Newton, M.G. (Feb. 22, 1843)
William Ford to Elvira Myers, Feb. 22, 1843.
 By A. Kiner, J.P. (Feb. 28, 1843)
James E. Sliger to Amanda Spradling, Feb. 27, 1843.
 By Neil Buttram, M.G. (Feb. 27, 1843)
Thomas C. Cantrell to Louisa Lawson, Mar. 1, 1843.
 By Hiram Ingram, M.G. (Mar. 1, 1843)
Aaron Southan to Lydia Johns, Mar. 2, 1843.
 By Justus Steed, J.P. (Mar. 2, 1843)
John Vance to Nancy Crows, Mar. 9, 1843.
 By J. H. Benton, J.P. (Mar. 9, 1843)
James N. Wilson to Delaney Triplett, Mar. 9, 1843.
 By Moses Swenny, Esq. (Mar. 9, 1843)
Jesse Mason to Nancy Norman, Mar. 11, 1843.
 (no returns)
John Green to Mahala Bledsoe, Mar. 13, 1843.
 (no returns)
Daniel W. Ahl to Emaline Wilson, Mar. 15, 1843.
 By John Jenkins, J.P. (Mar. 17, 1843)
McCamy N. Dorcy to Rebecca Newman, Mar. 15, 1843.
 By John Scruggs, M. (Mar. 15, 1843)
Johnson Crewse to Mary McGuire, Mar. 20, 1843.
 By W. H. Ballew, J.P. (Mar. 23, 1843)
David Niel to Elizabeth A. Shults, Mar. 29, 1843.
 (no returns)
John H. Long to Milly Gray, Apr. 1, 1843.
 By M. A. Cass, J.P. (Apr. 2, 1843)
Jefferson Hooser to Margaret Hix, Apr. 3, 1843.
 By M. A. Cass, J.P. (Apr. 3, 1843)
John Sarlin to Mary O. Daniel, Apr. 8, 1843.
 By A. Carlock, J.P. (Apr. 9, 1843)
William E. Martin to Nancy W. Dodson, Apr. 18, 1843.
 By Wilson Chapman, M.G. (Apr. 20, 1843)
Richard M. Fisher to Ann M. Gettys, Apr. 20, 1843.
 By L. T. Morrison, V.D.M. (Apr. 20, 1843)
James Kelly to Lois A. Bridges, Apr. 26, 1843.
 By L. R. Morrison, V.D.M. (Apr. 26, 1843)
William L. Rice to Elizabeth A. Rayburn, May 3, 1843.
 By W. F. Forest, M.G. (May 3, 1843)
James H. Dugan to Mary E. Barnett, May 9, 1843.
 By Wilson Chapman, M.G. (May 25, 1843)

McMINN COUNTY MARRIAGES

Richard B. Campbell to Isabella Bridges, May 25, 1843.
  By L. R. Morrison, V.D.M. (May 25, 1843)
D. C. McMillin to Mary S. Campbell, May 24, 1843.
  By L. R. Morrison, V.D.M. (May 24, 1843)
Nimrod Dodson to Margaret Ann Grigsby, June 5, 1843.
  By W. F. Forrest, M.G. (June 6, 1843)
John H. Colville to Janett V. Lide, June 6, 1843.
  By A. Slover, M.G. (June 6, 1843)
John Wallen to Emily Dellon, June 12, 1843.
  By Elisha Hays, J.P. (June 12, 1843)
William H. Gibbs to Martha Rudd, June 13, 1843.
  By Hiram Ingram, M.G. (June 16, 1843)
William Howard to Elizabeth Henderson, June 14, 1843.
  (no returns)
John W. Langford to Eliza E. Sharp, June 17, 1843.
  By B. E. Blain, J.P. (June 17, 1843)
Gibson Langford to Sarah Wray, June 27, 1843.
  (no returns)
Looney Grisham to Eliza Peters, July 7, 1843.
  By W. H. Ballew, J.P. (July 7, 1843)
James M. Rutherford to Nancy Cantrell, July 13, 1843.
  By A. Carlock, J.P. (July 15, 1843)
Blasengame Buck to Mary Morgan, July 14, 1843.
  (no returns)
Thomas Hemphill to Melvina Morris, July 18, 1843.
  By M. D. Anderson, J.P. (July 18, 1843)
Abner L. Coffman to Sarah Couch, July 20, 1843.
  (no returns)
Robert Langford to Mary Hughs, July 20, 1843.
  By J. H. Benton, J.P. (July 26, 1843)
William Poe to Jane Hillard, July 25, 1843.
  (no returns)
Benjamin John to Mary Baker, July 27, 1843.
  By Moses Sweny, Esq. (July 27, 1843)
Solomon Cole to Harriet Emory, July 27, 1843.
  By Asabel Carlock, J.P. (July 27, 1843)
Anderson Coffman to Louisa J. Campbell, July 29, 1843.
  By Rev. B. Buckner. (July 30, 1843)
Samuel Edgemon to Jane Allen, July 29, 1843.
  By J. W. Barnett, J.P. (July 30, 1843)
Green C. Trotter to Sinthey C. Triplett, Aug. 1, 1843.
  By William Newton, M.G. (Aug. 1, 1843)
Wilson Small to Hannah Lamor, Aug. 9, 1843.
  By D. Morris, M.G. (Aug. 10, 1843)
Eldred Lane to Armenia Miller, Aug. 9, 1843.
  By W. H. Ballew, J.P. (Aug. 9, 1843)
James Gilley to Mary Ann Sivils, Aug. 10, 1843.
  By M. D. Anderson, J.P. (Aug. 10, 1843)
James Lea (or Lee) to Lucinda Cantrell, Aug. 10, 1843.
  (no returns)
William Hafely to Jane Seay, Aug. 17, 1843.
  By J. H. Benton, J.P. (Aug. 17, 1843)
Madison Williams to Mary E. Clark, Aug. 22, 1843.
  By J. W. Barnett, J.P. (Aug. 22, 1843)

McMINN COUNTY MARRIAGES

John J. York to Matilda Luttrell, Aug. 27, 1843.
(no returns)
Isaac R. Thompson to Amanda Gray N(?), Aug. 30, 1843.
By Wm. F. Forest, M.G. (Aug. 31, 1843)
Archibald F. Smart to Isbell Farris, Aug. 31, 1843.
(no returns)
Tessy Buck to Elizabeth Walker, Spe. 11, 1843.
(no returns)
James Sisk to Mary King, Sep. 13, 1843.
By Tapley Gregory, J.P. (Sep. 17, 1843)
Joseph Monger to Jackabena Southard, Sep. 14, 1843.
By Justus Steed, J.P. (Sep. 14, 1843)
Greenberry Cate to Magdalena Cate, Sep. 20, 1843.
By Y. Rose, M.G. (Sep. 24, 1843)
John Sparks to Mary Ann Gallaher, Sep. 26, 1843.
By Green L. Reynolds, J.P. (Sep. 26, 1843)
John S. Raper to Mary Ann Robeson, Sep. 27, 1843.
By John Scruggs, J.P. (Sep. 28, 1843)
Jacob S. Miller to Edny Fair, Oct. 2, 1843.
By T. S. Rice, J.P. (Oct. 5, 1843)
Martin Onich to Eva Dobbs, Oct. 7, 1843.
By G. W. Wallis, J.P. (Oct. 8, 1843)
James M. White to Mary A. Dennis, Oct. 7, 1843.
By J. H. Benton, J.P. (Oct. 8, 1843)
David T. Shelton to Mary Terry, Oct. 7, 1843.
By M. Robert Gregory, M. Baptist. (Oct. 8, 1843)
Thomas J. Lowry to Nancy B. Smith, Oct. 9, 1843.
By J. Cunningham, M.G. (Oct. 11, 1843)
James W. Plank to Mary Ann Hays, Oct. 11, 1843.
By Neil Buttram, M.G. (Oct. 12, 1843)
Jefferson D. Murphy to Susan Orten, Oct. 13, 1843.
(no returns)
Peter Roberts to Clive Guffy, Oct. 14, 1843.
By Neil Buttram, M.G. (Oct. 15, 1843)
John N. Cracy to Nancy Rogers, Oct. 16, 1843.
By M. D. Anderson, J.P. (Oct. 17, 1843)
Daniel D. Holcomb to Glapha Ann Robertson, Oct. 17, 1843.
(no returns)
William R. Neil to Elizabeth Burnett, Oct. 25, 1843.
By G. W. Wallis, J.P. (Oct. 26, 1843)
G. W. Haney to Margaret Pangle, Oct. 25, 1843.
By Samuel Wilson, J.P. (Oct. 25, 1843)
Isaac Sherrell to Jane Cate, Oct. 26, 1843.
By John Gaston, M.G. (Oct. 26, 1843)
Pleasant M. Long to Elizabeth Long, Oct. 26, 1843.
By William F. Forest, M.G. (Oct. 26, 1843)
Robert McNelly to Ann T. Fisher, Oct. 26, 1843.
By Justus Steed, J.P. (Oct. 27, 1843)
George W. Haney to Margaret Pangle, Oct. 25, 1843.
By Samuel Wilson, J.P. (Oct. 25, 1843)
Alexander Baker to Prudence Womack, Oct. 31, 1843.
By Jonathan Thomas, J.P. (Nov. 14, 1843)
Wm. W. Heddleston to Mary Fairbanks, Oct. 28, 1843.
(no returns)

Lide W. Dobbs to Catherine Monroe, Nov. 1, 1843.
  By G. W. Wallis, J.P. (Nov. 2, 1843)
James McCoy to Emeline Southard, Nov. 6, 1843.
  By Rev. Edwin A. Allen. (Nov. 7, 1843)
Philip Cold to Eliza Smith, Nov. 8, 1843.
  (no returns)
James Rutherford to Rebecca A. Gamble, Nov. 11, 1843.
  By James Sewell, J.P. (Nov. 12, 1843)
Justus C. Steed to Sarah Jane Lasiter, Nov. 20, 1843.
  By Wilson Chapman, M.G. (Nov. 21, 1843)
Pleasant M. Reynolds to Elizabeth A. Oliver, Nov. 20,
  1843. (no returns)
Richard Spradling, Sr. to Mrs. Hannah West, Nov. 24,
  1843. By Neil Buttram, M.G. (Nov. 28, 1843)
John H. Luttrell to Susan Brock, Nov. 25, 1843.
  By M. I. Anderson, J.P. (Nov. 26, 1843)
William H. Patty to Ede Ferguson, Nov. 29, 1843.
  By Robert Gregory, M. Baptist. (Nov. 20, 1843(?)
Frankford W. Hafly to Elizabeth Says, Nov. 30, 1843.
  By R. A. McAdoo, J.P. (Nov. 30, 1843)
Robert Randolph to Jemima Miller, Dec. 2, 1843.
  By Wm. McKamy, J.P. (Dec. 3, 1843)
Daniel A. Toomey to Lucinda Stead, Dec. 6, 1843.
  By M. I. Anderson, J.P. (Dec. 7, 1843)
Wm. Scarborough to Deniz Cambright, Dec. 9, 1843.
  (no returns)
Oliver P. N. Caldwell to Lucinda J. Johnson, Dec. 12, 1843.
  By Joseph Peeler, M.G. (Dec. 12, 1843)
William Chamlee to Elizabeth Fair, Dec. 13, 1843.
  By T. L. Rice. (Dec. 19, 1843)
Edward W. Robeson to Catherine Campbell, Dec. 13, 1843.
  By James Carter. (Dec. 17, 1843)
Morris M. Smith to Amanda M. Jarnagin, Dec. 14, 1843.
  By William H. Ballew, J.P. (Dec. 14, 1843)
William S. S. Porter to Martha Dodson, Dec. 14, 1843.
  By Wm. McKamy, J.P. (Dec. 17, 1843)
Robert Cate to Elizabeth Brown, Dec. 15, 1843.
  By R. A. McAdoo, J.P. (Dec. 15, 1843)
John Queener to Mable Gregg, Dec. 12, 1843.
  By Hiram Ingram, M.G. (Dec. 14, 1843)
John McMillan to Susan Reneau, Dec. 17, 1843.
  By Daniel McPhail, Esq. (Dec. 17, 1843)
James F. Benton to Nancessa White, Dec. 20, 1843.
  By Moses A. Cass, J.P. (Dec. 21, 1843)
Tapley Gregory to Eleanor Snodgrass, Dec. 20, 1843.
  By R. A. McAdoo, J.P. (Dec. 21, 1843)
Thomas M. Isbell to Sarah Ann Terry, Dec. 21, 1843.
  By A. Slover, M.G. (Dec. 21, 1843)
Charles Dennis to Nancy Dennis, Dec. 23, 1843.
  By Tapley Gregory, M.G. (Dec. 24, 1843)
Silas Morgan to Christen Moore, Dec. 23, 1843.
  (no returns)
John Kinser to Rachel Barb, Dec. 27, 1843.
  By J. Cunningham, J.P. (Dec. 27, 1843)

John M. Hunt to Margaret N. Tunnell, Dec. 28, 1843.
  By Moses Sweeney, J.P. (Dec. 28, 1843)
Charles H. Carrigan to Mary E. Benton, Dec. 30, 1843.
  By C. Sanders, M.G. (Dec. 31, 1843)
Ransom A. Marcum to Jane Matthews, Dec. 30, 1843.
  By M. D. Anderson, J.P. (Dec. 31, 1843)
Christian Peters to Ellen Grisham, Jan. 9, 1844.
  By Wm. H. Ballew, J.P. (Jan. 9, 1844)
Rosevell P. Burke to Catherine J. Wilson, Jan. 10, 1844.
  By M. D. Anderson, J.P. (Jan. 10, 1844)
William F. Peck to Sarah E. Workman, Jan. 22, 1844.
  By T. Wetten, M.G. (Jan. 23, 1844)
James T. Eaton to Jane Wengewood, Jan. 20, 1844.
  By B. E. Blain, J.P. (Jan. 21, 1844)
Enoch Harrel to Elizabeth Miller, Jan. 25, 1844.
  By J. W. Barnett, J.P. (Jan. 25, 1844)
Arthur Newman to Louisa Reneau, Jan. 27, 1844.
  By B. E. Blain, J.P. (Jan. 28, 1844)
James Wilson to Barbara Marcum, Feb. 3, 1844.
  By John Gaston, M.G. (Feb. 4, 1844)
John Cruse to Elizabeth Ann Cate, Feb. 7, 1844.
  By J. H. Benton, J.P. (Feb. 7, 1844)
Adolphus H. Crow to Emeline Glaze, Feb. 3, 1844.
  By A. Slover, M.G. (Feb. 8, 1844)
William Shipley to Ann E. Brandon, Feb. 18, 1844.
  By James Sewell, M.G. (Feb. 18, 1844)
Thomas Martin to Polly A. Lawson, Feb. 17, 1844.
  By E. P. Blom, J.P. (Feb. 18, 1844)
B. W. Smith to L. G. Prigmore, Feb. 20, 1844.
  (no returns)
S. Swafford to Martha C. Wilson, Feb. 21, 1844.
  (no returns)
Saml McSpadden to Charity Cunningham, Feb. 22, 1844.
  (no returns)
Samuel Hughes to Easter Roe, Feb. 27, 1844.
  (no returns)
Elias Buchannon to Scyntha Lewis, March 4, 1844.
  (no returns)
W. C. Henly to Mary Owen, Mar. 7, 1844.
  By M. D. Anderson, J.P. (Mar. 7, 1844)
J. L. Carmichael to Ruth K. Prigmore, Mar. 12, 1844.
  By Thos. H. Small, M.G.C.P.C. (Apr. 24, 1845)
G. W. Hughs to Elize Cate, Mar. 13, 1844.
  By J. H. Benton, J.P. (Mar. 17, 1844)
Warren Moss to Patsy Cloud (Mar. 14, 1844.
  By M. C. Sanders, J.P. (Mar. 14, 1844)
Elias Henderson to Sarah Boon, Mar. 22, 1844.
  By John Scruggs, M.G. (Mar. 26, 1844)
Squire North to Eliza Herd, Mar. 25, 1844.
  By Samuel Wilson, J.P. (Mar. 25, 1844)
James C. Massengale to Elizabeth Morris, Mar. 30, 1844.
  By E. P. Bloom, J.P. (Mar. 31, 1844)
C. W. Rice to Julia C. Cobb, Apr. 1, 1844.
  By Hiram Ingram, M.G. (Apr. 2, 1844)

McMINN COUNTY MARRIAGES

Absolem Maples to Sarah Maples, Apr. 4, 1844.
By John Hoyl, M.G. (Apr. 4, 1844)
Wm. R. Wright to Lucy Moon, Apr. 6, 1844.
By Tapley Gregory, J.P. (Apr. 7, 1844)
Peter Shook to Elizabeth Brad, Apr. 6, 1844.
By J. H. Benton, J.P. (Apr. 7, 1844)
John Webb to Elizabeth Maris, Apr. 16, 1844.
By J. H. Benton, J.P. (Apr. 18, 1844)
John D. Sweeny to Jane M. Underdown, Apr. 18, 1844.
By John Hays, J.P. (Apr. 18, 1844)
William Wyrick to Nancy Renfro, Apr. 18, 1844.
By T. S. Rice, J.P. (Apr. 18, 1844)
John Chambers to Frances Carny, Apr. 22, 1844.
By M. S. Cass, J.P. (Apr. 24, 1844)
Mitchell Johnson to Lucinda Presly, Apr. 22, 1844.
By Justice Steed, J.P. (Apr. 24, 1844)
Maredeth Hart to Julian Nance, Apr. 23, 1844.
(no returns)
Samuel W. Thomas to Mary C. Davis, May 9, 1844.
By M. C. Hawk, M.G. (May 9, 1844)
Lindley M. Johnson to Eliza Jane Barnett, May 14, 1844.
By G. W. Wallis, J.P. (May 24, 1844)
Joseph Smith to Visa Askins, May 23, 1844.
By M. C. Atchley, M.G. (May 23, 1844)
Uriah Thompson to Susan Largent, May 27, 1844.
(Returned by Thompson, not executed June 24, 1844)
William Roberts to Harriet Owens, June 1, 1844.
By J. H. Venton, J.P. (June 2, 1844)
Lycander N. Johnson to Mira McDaniel, June 4, 1844.
By G. W. Rice, J.P. (June 4, 1844)
James Hester to Eliza Wordon, June 11, 1844.
By John Hoyl, M.G. (June 13, 1844)
Isaac Swinford to Keziah Woods, June 12, 1844.
By L. L. Ball, J.P. (June 13, 1844)
Jonathan F. Pugh to Elizabeth Reed, June 18, 1844.
By L. L. Ball, J.P. (July 7, 1844)
P. B. Elliott to Emeline Kelly, June 20, 1844.
By M. A. Cass, J.P. (June 20, 1844)
O. S. Myrick to Jane Grisham, July 3, 1844.
By Tapley Gregory, J.P. (July 4, 1844)
Hiram Robeson to Sally Ketron, July 4, 1844.
By Daniel McPhail, J.P. (July 4, 1844)
Russel Boren to Nancy Rhea, July 9, 1844.
By Moses A. Cass, J.P. (July 11, 1844)
John Clark to Nancy Hampton, July 10, 1844.
By John Jenkins, J.P. (Aug. 13, 1844)
Jacob Moon to Arrena Newton, July 10, 1844.
(no returns)
William Cannon to Matilda Crawford, July 12, 1844.
By Daniel McPhail, J.P. (July 14, 1844)
G. W. Sims to Caldena Lawson, July 15, 1844.
By J. B. Fryor, M.G. (July 17, 1844)
Uriah Payne to Nancy Atkinson, July 16, 1844.
By C. R. Hoyl, J.P. (July 17, 1844)

Thomas C. Roberts to Nancy Miller, July 24, 1844.
By C. A. Smith, M.G. (July 25, 1844)
A. S. Gibbs to Sophrona Rudd, July 30, 1844.
By John Jenkins, J.P. (July 30, 1844)
James Ginon to Emeline Robeson, July 31, 1844.
By James A. Gunn, M.G. (Aug. 4, 1844)
Hiram Cox to Luzireen Senter, Aug. 1, 1844.
By John Jenkins, J.P. (Aug. 13, 1844)
Jno. Mayfield to Jane Poe, Aug. 1, 1844.
By William Walsh, J.P. (Aug. 1, 1844)
James Buttram to Jane Rothrons, Aug. 3, 1844.
By Lewis Carter, M.G. (Aug. 8, 1844)
R. B. Cobb to Catherine J. Baker, Aug. 7, 1844.
(no returns)
John Inman to Sally C. Riddle, Aug. 7, 1844.
By Neil Butram, M.G. (Aug. 8, 1844)
T. J. Armstrong to Mary Ann Baker, Aug. 17, 1844.
(no returns)
John P. Patton to Mary O. Barrett, Aug. 20, 1844.
By B. L. Smith, V.D.M. (Aug. 20, 1844)
James W. Shelton to Sarahann Lane, Aug. 21, 1844.
By Rusel Lane, J.P. (Aug. 22, 1844)
John R. Fitzgerald to Mary J. Jameson, Aug. 21, 1844.
By Obed Pearson, M.G. (Aug. 22, 1844)
James Mizell to Maryilla Peters, Aug. 29, 1844.
(no returns)
Alexander Shipley to Naomy Gibson, Sep. 3, 1844.
By M. C. Hawk, M.G. (Sep. 5, 1844)
R. A. McMillan to M. A. Isbell, Sep. 3, 1844.
By A. Slover, M.G. (Sep. 3, 1844)
M. J. Shipley to Eveline Dyer, Sep. 11, 1844.
By Daniel McPhail, J.P. (Sep. 11, 1844)
Andrew Foster to Elizabeth Goss, Sep. 12, 1844.
By G. W. Walis, J.P. (Sep. 12, 1844)
David G. Fry to Zeporah Harris, Sep. 13, 1844.
By J. W. Barnett, J.P. (Sep. 13, 1844)
Joseph W. Gibson to Sarah Matlock, Sep. 14, 1844.
By M. D. Anderson, J.P. (Sep. 17, 1844)
John R. Baulding to Nancy A. Barnett, Sep. 16, 1844.
By Robert Gregory, M. Baptist. (Sep. 17, 1844)
A. H. Rutherford to Lucinda Harris, Sep. 17, 1844.
By Samuel Snoddy, J.P. (Sep. 19, 1844)
J. A. Long to M. J. Newman, Sep. 18, 1844.
By R. W. Patty, M. Methodist. (Sep. 20, 1844)
John Boofer to Mary Wassom, Sep. 18, 1844.
By G. W. Wallis, J.P. (Sep. 19, 1844)
R. B. Brabson to Sarah M. Keith, Sep. 24, 1844.
By John Scruggs, M.G. (Sep. 24, 1844)
Robert Mantooth to Martha J. Burnett, Sep. 25, 1844.
(no returns)
John McBrien to Margaret Barnes, Sep. 25, 1844.
By J. Scarbrough, J.P. (Sep. 26, 1844)
C. B. Gibbs to S. A. Walker, Oct. 3, 1844.
By W. H. Ballew, J.P. (Oct. 3, 1844)

McMINN COUNTY MARRIAGES

Eli S. Pangle to H. J. Wiate, Oct. 6, 1844.
  By Wilson Chapman, M.G. (Oct. 6, 1844)
John F. Lane to Paralee C. Miller, Oct. 7, 1844.
  By W. H. Ballew, J.P. (Oct. 7, 1844)
Robert M. Newman to Sarah E. Jones, Oct. 15, 1844.
  By Green L. Reynolds, J.P. (Oct. 16, 1844)
Robert C. Cantrell to Esther J. Stansberry, Oct. 22, 1844.
  By Moses A. Cass, J.P. (Oct. 24, 1844)
William Thompson to Mary J. Hunter, Oct. 24, 1844.
  By L. R. Morrison, V.D.M. (Oct. 24, 1844)
Jesse Rucker to Minnda Gregory, Oct. 26, 1844.
  By R. A. McAdoo, J.P. (Oct. 26, 1844)
Gottlick Basalm to Eliza C. Gilton, Oct. 31, 1844.
  By S. M. Kelley, M.G. (Oct. 31, 1844)
George Parsons to Maryann Gilbert, Oct. 31, 1844.
  By S. M. Kelly, M.G. (Oct. 31, 1844)
John W. Knox to E. C. G. Stanton, Nov. 1, 1844.
  By J. H. Benton, J.P. (Nov. 2, 1844)
R. F. Hampton to Mary I. Isbell, Nov. 5, 1844.
  By A. Slover, M.G. (Nov. 5, 1844)
Nathan Lowe to Sarah M. Barnett, Nov. 9, 1844.
  By Thomas H. Small, M.G.C.P.C. (Apr. 24, 1845)
R. J. Patty to Pelina Reynolds, Nov. 11, 1844.
  By Robert Gregory, M. Baptist. (Nov. 12, 1844)
Reuben Lammons to Matilda Woodall, Nov. 12, 1844.
  By John Jenkins, J.P. (Nov. 17, 1844)
Wm. S. Foster to Mary P. Handly, Nov. 14, 1844.
  By J. H. Benton, J.P. (Nov. 14, 1844)
Jefferson Llarmer to Francis Dodson, Nov. 16, 1844.
  (no returns)
Matthew Stallion to N. A. Goins, Nov. 17, 1844.
  By Samuel Snoddy, J.P. (Nov. 17, 1844)
Joseph Cobb to Caroline Lolleman, Nov. 17, 1844.
  By F. McGonigal, M.G. (Nov. 17, 1844)
L. P. Basinger to Nasamond Bruer, Nov. 17, 1844.
  By John Jenkins, J.P. (Nov. 17, 1844)
James F. Eldridge to Malissa Hambright, Nov. 19, 1844.
  By Henry Price, M.G. (Nov. 20, 1844)
William Snoddy to Eveline Mizell, Nov. 21, 1844.
  By John Jenkins, J.P. (Dec. 17, 1844)
James Prince to L. L. Hayes, Nov. 21, 1844.
  By Matthew R. Gibson, J.P. (Nov. 21, 1844)
A. G. Derrick to Sarah A. Smith, Nov. 22, 1844.
  By Green L. Reynolds, J.P. (Nov. 25, 1844)
W. C. Brittain to Jane Robeson, Nov. 26, 1844.
  (no returns)
Calloway Melton to Eliza Tucker, Nov. 30, 1844.
  By Wm. Rucker, J.P. (Dec. 20, 1844)
H. C. Reynolds to Elizabeth Lee, Dec. 4, 1844.
  By Robert Gregory, M. Baptist. (Dec. 5, 1844)
Samuel Thomas to Abigail A. Peace, Dec. 5, 1844.
  (no returns)
Thomas M. Hogan to Juletts Sloop, Dec. 5, 1844.
  By M. D. Anderson, J.P. (Dec. 5, 1844)

McMINN COUNTY MARRIAGES

J. A. Baker to Elizabeth M. Derrick, Dec. 10, 1844.
  By E. P. Bloom, J.P. (Dec. 12, 1844)
Hugh Rogers to Elizabeth Amos, Dec. 17, 1844.
  By Willis M. Newton, M.G. (Dec. 17, 1844)
N. I. Peters to Permelia Frazier, Dec. 18, 1844.
  (no returns)
Michael McGeecie to Sarah O. Deaton, Dec. 18, 1844.
  By W. H. Ballew, J.P. (Dec. 18, 1844)
Robert Bryan to Eliza T. Harless, Dec. 21, 1844.
  By Justice Steed, J.P. (Dec. 22, 1844)
Benjamin Knoxx to Celia Bingman, Dec. 23, 1844.
  By R. A. McAdoo, J.P. (Dec. 24, 1844)
Philip Frazier to Nancy Wear, Dec. 24, 1844.
  By W. F. Forrest, M.C.G. (Dec. 24, 1844)
Madison Chapman to Zilpha Lee, Dec. 24, 1844.
  (no returns)
Daniel White to Maranda Fox, Dec. 24, 1844.
  (no returns)
Robert Pendergrass (or Pendergast) to Matilda Bell,
  Dec. 24, 1844. (no returns)
Joseph Sliger to Nancy Butram, Dec. 28, 1844.
  By Neil Buttram, M.G. (Dec. 29, 1844)
Jas. T. Smith to Nancy Wilson, Dec. 28, 1844.
  By James Sewell, M.G. (Dec. 29, 1844)
C. E. Neils to M. M. Suthard, Dec. 28, 1844.
  By M. D. Anderson, J.P. (Dec. 28, 1844)
Matthew Gwinn to Margaret Maddan, Dec. 30, 1844.
  By D. A. Cobb, M.G. (Dec. 30, 1844)
W. C. Owen to Jane Reed, Dec. 31, 1844.
  By M. D. Anderson, J.P. (Dec. 31, 1844)
Peter Ingals to Narcissa Hambrick, Jan. 1, 1845.
  By R. A. McAdoo, J.P. (Jan. 2, 1845)
M. L. Myers to Nancy L. C. Bowerman, Jan. 7, 1845.
  By John Jenkins, J.P. (Jan, 7, 1845)
Austin Lowden to Nancy Falkner, Jan. 14, 1845.
  By G. W. Wallis, J.P. (Jan. 16, 1845)
John Allen to May Perry, Jan. 15, 1845.
  By Tapley Gregory, J.P. (Jan. 15, 1845)
John T. Dixon to Elvira Bird, Jan. 16, 1845.
  By Samuel Wilson, J.P. (Jan. 16, 1845)
John C. Phillips to Hily Reggins, Jan. 16, 1845.
  By T. Gregory, J.P. (Jan. 16, 1845)
John I. Parker to Chrisada McMinn, Jan. 21, 1845.
  By E. P. Bloom, J.P. (Jan. 21, 1845)
Daniel Plumly (or Plumlee) to Amanda Cunningham, Jan. 23,
  1845. By Thomas Russell, M.G. (Jan. 23, 1845)
G. M. Peper to Clarrysa J. Lyle, Feb. 11, 1845.
  By L. R. Morrison, V.D.M. (Feb. 11, 1845)
John Printwood to Mary Ann I. F. Johnson, Feb. 13, 1845.
  By Justus Steed, J.P. (Feb. 13, 1845)
John Reid to Sarah Burnett, Feb. 18, 1845.
  (no returns)
John Hix to Ann Long, Feb. 22, 1845.
  By D. A. Cobbs, M.G. (Feb. 23, 1845)

McMINN COUNTY MARRIAGES

James Carson to Attaline Cooke, Feb. 26, 1845.
  By John Scruggs, M.G. (Feb. 27, 1845)
Jarrett Johnson to Mary McConnell, Mar. 1, 1845.
  By James Douglas, M.G. (Mar. 9, 1845)
Jordan Calhoun to Jane Matlock, Mar. 1, 1845.
  By H. Ingram, M.G. (Mar. 3, 1848(?))
John Pierce to Sarah M. Lawson, Mar. 1, 1845.
  By Moses A. Cass, J.P. (Mar. 2, 1845)
A. J. Smart to Tabitha Benson, Mar. 8, 1845.
  By M. C. Stahly, Ord. Minister. (Mar. 9, 1845)
Marcellis B. Johnson to Margaret C. Hess, Mar. 12, 1845.
  By Justus Steed, J.P. (Mar. 13, 1845)
William Sheets to Lotty Townsend, Mar. 19, 1845.
  By William Newton, M.G. (Mar. 20, 1845)
Mark Hale to Jane Long, Mar. 24, 1845.
  (no returns)
C. W. B. Howard to Mariah J. Morris, Mar. 25, 1845.
  By J. Douglas, M.G. (Mar. 27, 1845)
George Louder to Judah McCall, Apr. 2, 1845.
  (no returns)
Wm. Johnson to Dicy Maples, Apr. 9, 1845.
  By John Hoyl, M.G. (Apr. 9, 1845)
H. M. Davis to Jane T. Watson, Apr. 10, 1845.
  By Wm. Rucker, J.P. (Apr. 10, 1845)
William Bolding to Tabitha Browder, Apr. 10, 1845.
  By R. A. McAdoo, J.P. (Apr. 10, 1845)
Wm. Phillips to Katharine Miller, Apr. 21, 1845.
  By Wilson Chapman, M.G. (Apr. 21, 1845)
James B. Taylor to Rebecca Moss, Apr. 30, 1845.
  By T. K. Munsey, M.G.
J. H. Hawk to Amanda Crawford, May 3, 1845.
  By O. F. Cunningham, M.G. (May 29, 1845)
E. M. Newton to Rebecca M. Allison, May 6, 1845.
  By William Newton, M.G. (May 11, 1845)
Thomas T. Young to Rebecca W. Gammon, May 6, 1845.
  By O. F. Cunningham, M.G. (May 6, 1845)
Thomas H. Jones to Susan O. Hoyl, May 13, 1845.
  By O. F. Cunningham, M.G. (May 14, 1845)
John Glass to E. Strattin, May 19, 1845.
  By Wm. McKamy, J.P. (May 20, 1845)
Phillip Hess to Susan Johnson, May 29, 1845.
  By Justus Steed, J.P. (May 29, 1845)
Ensly Wan (or Van) to Mary White, May 29, 1845.
  By Heil Buttram, M.G. (May 29, 1845)
Benjamin T. Wason to Mary J. Bryan, June 7, 1845.
  By Wm. Rucker, J.P. (June 10, 1845)
Calvin Giles to Elender Carter, June 19, 1845.
  By James Sewell, M.G. (June 20, 1845)
Samuel Douthil to Girsey Turk, June 21, 1845.
  By M. C. Hawk, M.G. (June 22, 1845)
Daniel L. Boyd to Sarah E. Barb, June 26, 1845.
  By Jonathan Thomas, J.P. (June 26, 1845)
James Pearce to Elizabeth Galleon, June 28, 1845.
  By C. Sanders, M.G. (June 30, 1845)

Jonathan F. Franklin to Sarah Collier, July 5, 1845.
  By J. H. Benton, J.P. (July 6, 1845)
Jell Tagris to Holly McCarroll, July 8, 1845.
  By M. A. Cass, J.P. (July 10, 1845)
Elias Kibble to Martha C. Jones, July 1, 1845.
  (no returns)
John Grisham to Gemima Kinchlow, July 10, 1845.
  By Edward Newton, M.G. (July 10, 1845)
John Goodner to Nancy Long, July 16, 1845.
  By Green L. Reynolds, J.P. (July 16, 1845)
C. A. Dodson to Rachel C. Forrest, July 19, 1845.
  By Wm. F. Forrest, M.G. (July 22, 1845)
Terrell Cantrell to Maranda J. Manery, July 1, 1845.
  By M. A. Cass, J.P. (July 8, 1845)
Joseph Reeding to Eliza Newman, July 30, 1845.
  By Daniel McPhail, J.P. (July 31, 1845)
G. W. Brown to Elizabeth Herald, July 28, 1845.
  By J. W. Barrett, J.P. (July 28, 1845)
Parker Rudd to Malisa Jane Hughes, July 31, 1845.
  By Wm.H. Ballew, J.P. (July 31, 1845)
Wm. M. Carter to Elizabeth Couch, Aug. 4, 1845.
  By Wm. Rucker, J.P. (Aug. 7, 1845)
Elijah Rector to Martha Liles, Aug. 4, 1845.
  By J. H. Benton, J.P. (Aug. 4, 1845)
John Lowden to Catherine McCall, Aug. 4, 1845.
  (no returns)
William C. Marshall to P. M. M. Hickman, Aug. 6, 1845.
  (no returns)
Turner Sharp to Winney Bicknele, Aug. 7, 1845.
  By B. E. Blain, J.P. (Aug. 9, 1845)
Lewis Erwin to Barbay Ellison, Aug. 8, 1845.
  By McAtchley(?), Minister. (Aug. 8, 1845)
Henry M. Simpson to Elizabeth Ann Woody, Aug. 14, 1845.
  By L. R. Morrison, V.D.M. (Aug. 14, 1845)
Robert M. Maxwell to Eliza Jane Haney, Aug. 16, 1845.
  By Samuel Wilson, J.P. (Aug. 19, 1845)
Harry Morgan to Polly Kinchelo, Aug. 18, 1845.
  (no returns)
T. W. Jones to Sarah E. Morgan, Aug. 18, 1845.
  (no returns)
Thomas Parrett to Sarah Ann Grayson, Aug. 19, 1845.
  By Green L. Reynolds, J.P. (Aug. 20, 1845)
Albert Coffman to Elizabeth Kinser, Aug. 20, 1845.
  By L. L. Dall, J.P. (Aug. 21, 1845)
R. H. Hickey to Elizabeth Amursin, Aug. 22, 1845.
  By Justus Steed, J.P. (Aug. 24, 1845)
Charles Orten to Milly Olden, Aug. 22, 1845.
  By R. A. McAdoo, J.P. (Aug. 26, 1845)
Joseph Hughes to Elizabeth Knox, Aug. 30, 1845.
  By J. H. Benton, J.P. (Aug. 31, 1845)
Robert Atchley to Nancy M. Butler, Aug. 30, 1845.
  By Jonathan Thomas, J.P. (Sep. 11, 1845)
James Allen to Lithey L. Myers, Sep. 1, 1845.
  (no returns)

McMINN COUNTY MARRIAGES

Montraville Reynolds to Rachel Bond, Sep. 1, 1845.
  By L. R. Morrison, V.D.M. (Sep. 2, 1845)
H. B. Brandon to Louisa Waide, Sep. 1, 1845.
  By Heil Buttram, M.G. (Sep. 1, 1845)
McCamy Largent to Eliza Lafforty, Sep. 3, 1845.
  By M. C. Hawk, M.G. (Sep. 4, 1845)
Wm. Wilson to Sidney A. Roberts, Sep. 4, 1845.
  By Wm. Rucker, J.P. (Sep. 4, 1845)
Maximillan Rector to Mary Elizabeth Dethroe, Sep. 4, 1845.
  By J. H. Benton, J.P. (Sep. 4, 1845)
John Guffy to P. Lowry, Sep. 6, 1845.
  (no returns)
Joseph Baker to Nancy E. Hickey, Sep. 21, 1845)
Nelson Pennington to Nancy Ann Lurena Bigham, Sep. 1, 1845.
  By Wm. McKamy, J.P. (Sep. 20, 1845)
Clemmons Sanders to Caroline Peoples, Sep. 23, 1845.
  (no returns)
Wm. J. Rutherford to Mira Heenysheys, Oct. 1, 1845.
  By Samuel H. Jordan, J.P. (Oct. 1, 1845)
Vincent Haynes to Caroline Templeton, Oct. 2, 1845.
  By M. D. Anderson, J.P. (Oct. 2, 1845)
John Benton to Sarah Davis, Oct. 2, 1845.
  By R. A. McAdoo, J.P. (Oct. 2, 1845)
John W. Griffith to Mariah Wight, Oct. 3, 1845.
  (no returns)
Calvin Kirby to Elizabeth Sanders, Oct. 9, 1845.
  By Moses A. Cass, J.P. (Oct. 9, 1845)
Jacob K. Starnes to A. N. Cofman, Oct. 20, 1845.
  By Wm. Rucker, J.P. (Oct. 23, 1845)
John A. Ware to C. J. Smith, Oct. 15, 1845.
  By Samuel Snoddy, J.P. (Oct. 15, 1845)
Elijah Knox to Jennett Nance, Oct. 22, 1845.
  By R. A. McAdoo, J.P. (Oct. 23, 1845)
Francis A. Holt to Sarah D. Yearwood, Oct. 26, 1845.
  By A. Slover, M.G. (Oct. 26, 1845)
Samuel H. Parker to Emily Templeton, Oct. 27, 1845.
  By James Blair, M.G. (Oct. 28, 1845)
John Manery to Lucy Ann Floyd, Oct. 29, 1845.
  By J. Jack, M.G. (Oct. 30, 1845)
John P. Bayless to Martha Jane Franklin, Oct. 30, 1845.
  By A. Slover, M.G. (Oct. 30, 1845)
William Griffith to Elisabeth Cook, Nov. 5, 1845.
  By Samuel Wilson, J.P. (Nov. 6, 1845)
Noah Williams to Mary Champlin, Nov. 8, 1845.
  By A. Slover, M.G. (Nov. 8, 1845)
John J. Haney to Keziah Rowan, Nov. 12, 1845.
  By I. W. Barnett, J.P. (Nov. 12, 1845)
John H. Young, E. J. Barnett, Nov. 18, 1845.
  By Robert Gregory, M.G. (Nov. 27, 1845)
Nathaniel Knox to Julian Smith, Nov. 25, 1845.
  By J. W. Benton, J.P. (Nov. 27, 1845)
I. B. Miller to Mary Smith, Nov. 27, 1845.
  By Green L. Reynolds, J.P. (Nov. 27, 1845)
William White to Eliza Jane Daugherty, Dec. 12, 1845.
  By Robert Mansel, M.G. (Dec. 14, 1845)

William Wason to Jane Bedford, Dec. 13, 1845.
  By W. Rucker, J.P. (Dec. 21, 1845)
James S. McCroskey to Eliza Flinn, Dec. 20, 1845.
  By W. F. Forrest, M.G. (Dec. 21, 1845)
Arden Sanders to Elizabeth Lile, Dec. 22, 1845.
  (no returns)
Joseph A. Zegler to Mary Ann Cate, Dec. 22, 1845.
  By W. Rucker, J.P. (Dec. 23, 1845)
Leonard Hix to Mary Ann Robeson, Dec. 23, 1845.
  By D. A. Cobbs. (Feb. 2, 1845)
F. M. Edens to Elisabeth Bedford, Dec. 27, 1845.
  By W. Rucker, J.P. (Jan. 1, 1845)
Wiley Lasater to Elizabeth Ross, Dec. 31, 1845.
  By John Key, M.G. (Jan. 1, 1845)
Robert F. Browder to Aminda Q. Erwin, Dec. 31, 1845.
  By M. C. Hawk. (Jan. 1, 1845)
John M. Workman to Martha Ann Workman, Jan. 1, 1846.
  By M. C. Hawk. (Jan. 1, 1846)
Thos. Rogers to Letticia Wallin, Jan. 7, 1846.
  By M. C. Hawk. (Jan. 8, 1846)
Adison Jenkins to Elisabeth Dodson, Jan. 9, 1846.
  By W. Chapman, M.G. (Jan. 18, 1846)
Daniel Fox to Carline Stone, Jan. 9, 1846.
  By F. McGonegal, M.G. (Jan. 9, 1846)
Samuel M. Knox to Mary E. Gulls, Jan. 11, 1846.
  By W. F. Forrest, M.G. (Jan. 15, 1846)
I. T. Davis to Catherine Hinkler, Jan. 12, 1846.
  By W. F. Forrest, M.G. (Jan. 13, 1846)
Joseph C. Wear to Sally Colville, Jan. 15, 1846.
  By Wm. McKamy, J.P. (Jan. 15, 1846)
Solomon L. Stowe, Jr. to Mary Ann Godard, Jan. 16, 1846.
  By James Sewell, M.M. (Jan. 20, 1846)
C. H. Guthey to Elizabeth Crisman, Jan. 19, 1846.
  (no returns)
M. V. Blain to Mary Fields, Jan. 21, 1846.
  By Daniel McPhail, J.P. (Jan. 29, 1846)
Chas. McCullum to Elizabeth Jane Marnoe, Jan. 28, 1846.
  By Heil Buttram, M.G. (Jan. 28, 1846)
James H. Bench to Avy E. Bench, Jan. 29, 1846.
  By Justus Steed, J.P. (Jan. 29, 1846)
Andrew Cooley to Lidia Cooley, Feb. 5, 1846.
  By McC. Atchley, M. (Feb. 5, 1846)
Thomas Mesimores to E. S. Torbett, Feb. 4, 1846.
  By Robert Gregory, M. Baptist. (Feb. 5, 1846)
John Douglas to Susan Barker, Feb. 6, 1846.
  By E. Newton, M.G. (Feb. 8, 1846)
Eli A. Eaton to Nancy M. Lunull, Feb. 7, 1846.
  By M. Swenney. (Feb. 8, 1846)
Noah Higdon to Lidia Ann Rutherford, Feb. 12, 1846.
  By Wm. C. Lee, M.G. (Feb. 16, 1846)
Johnson Smith to Savanah Lawson, Feb. 16, 1846.
  By Jas. Douglass, M.G. (Feb. 16, 1846)
W. Cannon to Mary Doss, Feb. 16, 1846.
  By A. Swafford, J.P. (Feb. 16, 1846)

McMINN COUNTY MARRIAGES

Daniel Womack to Mary Benson, Feb. 20, 1846.
   By R. S. McAdoo, J.P. (Jeb. 20, 1846)
James Winsant to Elisabeth Hill, Feb. 21, 1846.
   By John Walker, J.P. (Feb. 21, 1846)
Nimrod Ford to Amandia Anderson, Feb. 21, 1846.
   By A. Slover, M.G. (Mar. 5, 1846)
Wm. Rutherford to Frances Atkinson, Feb. 25, 1846.
   By C. R. Hoyl, J.P. (Feb. 26, 1846)
H. W. Breazeale to Catherine Foster, Feb. 25, 1846.
   By G. W. Wallis, J.P. (Feb. 26, 1846)
Thomas K. Cantrell to Sarah Rigg, Feb. 24, 1846.
   By M. A. Cass, J.P. (Mar. 5, 1846)
D. F. Scoggins to Margaret Buttram, Mar. 5, 1846.
   By James Sewell, M.M.(?) (Mar. 12, 1846)
Thomas Townsend to Margora Hays, Mar. 9, 1846.
   By John Scarbrough, J.P. (Mar. 9, 1846)
William Philpot to Rachel Nations, Mar. 9, 1846.
   By C. Sanders, M.G. (Mar. 10, 1846)
Jonathan T. Smith to Elizabeth Shipley, Mar. 10, 1846.
   By Russell Lane, J.P. (Mar. 10, 1846)
James Gregory to Elizabeth Bonnis, Mar. 16, 1846.
   By McAtchley, M. (Mar. 19, 1846)
Noah Maples to Sarahann Greenway, Mar. 18, 1846.
   By W. F. Forrest. (Mar. 18, 1846)
S. P. Riggs to Nancy Elliott, Mar. 19, 1846.
   By M. A. Cass, J.P. (Mar. 19, 1846)
W. C. Adams to Malissa B. Crawford, Mar. 28, 1846.
   (no returns)
James Landers to Rachel Maynor, Mar. 30, 1846.
   By C. Sanders, M.G. (Mar. 30, 1846)
Samuel A. Smith to Martha E. McCarty, Apr. 1, 1846.
   By M. C. Hawk, M.G. (Apr. 2, 1846)
Adam McCalley to Anna Jane Fry, Apr. 3, 1846.
   By Russell Lane, J.P. (Apr. 3, 1846)
William Parris to M. Ann Porter, Apr. 3, 1846.
   By Robert Mansell, M.G. (Apr. 10, 1846)
John B. Sherrell to Mary Shook, Apr. 8, 1846.
   By M. D. Anderson, J.P. (Apr. 9, 1846)
James K. Boeils to Dear Jane Templeton, Apr. 11, 1846.
   (no returns)
George Bush to Catherine Prince, Apr. 11, 1846.
   By S. H. Jordan, J.P. (Apr. 13, 1846)
William Casada to Nancy Manerva Crisp, Apr. 16, 1846.
   (no returns)
Larkin Collins to Nancy Newkirk, Arp. 27, 1846.
   By Rev. Edwin A. Atlee. (May 3, 1846)
John T. Jones to Susan Eldridge, Apr. 28, 1846.
   By Samuel Wilson, J.P. (Apr. 29, 1846)
Joseph I. Culpepper to Polly Ann Wallin, Apr. 30, 1846.
   By Alfred Swafford, J.P. (Apr. 30, 1846)
I. M. Reynolds to Emily Copeland, Apr. 30, 1846.
   By Green L. Reynolds. (Apr. 30, 1846)
G. W. Fry to Elizabeth Ann Newkirk, May 1, 1846.
   By Rev. Edwin A. Atlee. (May 3, 1846)

McMINN COUNTY MARRIAGES

Bluford Smith to Eliza Jane Lennox, May 2, 1846.
By John Jenkins, J.P. (May 3, 1846)
Wm. R. Morgan to Caroline Boring, May 8, 1846.
By Thomas J. Russel, M. Baptist. (May 18, 1846)
John White to Mary McCarroll, May 11, 1846.
By M. A. Cass, J.P. (May 11, 1846)
A. T. Blair to Eliza Ann Reynolds, May 21, 1846.
By Green L. Russell, J.P. (May 21, 1846)
Elijah Rawlings to Catharine Vinsen, May 24, 1846.
By John Scarbrough, J.P. (May 24, 1846)
Joseph L. Whaley to Sarah L. Huddleston, June 1, 1846.
By M. C. Atchley, M. (June 1, 1846)
C. W. Whaley to Becksey Fulgam, June 1, 1846.
(no returns)
Nathan Melton to Susannah Melton, June 4, 1846.
By John Hoyl, M.G. (June 4, 1846)
T. J. Campbell to Frances E. Bridges, June 11, 1846.
By L. R. Morrison, V.D.M. (June 11, 1846)
Andrew Lunsford (or Luntsford) to Martha C. Ferrell,
June 18, 1846. By A. Slover, M.G. (June 18, 1846)
James Riddle to Mary Read, June 27, 1846.
By J. H. Benton, J.P. (June 28, 1846)
Henry Slater to Sarah A. Parks, July 12, 1846.
By John Jenkins, J.P. (July 13, 1846)
Peter L. Byran to Anna Horton, July 13, 1846.
By Wm. Rucker, J.P. (July 14, 1846)
George W. Childers (or Childress) to Catherine Robertson,
July 4, 1846. By David F. Jamerson, J.P. (July 16, 1846)
James C. Triplet to Mahala Melton, July 22, 1846.
By James Douglass, M.G. (July 22, 1846)
Robert Reynolds to Mary Jane Dodson, July 22, 1846.
By Wilson Chapman, M.G. (July 23, 1846)
Thomas C. Henley to Mary Ann F. Swenney, July 23, 1846.
By Wm. H. Ballew, J.P. (July 23, 1846)
Joseph R. Ware to Martha Ann Cobb, July 23, 1846.
(no returns)
C. W. Cobb to Elizabeth Reynolds, July 23, 1846.
By A. Templeton, M.G. (July 28, 1846)
Noah C. Cantrell to Mary Derrick, July 25, 1846.
By E. P. Bloom, J.P. (July 26, 1846)
John M. Burger to Manda Caves, July 30, 1846.
By M. A. Cass, J.P. (July 30, 1846)
John M. Wright to Milley Rivers, Aug. 1, 1846.
By R. A. McAdoo, J.P. (Aug. 9, 1846)
John Butter to Prisila Atchley, Aug. 7, 1846.
By J. THomas, J.P. (Aug. 10, 1846)
James More to Catherine Hall, Aug. 8, 1846.
By R. A. McAdoo, J.P. (Aug. 8, 1846)
Carroll C. Lewis to Elizabeth D. Smith, Aug. 10, 1846.
By William Newton, M.G. (Aug. 20, 1846)
James Lewis to Mary Kile, Aug. 10, 1846.
By Green L. Reynolds, J.P. (Aug. 12, 1846)
Geo. M. McCulley to Ann A. Porter, Aug. 19, 1846.
By Archibald A. Mathis, M.G. (Aug. 20(?), 1846)

James Ellis to Nancy Pearson, Aug. 19, 1846.
By Daniel McPhail, J.P. (Aug. 23, 1846)
James Hay to Sarah Cecil, Aug. 20, 1846.
By Leander Wilson, M.G. (Aug. 20, 1846)
Thos. A. Underdown to Catherine A. Barker, Aug. 26, 1846.
By Wm. H. Ballew, J.P. (Aug. 27, 1846)
William Hicks to Elizabeth Cesil, Aug. 29, 1846.
By Leander Wilson, M.G. (Sep. 3, 1846)
Moses Hayl to June Baker, Aug. 31, 1846.
By J. H. Benton, J.P. (Aug. 31, 1846)
Marcus E. L. Sewell to Vina Darr, Sep. 2, 1846.
By M. C. Atchley, M. (Sep. 2, 1846)
William Dodd to Eliza Ann Fry, Sep. 2, 1846.
By G. W. Wallis, J.P. (Sep. 3, 1846)
Alfred P. Stout to Anna Brock, Sep. 3, 1846.
By William Rucker, J.P. (Sep. 3, 1846)
Luke L. Miller to Jane C. Vinson, Sep. 3, 1846.
By G. C. Metcalf, Eret. (Sep. 3, 1846)
Samuel D. Browder to Nancy Triplet, Sep. 10, 1846.
By C. D. Smith, M.G. (Sep. 10, 1846)
Thomas Haney to Nancy Haney, Sep. 16, 1846.
(no returns)
David H. Coffman to Mary C. Sterns, Sep. 17, 1846.
By Wm. Rucker, J.P. (Sep. 17, 1846)
William C. Hudson to Mary Ann Lawson, Sep. 23, 1846.
By J. H. Benton, J.P. (Sep. 24, 1846)
Charles Haley to Margaret Smith, Sep. 29, 1846.
(no returns)
Langden C. Rentfrel to Nancy Parlinson, Oct. 1, 1846.
By Wm. F. Forrest, M.G. (Oct. 1, 1846)
Matthew G. McNabb to Sarah Hunt, Oct. 1, 1846.
By Wm. Rucker, J.P. (Oct. 1, 1846)
David L. Harris to Eliza M. Pike, Oct. 6, 1846.
By M. D. Anderson, J.P. (Oct. 6, 1846)
David A. Wilson to Amanda M. Burk, Oct. 8, 1846.
By M. D. Anderson, J.P. (Oct. 8, 1846)
Parris L. Dobbs to Lucinda Fields, Oct. 10, 1846.
By G. W. Wallis, J.P. (Oct. 11, 1846)
Embre Buttram to Sarah Wattenbarger, Oct. 12, 1846.
By Heil Buttram, M.G. (Oct. 15, 1846)
Joseph Eldredge to Susan Rice, Oct. 15, 1846.
By A. Slover, M.G. (Oct. 15, 1846)
William Wooddall to Eliza Hetterbrand, Oct. 17, 1846.
By J. C. Weir, J.P. (Oct. 18, 1846)
Montgomery Hass (or Hess) to Sarah Bicknels, Oct. 18, 1846.
By Hellery Patrick, M.G. (Oct. 19, 1846)
Flemming S. Norman to Susan Miller, Oct. 21, 1846.
By R. A. McAdoo, J.P. (Oct. 20, 1846)
Isaac Morris to Susan Peters, Oct. 20, 1846.
By John Hoyl, M.G. (Oct. 20, 1846)
Joseph Hame to Sarah Reese, Oct. 21, 1846.
(no returns)
Valentine Martin to Vashtie Boon, Oct. 31, 1846.
By E. P. Bloom, J.P. (Nov. 1, 1846)

William Newton to Elizabeth H. Roberts, Nov. 2, 1846.
By Wm. Rucker, J.P. (Nov. 3, 1846)
Willias B. Carr to Clarrinda Linos, Nov. 2, 1846.
By Wm. Newton, M.G. (Nov. 3, 1846)
William Daugherty to Nanny Riggs, Nov. 5, 1846.
By M. A. Cass, J.P. (Nov. 5, 1846)
Alfred W. Cate to Mary Gregory, Nov. 7, 1846.
By Wm. Rucker, J.P. (Nov. 12, 1846)
Joseph Roberts to Lucy Mafield, Nov. 7, 1846.
By Heil Buttram, M.G. (Nov. 8, 1846)
James Caslowe to Sarah Rumedy, Nov. 9, 1846.
By Wm. Newton, M.G. (Nov. 12, 1846)
David Weeks to Isabel Clark, Nov. 1, 1846.
By John Jenkins, J.P. (Nov. 9, 1846)
John Karl Winsch to Rebecca Fisher, Nov. 11, 1846.
By A. Slover, M.G. (Nov. 11, 1846)
Alfred M. Collins to Sarah Melton, Nov. 12, 1846.
By John Jenkins, J.P. (Nov. 13, 1846)
James Williams to Jenny Bunch, Nov. 12, 1846.
By M. C. Atchley, Ord. Min. (Nov. 12, 1846)
Nelson Lawson to Joanna Martin, Nov. 13, 1846.
(no returns)
Flemmings G. Gibbs to Jane Eaton, Nov. 18, 1846.
(no returns)
Soloman Cate to Eliza McCariel, Nov. 19, 1846.
By J. Jack, M.G. (Nov. 19, 1846)
William W. Dobbs to Sarah I. Sellers, Nov. 23, 1846.
By G. Wallis, J.P. (Nov. 26, 1846)
Emery Choate to Elizabeth Bottoms, Nov. 24, 1846.
By J. C. Weir, J.P. (Nov. 24, 1846)
Benj. Riddle to Elizabeth J. Fairell, Dec. 3, 1846.
By R. A. McAdoo, J.P. (Dec. 3, 1846)
Edward Price to Eliza Jamison, Dec. 7, 1846.
By B. E. Blain, J.P. (Dec. 10, 1846)
Clenton B. Newman to Clementine Cantrell, Dec. 9, 1846.
By W. Chapman, M.G. (Dec. 9, 1846)
William Campbell to Elizabeth Ballard, Dec. 14, 1846.
By David F. Jameson, J.P. (Dec. 14, 1846)
Frederick Michael to Charlotte R. Courtney, Dec. 14, 1846.
By J. M. Courtney, M.G. (Dec. 16, 1846)
Martin V. Shipley to Polly Sivels, Dec. 16, 1846.
By M. C. Hawk, M.G. (Dec. 23, 1846)
William Dennis to Sophia Moore, Dec. 16, 1846.
By Thomas B. Weller, M.G. (Dec. 17, 1846)
William Deaton to Sarah McGuire, Dec. 16, 1846.
By Wm. H. Ballew, J.P. (Dec. 18, 1846)
William Nations to Nancy Higdon, Dec. 16, 1846.
By C. Sanders, M.G. (Dec. 17, 1846)
Peter Maples to Elizabeth Henson, Dec. 16, 1846.
By Robert Gregory, M. Baptist. (Dec. 16, 1846)
Robert King to Elizabeth Guthrie, Dec. 18, 1846.
By John Tate, M.G. (Dec. 20, 1846)
Willis Wright to Mahala Newton, Dec. 23, 1846.
By B. K. Stewart, M.G. (Feb. 29, 1846)

McMINN COUNTY MARRIAGES

James Edens to Catherine Bedford, Dec. 26, 1846.
  By R. A. McAdoo, J.P. (Dec. 31, 1846)
Isaac Tinney to Mary Moore, Dec. 21, 1846.
  (no returns)
Hamilton Watson to Rachael M. Rucker, Jan. 7, 1847.
  By Wm. Rucker, J.P. (Jan. 7, 1847)
J. W. Sellers to Nancy Nasom, Jan. 7, 1847.
  By G. W. Wallis, J.P. (Jan. 7, 1847)
James H. West to Elisabeth Bond, Jan. 9, 1847.
  By Samuel Wilson, J.P. (Jan. 21, 1847)
Wm. C. Vaughn to Mary Ann Chesnut, Jan. 12, 1847.
  By W. F. Forrest, M.G. (Jan. 12, 1847)
Daniel Dobbs to Bartheny Watts, Jan. 13, 1847.
  By G. W. Wallis, J.P. (Jan. 14, 1847)
Jacob M. Collins to Catherine Franklin, Jan. 16, 1847.
  By J. H. Benton, J.P. (Jan. 17, 1847)
Eli Dixon to Malissa Randolph, Jan. 18, 1847.
  By W. F. Forrest, M.G. (Jan. 21, 1847)
James M. Sellers to Martha Watson, Jan. 18, 1847.
  By G. W. Wallis, J.P. (Jan. 21, 1847)
John Benton to Matilda C. Bolding, Jan. 20, 1847.
  By E. P. Bloom, J.P. (Jan. 27, 1847)
John J. Copeland to Sarah Katharine Rily, Jan. 29, 1847.
  By J. Jack, M.G. (Jan. 31, 1847)
Joseph League to Malinda Kelly, Jan. 31, 1847.
  By J. Jack, M.G. (Jan. 31, 1847)
Donnie M. Bayles to Hannah Benton, Feb. 6, 1847.
  By R. A. McAdoo, J.P. (Feb. 7, 1847)
Israel Canseller to Ellen Levina Cunningham, Feb. 10, 1847.
  By Samuel Wilson, J.P. (Feb. 11, 1847)
Thomas Elliott to Mary J. Rutherford, Feb. 10, 1847.
  By M. A. Cass, J.P. (Feb. 11, 1847)
John Dixon to Martha Riddle, Feb. 11, 1847.
  By B. E. Blain, J.P. (Feb. 11, 1847)
John Doss to Sarah Willing, Feb. 12, 1847.
  By A. Swafford, J.P. (Feb. 14, 1847)
Isaac Rolin to Rebecca Melins, Feb. 14, 1847.
  (no returns)
Thomas W. Elliott to Amy Thompson, Feb. 17, 1847.
  By M. A. Cass, J.P. (Feb. 18, 1847)
Martin Faire to Manervia Haney, Feb. 19, 1847.
  (no returns)
William J. Gentry to Mary M. Suntan, Feb. 20, 1847.
  (no returns)
James M. Corrigin to Martha Ann Head, Feb. 21, 1847.
  By Joseph Cobbs, J.P. (Feb. 21, 1847)
Jesse W. Flinn to Nancy M. Smith, Feb. 26, 1847.
  By W. F. Forrest, M.G. (Feb. 26, 1847)
Lorenzo Dow Ward to Nancy Jane Maynor, Mar. 1, 1847.
  By M. C. Atchley, Ord. Min. (Mar. 1, 1847)
Walter Howard to Eliza Sallee, Mar. 4, 1847.
  By A. Slover, M.G. (Mar. 4, 1847)
William Reno (or Reneau) to Matilda Naney, Mar. 5, 1847.
  By Thomas Witten, M.G. (Mar. 10, 1847)

John S. Reid to Lorinda Dearin, Mar. 6, 1847.
  By J. H. Benton, J.P. (Mar. 7, 1847)
W. G. Barker to Margaret Ann Barker, Mar. 10, 1847.
  By Wm. A. Ballew, J.P. (Mar. 11, 1847)
David Green to Abigale Sivley, Mar. 13, 1847.
  (no returns)
Columbus E. Walsh to Frances Doss, Mar. 24, 1847.
  (no returns)
John J. Ritchie to Frances Henly, Mar. 24, 1847.
  By Wm. H. Ballew, J.P. (Mar. 25, 1847)
Thomas Shipley to Nancy Jane Wattenbarger, Apr. 6, 1847.
  By Thos. Witten, M.G. (Apr. 6, 1847)
James Long to Margaret Henderson, Apr. 12, 1847.
  By Robert Gregory, M. Baptist. (Apr. 12, 1847)
J. D. Chattin to Susan Cooke, Apr. 12, 1847.
  (no returns)
Samuel T. Sharp to Mary Rhea, Apr. 11, 1847.
  By Wilson Chapman, M.G. (Apr. 14, 1847)
William Thompson to Matilda Gregory, Apr. 25, 1847.
  By M. A. Cass, J.P. (Apr. 25, 1847)
John P. Moor to Mary C. King, May 12, 1847.
  By W. G. E. Cunningham, M.G. (May 13, 1847)
Ezekiel Bates to Elizabeth J. Douglas, May 14, 1847.
  By Leander Wilson, M.G. (May 17, 1847)
James Reed to Margaret Young, May 22, 1847.
  By R. A. McAdoo, J.P. (Apr. 23, 1847)
Harvey Fry to Alphy Rutherford, May 29, 1847.
  By G. W. Wallis. (Jan. 3, 1849)
John C. Crawford to Elizabeth E. Pain, May 31, 1847.
  By David F. Jamerson, J.P. (June 3, 1847)
Madison Carney to Martha Jane Helms, June 22, 1847.
  By J. C. Weir, J.P. (June 24, 1847)
John Martin to Harriet E. Greenway, June 24, 1847.
  By W. F. Forrest, M.G. (June 24, 1847)
Thos. Dye to Judy Dye, June 29, 1847.
  By Tapley Gregory, J.P. (July 1, 1847)
Thomas T. Paul to Mary Washam, July 4, 1847.
  By G. W. Kirksey, J.P. (July 4, 1847)
Allen Christian to Martha Jane Lile, July 10, 1847.
  By T. S. Rice, J.P. (July 10, 1847)
Samuel Hall to Delila Emmerson, July 13, 1847.
  By Russell Lane, J.P. (July 14, 1847)
Jeremiah Young to Rosanah Blanton, July 19, 1847.
  By Tapley Gregory, J.P. (July 21, 1847)
Robert L. Shipley to Anna R. Gore, July 22, 1847.
  By D. A. Cobbs, M.G. (July 22, 1847)
John Harris to Jane Shelton, July 31, 1847.
  By M. A. Cass, J.P. (July 31, 1847)
William F. Young to Nancy Ann Bolton, July 31, 1847.
  By J. W. Barnett, J.P. (Aug. 22, 1847)
James Grisham to Polly Newton, Aug. 2, 1847.
  By Wm. Newton, M.G. (Aug. 3, 1847)
Hiram Weeks to Nancy Ann Helms, Aug. 2, 1847.
  By John Scarbrough, J.P. (Aug. 3, 1847)

McMINN COUNTY MARRIAGES

Nelson Grigg to Elizabeth Ann Ware, Aug. 2, 1847.
    (no returns)
Elisha Melton to Rebecca M. Cate, Aug. 5, 1847.
    By Jas. Douglass, M.G. (Aug. 5, 1847)
Wm. A. Smith to Phebe J. Liner, Aug. 17, 1847.
    By Wm. Newton, M.G. (Aug. 19, 1847)
James C. Barnes to Elizabeth Flatford, Aug. 17, 1847.
    (no returns)
Jacob Sharp to Vilana Graves, Aug. 21, 1847.
    (no returns)
Benjamin Shell to Malissa Moore, Aug. 25, 1847.
    By Tapley Gregory, J.P. (Sep. 2, 1847)
John Grisham to Elizabeth Wolff, Aug. 30, 1847.
    By M. R. Gibson, J.P. (Aug. 30, 1847)
Jackson McGuire to Milly Craige, Aug. 31, 1847.
    (no returns)
Hiram James to Nancy Ann Bradley, Sep. 9, 1847.
    (no returns)
Benjamin Eldridge to Rebecca Middleton, Sep. 14, 1847.
    By Samuel Wilson, J.P. (Sep. 16, 1847)
Perry Triplett to Elizabeth Hunt, Sep. 15, 1847.
    By W. F. Forrest, M.G. (Sep. 16, 1847)
James McCall to Rebecca E. Jimmison, Sep. 16, 1847.
    By B. E. Blain, J.P. (Sep. 16, 1847)
Henry Harris to Nancy Nations, Sep. 18, 1847.
    By J. Jack, M.G. (Sep. 21, 1847)
John Shields to Ann Shook, Sep. 19, 1847.
    By S. H. Jordan, J.P. (Sep. 21, 1847)
Wm. Hull to Hannah E. Wright, Sep. 23, 1847.
    By R. A. McAdoo, J.P. (Sep. 23, 1847)
Thomas B. Mayfield to Sarah Jane Rudd, Sep. 12, 1847.
    (no returns)
Madison Atkins to Maryann Thomas, Oct. 2, 1847.
    By John Gaston, M.G. (Oct. 3, 1847)
John Higdon to Mary Ann Rivers, Sep. 30, 1847.
    By Thomas B. Miller, M.G. (Oct. 1, 1847)
John Grubb to Nancy A. Robinson, Oct. 19, 1847.
    By Samuel Wilson, J.P. (Oct. 19, 1847)
A. R. Smider (or Snider) to Mahaley Lemare, Oct. 20, 1847.
    By G. C. Matcalf, Esq. (Oct. 22, 1847)
Allen Stephens to Elizabeth Rodden, _____, 1847.
    By G. W. Kirksey, J.P. (Oct. 14, 1847)
Martin Cook to Eliza Jane Eddington, Oct. 21, 1847.
    By G. C. Metcalf, Esq. (Oct. 22, 1847)
Reuben Melton to Elizabeth Jane Smith, Oct. 21, 1847.
    By Samuel Snoddy, J.P. (Oct. 22, 1847)
John P. Ferguson to Mary A. Miller, Oct. 21, 1847.
    By Robert Randolph, E.C.E. (Oct. 21, 1847)
Jas. M. Hicks to Elender J. Sanders, Oct. 23, 1847.
    By J. W. Barnet, J.P. (Oct. 24, 1847)
John M. Burnet to Franky L. McCray, Oct. 28, 1847.
    By A. Slover, M.G. (Oct. 28, 1847)
Daniel Ward to Elizabeth McNabb, Nov. 3, 1847.
    By R. A. McAdoo, J.P. (Nov. 4, 1847)

McMINN COUNTY MARRIAGES

Wm. R. Long to Sarah E. Atlee, Nov. 4, 1847.
  By J. Atkins, M.G. Methodist. (Nov. 4, 1847)
A. M. Lowry to Emeline Smith, Nov. 16, 1847.
  By A. Slover, M.G. (Nov. 16, 1847)
Frishy(?) J. Gollahon to Katharine Brookshire, Nov. 17,
  1847. (no returns)
John E. Williams to Louisa Jane Hall, Nov. 18, 1847.
  By Wm. F. Forrest, M.G. (Nov. 18, 1847)
Greenbery Norwell to Sarah Dobbins, Nov. 24, 1847.
  By John Jenkins, J.P. (Nov. 25, 1847)
Robert Melton to Elisabeth Eliott, Nov. 24, 1847.
  (no returns)
Andrew Boyd to Martha Phillips, Nov. 25, 1847.
  By Wm. Rucker, J.P. (Nov. 25, 1847)
Robert A. Anderson to Martha A. Templeton, Nov. 25, 1847.
  (no returns)
William C. Britton to Jane Robison, Nov. 25, 1847.
  By Wm. H. Ballew, J.P. (Nov. 25, 1847)
Jonathan H. Sweeny to Sarah Cate, Dec. 12, 1847.
  By Daniel L. Yearout, J.P. (Dec. 12, 1847)
Sarah Detherow to Elisabeth Gibson, Dec. 16, 1847.
  By John Jenkins, J.P. (Dec. 23, 1847)
James G. Willson to Martha Cansler, Dec. 2, 1847.
  By Samuel Wilson, J.P. (Dec. 20, 1847)
William Stephenson to Nancy Elder, Dec. 23, 1847.
  By Robert Gregory, M. Baptist. (Dec. 23, 1847)
John Armstrong to Malinda James, Dec. 21, 1847.
  By E. P. Bloom, J.P. (Dec. 21, 1847)
Michael M. Lower to Amanda Hoozier, Dec. 22, 1847.
  By J. Jack, M.G. (Dec. 23, 1847)
Joshua Low to Mary Jane Lowry, Dec. 23, 1847.
  By J. Cunningham, M.G.
Bryant Thompson to Margaret Miller, Dec. 23, 1847.
  By Tapley Gregory, J.P. (Dec. 23, 1847)
J. W. Emerson to Sarah Jane Bayless, Dec. 24, 1847.
  By W. F. Forrest, M.G. (Dec. 24, 1847)
James Lemmons to Anna Blackwell, Dec. 25, 1847.
  By John Scarbrough, J.P. (Dec. 26, 1847)
Newton Smith to Eliza Smith, Dec. 27, 1847.
  By W. F. Forrest, M.G. (Dec. 27, 1847)
Benjamin Y. Brock to Rheda Mannery, Dec. 28, 1847.
  By J. Jack, M.G. (Dec. 30, 1847)
Robert Powers to Mary Light, Jan. 1, 1848.
  By David F. Jamison, J.P. (Jan. 5, 1848)
William Y. Gibson to Nancy Detherow, Jan. 3, 1848.
  By J. Jenkins, J.P. (Jan. 4, 1848)
Caleb G. Hale to Elizabeth Foster, Jan. 8, 1848.
  (no returns)
Wilbert Crisman to Elizabeth Smith, Jan. 11, 1848.
  By B. C. Blair, J.P. (Jan. 13, 1848)
William Suddard to Lemgra Wilson, Jan. 12, 1848.
  By Wm. H. Ballew, J.P. (Jan. 12, 1848)
James Myers to Sarah C. Snoddy, Jan. 14, 1848.
  By J. Jenkins, J.P. (Jan. 14, 1848)

David Marshall to Elizabeth Jane Hickman, Jan. 18, 1848.
By James Coffer, J.P. (Jan. 18, 1848)
Rufus Witt to Margaret Jane West, Jan. 19, 1848.
By Reuben Falkner, J.P. (Jan. 20, 1848)
John Yount to Sarah K. Fry, Jan. 20, 1848.
By Rev. Edwin A. Atlee. (Jan. 20, 1848)
William Moss to Elizabeth Lover, Jan. 20, 1848.
By J. Jack. (Jan. 20, 1848)
Thos. C. Carson to Martha A. E. Trotter, Jan. 31, 1848.
By J. Jenkins, J.P. (Jan. 31, 1848)
John W. Miller to Nancy McDaniel, Feb. 2, 1848.
By T. S. Rice, J.P. (Feb. 8, 1848)
G. W. Newton to Mary T. Wilson, Feb. 2, 1848.
By Ed Newton, M.G. (Feb. 3, 1848)
Thomas Dixon to Emeline Riddle, Feb. 3, 1848.
By Heil Buttram, M.G. (Feb. 3, 1848)
Thomas Galloway to M. C. Rothwell, Feb. 7, 1848.
(no returns)
Thos. Nichols to Lucy Cofman, Feb. 8, 1848.
By Wm. Rucker, J.P. (Feb. 10, 1848)
Malchiah Campbell to Margaret McCalley, Feb. 16, 1848.
By David F. Jamison, J.P. (Feb. 17, 1848)
Joel Roberts to Mary Spearman, Feb. 16, 1848.
By Wm. McKamy, J.P. (Feb. 17, 1848)
Thomas Worthy to Mahaley Boands, Feb. 22, 1848.
(no returns)
Henry J. Eaton to Sarah L. Jarnagan, Feb. 24, 1848.
By Wm. H. Ballew, J.P. (Feb. 24, 1848)
James R. Walker to Evanna Turnmill, Feb. 24, 1848.
(no returns)
Alexander Henderson to Jane Robison, Feb. 24, 1848.
By Wm. H. Ballew, J.P. (Feb. 24, 1848)
Wm. White to Stalin Cauldwell, Feb. 29, 1848.
By Tapley Gregory, J.P. (Mar. 2, 1848)
Wm. Smith to Malinda McGeho, Mar. 7, 1848.
By George Monroe(?), M.G. (Mar. 9, 1848)
William Shook, Jr. to Margaret Robeson(?), Mar. 9, 1848.
(no returns)
John R. Neil to Eleanor J. Wallis, Mar. 16, 1848.
(no returns)
William Ashley to Sarah Mayriod (or Mayniad), Mar. 16, 1848.
(no returns)
Jesse Givins to Mary Firestone, Mar. 21, 1848.
(no returns)
Samuel Cook to Jane Young, Mar. 25, 1848.
(no returns)
Thos. B. Dearman to Sarah Clark, Mar. 28, 1848.
(no returns)

McMINN COUNTY MARRIAGES

Book "D" 1848-1859

Josiah Pugh to Martha Morris, Apr. 3, 1848.
(no returns)
Isaac Brock to Mary Irene Sanndry, Apr. 10, 1838(?)
By J. Jack, M.G. (Apr. 10, 1838(?)
John A. Rowly to Rebecca Elizabeth McCallia, Apr. 15, 1848.
By M. C. Hawk, M.G. (Apr. 16, 1848)
James A. Briant to Armena Williams, Apr. 25, 1848.
By John Jenkins, J.P. (Apr. 25, 1848)
William A. Rhodes to Sarah Douglas, Apr. 26, 1848.
By John Jenkins, J.P. (Apr. 27, 1848)
Geo. W. Bridges to Margaret D. Gettys, Apr. 27, 1848.
By John B. Meek, M.G. (Apr. 27, 1848)
Payton T. Nance to Polly Ann Womack, May 2, 1848.
By Thos. B. Miller, M.G. (May 3, 1848)
McMillan Dodson to Sarah D. Cunningham, May 9, 1848.
By G. W. Alexander, M.G. (May 9, 1848)
Wesley Ghaston to Laura Jane Peck, May 9, 1848.
By A. F. Shanon, M.G. (May 11, 1848)
James Hambrick to Cinthia Malissa Richards, May 11, 1848.
By Daniel McPhale, J.P., McMinn Co. (May 11, 1848)
James Brown to Nancy George, May 13, 1848.
By S. C. Bryan, J.P. (May 17, 1848)
Elisha Crawley to Sarah D. Dorsey, May 16, 1848.
By Uriah Johnston, J.P. (May 16, 1848)
Andrew Jackson Johnston to Elizabeth West, May 18, 1848.
By Rupall Pane, J.P. (May 18, 1848)
Columbus A. W. Jordan to Mary Jane Young, May 18, 1848.
(no returns)
Alfred Carson to Caroline Lowe, May 25, 1848.
By J. Jack, M.G. (May 28, 1848)
John Grisham to Nancy McCrary, May 25, 1848.
By W. H. Ballew, J.P. (May 25, 1848)
William H. Smith to Frances Jane Wilson, June 7, 1848.
By John Key, M.G. (June 7, 1848)
Thomas P. Phillips to Sarah Elizabeth Dyer, June 7, 1848.
By James Sewell, M.G. (June 7, 1848)
J. H. Effert to M. A. W. Hawk, June 7, 1848.
By M. C. Hawk, M.G. (June 8, 1848)
William B. Johnston to Mary Isabella McCarty, June 8, 1848.
By Henry Price, M.G. (June 16, 1848)
C. H. Eaton to Rebecca Cate, June 22, 1848.
By James D. Henley, J.P. (Aug. 22, 1848)
John Thompson to Elizabeth Campbell, June 24, 1848.
By Thomas L. Russell, M.G. (June 29, 1848)
Jessie Elliot to Elizabeth Nation, June 24, 1848.
By Robt. T. Henderson, M.G. (July 2, 1848)
Thomas Rentfro to Katharine Wyrick, June 30, 1848.
(no returns)
Matthew Aulford to Martha C. Young, July 2, 1848.
By W. H. Ballew, J.P. (July 2, 1848)
Jackson C. Wilson to Sarah Martin, July 10, 1848.
By W. W. Haynes, Acting J.P. (July 11, 1848)

McMINN COUNTY MARRIAGES

William Dockery to Sarah Dockery, July 15, 1848.
   By G. W. Kirksey, J.P. (July 16, 1848)
Isaac P. Lynch to Elizabeth Jane Blankenship, July 20, 1848.
   By James J. Trott, M.G. (July 20, 1848)
John W. Burnett to Martha Katharine McGinty, July 26, 1848.
   (no returns)
Wm. Foster to Elizabeth Jane Bryant, Aug. 1, 1848.
   By David F. Jamison, J.P. (Aug. 2, 1848)
Allen Ellis to Malinda Foster, Aug. 1, 1848.
   By David F. Jamison, J.P. (Aug. 3, 1848)
Benjamin A. Ellis to Mary Ann Maples, Aug. 7, 1848.
   By William W. Haynes, J.P. (Aug. 8, 1848)
Marcus Gilbert to Nancy Maxwell, Aug. 8, 1848.
   By A. Swafford, J.P. (Aug. 9, 1848)
Enoch Miller to Saphrona Adaline Wilson, Aug. 10, 1848.
   (no returns)
Henry J. Dake to Lidia Lucindy Knox, Aug. 16, 1848.
   By Thomas B. Miller, M.G. (Aug. 17, 1848)
Henry Longforth to S. A. Morrison, Aug. 26, 1848.
   By Reuben Falkner, J.P., McMinn Co. (Aug. 27, 1848)
Elisha Melton to Anis Crabtree, Aug. 29, 1848.
   By Samuel Snoddy, J.P. (Aug. 30, 1848)
James Sherrill to Sarah Matilda Childress, Aug. 31, 1848.
   By A. F. Shannon, M.G. (Sep. 1, 1848)
Josiah R. Hardin to Elizabeth Cook, Aug. 31, 1848.
   By E. Newton, M.G. (Aug. 31, 1848)
Owen West Patty to Nancy Eveline Reynolds, Sep. 8, 1848.
   By Wilson Chapman, M.G. (Oct. 1, 1848)
Josiah Patty to Elizabeth Ann Black, Sep. 18, 1848.
   By David F. Jameson, J.P. (Oct. 5, 1848)
Dempsey Robison to Mary Lewis, Sep. 20, 1848.
   By Daniel McPhail, J.P. (Sep. 20, 1848)
Jacob Tribbue to Mahala Duff, Sep. 21, 1848.
   By A. L. Dugin, J.P. (Sep. 25, 1848)
Albert G. Small to Mary P. Burnett, Sep. 26, 1848.
   By Thos. H. Small, M.G. (Sep. 26, 1848)
Francis M. Rowan to Sidney Ann Lane, Sep. 26, 1848.
   By Wm. Call, M.G. (Sep. 28, 1848)
John Samples to Jemima Divine, Sep. 30, 1848.
   By S. C. Carlock, J.P. (Oct. 1, 1848)
Geo. W. Hughes to Nancy Young, Oct. 1, 1848.
   By A. L. Dugin, J.P. (Oct. 2, 1848)
John H. Wright to Sarah Ann Crittenden, Oct. 2, 1848.
   By Samuel Snoddy, J.P. (Oct. 2, 1848)
Hezekiah Blanton to Bedience Young, Oct. 4, 1848.
   By Tapley Grayson, J.P. (Oct. 5, 1848)
James Brown to Mary Carroll, Oct. 15, 1848.
   By A. Slover, M.G. (5th day of 1848(?)
John Cole to Polly Ann Dean, Oct. 7, 1848.
   (no returns)
Wm. G. Horton to P. C. Steed, Oct. 12, 1848.
   By M. A. Cass, M.G. (Oct. 12, 1848)
Thomas Scruggs to M. J. Hale, Oct. 13, 1848.
   By Nathaniel Barnett, M.G.

John Rodes to Tabitha Ann Richardson, Oct. 16, 1848.
By Urial Johnston, J.P. (Oct. 16, 1848)
Ignatious W. Cagle to Nancy Lemmons, Oct. 18, 1848.
By Samuel C. Bryan, J.P. (Oct. 20, 1848)
W. Culpepper to Sallie Armstrong, Oct. 19, 1848.
By A. Swafford, J.P. (Oct. 22, 1848)
James A. Moreland to Margaret Ronack, Oct. 19, 1848.
By T. O. Rice, J.P. (Oct. 19, 1848)
James Finney to Jane Wells, Oct. 25, 1848.
By J. C. Carlock, J.P. (Oct. 25, 1848)
George W. Morgan to Martha R. Mayo, Oct. 12, 1848.
By Hillary Patrick, M.G. (Oct. 26, 1848)
William M. Purcell to Martha Matlock, Nov. 2, 1848.
(no returns)
Henry W. Mize to Mary Elizabeth Stansberry, Nov. 2, 1848.
By M. A. Cass, M.G. (Nov. 2, 1848)
Edmond Roberts to Elizabeth C. Petitt, Nov. 2, 1848.
By Robert Gregory, M.G. (Nov. 2, 1848)
Samuel Vincent to Lucindy Martin, Nov. 4, 1848.
(no returns)
James Crawford to Susan Crawford, Nov. 6, 1848.
By Daniel McPhail, J.P. (Nov. 6, 1848)
Jessie Dodson to Ailsey Matamon, Nov. 7, 1848.
By Wilson Chapman, M.G. (Nov. 9, 1848)
John M. Anderson to Sarah Jane Ware, Nov. 9, 1848.
By Urial Johnston, J.P. (Nov. 9, 1848)
William A. Triplet to Hopy Duckworth, Nov. 9, 1848.
By Urial Johnston, J.P. (Nov. 9, 1848)
Thomas Worthy to Mary McMahan, Nov. 9, 1848.
By Wm. Walker, J.P. (Nov. 9, 1848)
Houston Giles to Susan A. Carter, Nov. 18, 1848.
By James Sewell, M.G. (Nov. 19, 1848)
Juna Janeway to Nancy Plank, Nov. 27, 1848.
By Nathaniel Barnett, M.G. (Nov. 30, 1848)
James E. Patterson to Caroline Sloop, Nov. 29, 1848.
By J. C. Carlock, J.P. (Nov. 30, 1848)
H. C. Basinger to M. R. Elliott, Nov. 30, 1848.
(no returns)
Pleasant B. Gibson to Nancy Kinchelow, Dec. 4, 1848.
By I. M. Spear, J.P., McMinn Co. (Dec. 7, 1848)
Thomas Morris to Julia Amanda Wells, Dec. 4, 1848.
By J. C. Carlock, J.P. (Dec. 5, 1848)
S. W. Royston to Elizabeth Parshall, Dec. 5, 1848.
By A. A. Mathis, M.G.
Hugh Jones to Margaret Keeling, Dec. 6, 1848.
By Russell Lucie, J.P. (Dec. 8, 1848)
Joel Dennis to Sarahan Roberts, Dec. 11, 1848.
By Thomas B. Weller, M.G. (Dec. 12, 1848)
Joseph Buchanan to Margaret Dobson, Dec. 11, 1848.
By I. W. Thompson, M.G. (Dec. 13, 1848)
Joseph Brown to Matilda Hicks, Dec. 12, 1848.
By Thomas T. Russell, M.G. (Dec. 12, 1848)
John Lewis to Elizabeth Patterson, Dec. 14, 1848.
By J. C. Carlock, J.P. (Dec. 14, 1848)

McMINN COUNTY MARRIAGES

M. G. Reynolds to Mary C. Hogs, Dec. 14, 1848.
By Wilson Chapman, M.G. (Dec. 15, 1848)
John E. T. Wilson to Jane M. Richardson, Dec. 14, 1848.
By Urial Johnston, J.P. (Dec. 14, 1848)
Calvin H. Center to Sarah Gage, Dec. 15, 1848.
(no returns)
William Matterson to Martha Station, Dec. 18, 1848.
By Joseph Cobb, J.P. (Dec. 19, 1848)
Joseph Walker to Sarah Bonner, Dec. 20, 1848.
By A. F. Thomas, M.G.
Jackson Scroggins (or Scoggins) to Julia Buttram, Dec. 20, 1848. (no returns)
Peter Staner to Almina Correy, Dec. 20, 1848.
By William Walker, J.P. (Dec. 25, 1848)
Wesley Avans to Artilessa Brock, Dec. 27, 1848.
(no returns)
William Doss to Jane Cannon, Jan. 1, 1849.
By Alfred Swafford, J.P. (Jan. 2, 1849)
Jackson Miller to Manada Ellis, Jan. 3, 1849.
By A. A. Mathis, M.G. (Jan. 1, 1849(?)
Henry Shutz to Theressa Loomey, Jan. 8, 1849.
By J. P. Robbs, J.P. (Jan. 11, 1849)
Aaron Dean to Charlotta Ward, Jan. 2, 1849.
(no returns)
James Emery to Sarah Graves, Jan. 9, 1849.
(no returns)
John Vanzant to Sarah Paris, Jan. 11, 1849.
By J. C. Carlock, J.P. (Jan. 11, 1849)
William Gordon to Tabitha Harden, Jan. 17, 1849.
By John Spears, J.P. (Jan. 18, 1849)
James K. Bales to Abigale Benton, Jan. 18, 1849.
By R. S. McAdoo, J.P. (Jan. 18, 1849)
Robert Elder to Elizabeth Caldwell, Jan. 19, 1849.
By T. B. Waller, M.G. (Jan. 20, 1849)
Jonathan H. Embree to Lina Kelly, Jan. 15, 1849.
By A. L. Dugan, J.P. (Jan. 16, 1849)
James L. Kinser to Judith Hunt, Jan. 30, 1849.
By Nathaniel Barnett, M.G. (Jan. 30, 1849)
Larkin Lewis to Eell(?) Mize, Jan. 30, 1849.
By T. L. Hoge, Local Preacher.
John L. Thomas to Maryann Wattenbarger, Jan. 31, 1849.
By Thos. B. Waller, M.G. (Feb. 1, 1849)
Wm. R. Bean to Mariah Thornton, Feb. 3, 1849.
By John Scruggs, M.G. (Feb. 4, 1849)
James Hall to Jane Johnson, Feb. 3, 1849.
By Robert Sneed, M.G. (Feb. 4, 1849)
John W. Liner to Jane Hampton, Feb. 7, 1849.
By A. Swafford, J.P. (Feb. 7, 1849)
Jeremiah Knox to Martha McAdoo, Feb. 7, 1849.
By A. Barb, J.P. (Feb. 8, 1849)
Stephen Taylor to Leremiah Hall, Feb. 8, 1849.
By Nathaniel Barnett, M.G. (Feb. 18, 1849)
William Davis to Caroline Blackwell, Feb. 12, 1849.
By John Jenkins, J.P. (Feb. 13, 1849)

Reynolds Cantrell to Sarah E. Vaughn, Feb. 14, 1849.
By W. F. Forrest, M.G. (Feb. 14, 1849)
Jacob Wattenbarger to Louisa Thomas, Feb. 21, 1849.
By T. B. Waller, M.G. (Feb. 22, 1849)
Jacob Womack to Catherine Beavers, Feb. 21, 1849.
By Tapley Gregory, J.P. (Feb. 21, 1849)
Stephen Hill to Mary Stewart, Feb. 21, 1849.
By Nathaniel Barnett, M.G. (Feb. 22, 1849)
Isaiah Garrison to Mahala Arnwine, Feb. 22, 1849.
By G. W. Wallace, J.P. (Feb. 22, 1849)
Emanuel Haney to Amanda Irwin, Feb. 23, 1849.
By James Dougherty, M.G. (_____, 1849)
Sterling Hill to Mary Ann Wallace, Feb. 24, 1849.
By Russell Lane, J.P. (Feb. 26, 1849)
W. H. Williams to Amanda C. Dethro, Feb. 4, 1849.
(no returns)
B. A. Proffat to Eunice Grigg, Mar. 5, 1849.
By J. C. Carlock, J.P. (Mar. 5, 1849)
James R. Ash to Elizabeth Walton, Mar. 8, 1849.
By Samuel Snoddy, J.P. (Mar. 8, 1849)
Geo. Hotchkisson to Martha Reed, Mar. 9, 1849.
By John Jenkins, J.P. (Mar. 9, 1849)
Joseph R. Barnett to Miss C. (or M.) A. Smith, Mar. 10,
1849. By Samuel Wilson, J.P. (Mar. 13, 1849)
Lee Sparks to Elizabeth Shook, Mar. 12, 1849.
By A. L. Dugan, J.P. (Mar. 12, 1849)
William Melton to Rebecca Hampton, Mar. 14, 1849.
By A. Swafford, J.P. (Mar. 14, 1849)
Plisha (or Elisha) Kimbrough (or Kimbrow) to Lemira Jane
Hickson, Mar. 15, 1849. (no returns)
Thomas F. Whaley to Mary A. Howel, Mar. 22, 1849.
By A. F. Shannon, M.G. (Apr. 5, 1849)
Isaac M. Brigham (or Bingham) to Charlotte Temple Doss,
Mar. 28, 1849. By John Jenkins, J.P. (Mar. 28, 1849)
E. W. Shell (or Schell) to C. C. Carroll, Mar. 29, 1849.
By R. A. McAdoo, J.P. (Apr. 1, 1849)
James J. Rayburn to Catherine Saunders, Mar. 31, 1849.
By A. L. Dugan, J.P. (Apr. 1, 1849)
William Elmore to Nancy L. Dixon, Apr. 7, 1849.
By Thomas T. Russell, M.G. (Apr. 10, 1849)
Harrison Dill to Nancy Rogers, (no date given)
By Sam Scarbrough, M.G. (Apr. 10, 1849)
Floyd McGougal to Nancy Dorsey, Apr. 23, 1849.
(no returns)
John Morgan to Polly Abbott, Apr. 28, 1849.
By W. R. Walker, J.P. (Apr. 28, 1849)
Robert Dye to Mary Hackrider, Apr. 28, 1849.
By John Spears, J.P. (Apr. 29, 1849)
Henry Alog to Susannah Gunter, May 2, 1849.
By E. Newton, M.G. (May 3, 1849)
James M. Creasman to Nancy Haymes, May 2, 1849.
By J. C. Dugan, J.P. (May 3, 1849)
John Ashley to Sarah Wesham, May 7, 1849.
By A. L. Dugan, J.P. (May 3, 1849(?)

David N. Varnell to Mary Lowry, May 17, 1849.
   By James Ackinson, M.G. (May 17, 1849)
William Hicks (or Hix) to Nancy Dorherty, May 17, 1849.
   By S. L. Aryan, J.P. (May 17, 1849)
Robert W. Gregg to Sarah Wilson, May 24, 1849.
   By R. M. Hickey, M.G. (May 24, 1849)
James M. Waide to Martha D. H. Bridges, May 31, 1849.
   By J. Atkinson, M.M.E.C.S. (May 31, 1849)
Columbus Brown to Abigale Sively, June 5, 1849.
   By C. Brown. (Returned, no property found the intend
   bridegroom.)
Lazarus Dodson to Rebecca L. Sullins, June 5, 1849.
   By Thos. H. Small, M.G.C.P.C. (June 4, 1849(?)
James Hughes to Rebecca Lenny, June 7, 1849.
   By Hile Buttram, M.G. (June 7, 1849)
John A. S. Fisher to Mary L. Cogghill, June 9, 1849.
   (no returns)
W. R. Walker to Amanda C. Wolf, June 20, 1849.
   By A. F. Shannon. (June 21, 1849)
James H. Bridges to Eliza _____, June 30, 1849.
   By John Spears, J.P., McMinn Co. (July 1, 1849)
William Knox to Martha Underwood, June 30, 1849.
   By Thos. B. Waller, M.G. (June 2, 1849(?)
Benjamin M. Martin to Nancy Jane Foster, July 9, 1849.
   By A. Barb, J.P. (July 12, 1849)
William Brookshire to Rebecca C. Brookshire, July 11, 1849.
   By Wm. Makarn, J.P. (July 17, 1849)
William Emerson to Lidia Long, July 16, 1849.
   By Wm. F. Forrest, M.G. (July 17, 1849)
Thomas A. Owen to Nancy P. Rice, July 17, 1849.
   By W. F. Forest, M.G. (July 17, 1849)
Wm. J. Y. Bennett to Mary E. Only, July 18, 1849.
   By William Walker, J.P. (July 19, 1849)
John K. Morgan to Polly Stainer, July 23, 1849.
   By W. R. Walker, J.P.
Adam Sliger to M. E. Bales, July 24, 1849.
   By Hile Buttram, M.G. (July 26, 1849)
Samuel Hauce to Martha Brown, Aug. 9, 1849.
   (no returns)
Joseph Neil to Elizabeth Glaize, Aug. 15, 1849.
   By Sam. C. Lee, M.G. (Aug. 16, 1849)
James L. Meadows to Susan Caster, Aug. 21, 1847.
   By David F. Jamison, J.P. (Aug. 23, 1849)
Ecana D. Horton to Mary C. Rucker, Aug. 23, 1849.
   (Aug. 23, 1849)
James M. Charles to Eliza Jane Dodson, Aug. 23, 1849.
   By Wm. F. Forest, M.G. (Aug. 23, 1849)
John Corey to Litty Lawson, Aug. 25, 1849.
   By Nat Barnett, M.G. (Aug. 25, 1849)
Gainey M. Gallaher to Sarah Lawson, Aug. 28, 1849.
   By Urial Johnston, J.P. (Aug. 28, 1849)
John A. Selph to Mary Ann McInturff, (no date given)
   By Andrew John, M.G. (Sep. 6, 1849)
Samuel D. Ryan to Mary L. McMalenta (no date given)
   By H. C. Cooke, M.G. (Sep. 11, 1849)

Charles H. Mills to Sarah C. Brown, (no date given).
By Thos. A. Small, M.G.C.P.C. (Sep. 6, 1849)
James C. Rucker to Virginia McDonald, Sep. 8, 1849.
By Jas. C. Bryan, J.P. (Sep. 9, 1849)
Lafayett Trim to Luramy S. Giles, Sep. 8, 1849.
Henry Morgan to Caroline Brock, Sep. 10, 1849.
By William R. Walker, J.P. (Sep. 11, 1849)
Jonathan N. Cate to Martha M. Maples, Sep. 11, 1849.
By H. Douglas, M. (Sep. 13, 1849)
Frances M. Reece to Amanda J. Armstrong, Sep. 13, 1849.
By Moses Riving, J.P. (Sep. 13, 1849)
James A. Deam to Clarissa Griffith, Sep. 18, 1849.
By J. A. Akins(?), M. (Sep. 18, 1849)
Jessie Grisham, Sr. to Mary Jane Erwin, Sep. 20, 1849.
By Wm. Burns, J.P.
William S. Ageman to Martha Hardy, Sep. 20, 1849.
By M. Southan, M.G. (Dec. 21, 1849)
William J. Ware to Anna Cauldwell, Sep. 20, 1849.
By Robert Gregory, M.B.C. (Sep. 20, 1849)
Milton Robertson to Mary Hardy, Sep. 20, 1849.
By M. Southard, M.G. (Sep. 20, 1849)
William S. Rogers to Rachel Thompson, Sep. 26, 1849.
By John Jenkins, J.M.(?) (Sep. 27, 1849)
John Michaels to Martha Adolff, Sep. 26, 1849.
By Wm. McKay, J.P., McMinn Co. (Sep. 27, 1849)
Jonathan Dorsey to Peggyann Jackson, Sep. 27, 1849.
(no returns)
William A. Hemphill to Milly Triplett, (no date given).
By N. Southard, M.G. (Sep. 30, 1849)
George M. Hutsell to Mary E. McSpadden, (no date given).
By R. M. Hacker, M.G. (Oct. 3, 1849)
Andrew Turner to Susan Hounsell, Oct. 2, 1849.
By R. M. Hacker, M.G. (Oct. 3, 1849)
Samuel Bollen to Clarissa Moss, Oct. 4, 1849.
By A. L. Dugan, J.P. (Sep. 4, 1849(?)
Andrew Rolling to Rachel Martin, Oct. 8, 1849.
By Samuel Snoddy, J.P. (Oct. 8, 1849)
Franklin Triplett to Martha Lawson, Oct. 9, 1849.
By Urial Johnston, J.P. (Oct. 9, 1849)
James Lewis to Elizabeth Emery, Oct. 11, 1849.
By J. C. Carlock, J.P. (Oct. 11, 1849)
James A. Carrol to Jane Lawson, Oct. 24, 1849.
By I. W. Miller, M.G. (Oct. 25, 1849)
Wm. W. Miller to Elizabeth Belcher, Oct. 24, 1849.
By R. A. McAdoo, J.P. (Oct. 24, 1849)
Addison Sharp to Mary D. Porter, Oct. 25, 1849.
By A. A. Matthews, M.G. (Oct. 25, 1849)
Daniel Bunch to Rachel Bennett, Oct. 29, 1849.
By J. C. Carlock, J.P. (Nov. 1, 1849)
James Heck to Sarah Ann Stansberry, Nov. 1, 1849.
(no returns)
Edmund C. Carson to Nancy C. Thomas, Nov. 1, 1849.
By Jacob D. Henly, J.P. (Nov. 1, 1849)
George W. Scott to Mary Fort, Nov. 5, 1849.
By George W. Kirksey, J.P. (Nov. 6, 1849)

McMINN COUNTY MARRIAGES

Isaac Widows to Anna Parsons, Nov. 7, 1849.
  By Tripley Gregory, J.P. (Nov. 8, 1849)
J. J. Largon to Julia A. Kinchelow, Nov. 12, 1849.
  By William R. Walker. (Nov. 14, 1849)
James A. Hornsby to Harriet C. Coleman, Nov. 14, 1849.
  By John L. Robinson, M.G. (Nov. 14, 1849)
John J. Chambers to Mariah Swinford, Nov. 14, 1849.
  By John L. Robinson, M.G. (Nov. 14, 1849)
David Brown to Elizabeth A. McKenzie, Nov. 15, 1849.
  By William Weather, J.P. (Nov. 15, 1849)
Robert H. Paris (or Parris or Pharis) to Mary Jane Jenkins,
  (no date given). By J. C. Pendergrass, M.G. (Nov. 22,
  1849)
William B. Brussell to Caroline Sallee, Dec. 22, 1849.
  By Wm. A. Ballew, J.P. (Nov. 22, 1849(?)
William Orr to Elizabeth Ann Copeland, Nov. 26, 1849.
  By Uriel Johnston, Esq. (Nov. 26, 1849)
Johnson Errickson to Edy Milton, Nov. 28, 1849.
  By Jas. C. Bryan, J.P. (Nov. 28, 1849)
Joseph Gilbreath to Jemimah Thompson, Nov. 28, 1849.
  By H. C. Cooke, M.G. (Nov. 28, 1849)
John Young to Sarah Blevins, Dec. 1, 1849.
  By R. A. McAdoo, J.P. (Dec. 6, 1849)
James Turner to Harriet Porter, Nov. 4, 1849.
  By John J. Robinson, M.G. (Nov. 4, 1849)
I. Hamilton Gant to Sarah Elizabeth Isbell, Dec. 4, 1849.
  (no returns)
John Baker to Elizabeth Hudgens, Dec. 4, 1849.
  (no returns)
F. M. Cantrell to Martha M. Sellers, Dec. 4, 1849.
  By C. R. Hoyl, M.G. (Dec. 27, 1849)
James W. McAffrey to Nancy McGuire, Dec. 5, 1849.
  (no returns)
Thomas McEnturff to Nancy Pugh, Dec. 5, 1849.
  By James Bonner, J.P. (Dec. 9, 1849)
Robert L. Stout to Mariam Watson, Dec. 6, 1849.
  By Wm. McKamy, J.P. (Dec. 6, 1849)
Henry S. Marshall to Mary Elizabeth Smith, Dec. 10, 1849.
  By J. Cunningham, M.G. (Dec. 13, 1849)
Joseph M. Fry to Mary Cicils, Dec. 12, 1849.
  By Leander Wilson, M.G. (Dec. 13, 1849)
J. B. Collins to Elizabeth Jane McCarty, Dec. 12, 1849.
  By Henry Price, M.G. (Dec. 15, 1849)
Henry Jackson Mize to Elizabeth Jane Cartright, Dec. 19,
  1849. By J. Jack, M.G. (Dec. 19, 1850(?)
Andrew L. Rogers to Chrokee A. Morgan, Dec. 20, 1849.
  By A. A. Matthews, M.G. (Dec. 20, 1849)
Vardra Brookshire to Mary Brookshire, Dec. 20, 1849.
  By Wm. McKamy, J.P.
Humphrey Shults to Isabella Terry, Dec. 20, 1849.
  By Thos. Cunningham, J.P. (Dec. 20, 1849)
Frances Alread to Serene Dorherty, Dec. 20, 1849.
  By J. Jack, M.G. (Dec. 20, 1850(?)
William Burris to Mahala Rudd, Dec. 27, 1849.
  By Samuel Snoddy, J.P.

M. H. Casteel to Mary N. Elbert, Jan. 1, 1850.
  By J. C. Pendergrass, M. Gospel of Christ. (Jan. __, 1850)
James Kibble to Mary Reed, Jan. 1, 1850.
  By William Walker, J.P. (Jan. 2, 1850)
David F. Shipley to Elizabeth Sharp, Jan. 2, 1850.
  By Hiel Buttram, M.G. (Jan. 6, 1850)
Elmore Brock to Mary Bonner, Jan. 2, 1850.
  By Wm. McKamy, J.P. (Jan. 3, 1850)
John R. Lenty to Elizabeth Matlock, Jan. 3, 1850.
  By Bracket Goldy, Traveling Elder in the M. E. Church,
  South Holston Conference. (Jan. 3, 1850)
Samuel Mizell to Synthia Stephenson, Jan. 3, 1850.
  By Samuel Snoddy, J.P. (Jan. 3, 1850)
Calven Lunsford to Sarah Jane Benoutt, Jan. 8, 1850.
  (no returns)
Russell Miller to Jane Wilson, Jan. 15, 1850.
  (no returns)
James Falkner to Susan Crow, Jan. 16, 1850.
  By Heil Buttram, P.G. (Jan. 17, 1850)
Wm. M. Hart to Rachel Lamare, Jan. 17, 1850.
  By Wm. Burns, J.P. (Jan. 17, 1850)
Levi Swinford to Nancy C. Rucker, Jan. 19, 1850.
  By Y. C. Bryan, J.P. (Jan. 19, 1850)
Jesse W. Dodson to Elizabeth J. McKamy, Feb. 1, 1850.
  By Wm. F. Forrest, M.G. (Feb. 5, 1850)
Randle Rutherford to Artimelia Dy, Feb. 9, 1850.
  (no returns)
David Pearce to Lucinda Evans, Feb. 11, 1850.
  By J. M. Scarbrough. (Feb. 18, 1850)
Moses Cunningham to Margaret A. Graves, Feb. 14, 1850.
  By John J. Robinson, M.G. (Feb. 14, 1850)
Patrick W. Wilson to Mary C. Barnett, Feb. 14, 1850.
  By Thomas T. Russell, M.G. (Feb. 15, 1850)
William Poe to Susannah Largent, Feb. 15, 1850.
  (no returns)
George Kirby to Sarah Nanry (or Manry), Feb. 18, 1850.
  By A. L. Dugan, J.P. (Feb. 18, 1850)
Elmadoras R. Johnston to Malorina Sloop, Feb. 21, 1850.
  By Moses Sweney, J.P. (Feb. 21, 1850)
George W. Trew to Polly T. Walton, Feb. 22, 1850.
  (no returns)
William Shoemaker to Elizabeth Cannon, Feb. 24, 1850.
  By John Jenkins, J.P. (Feb. 25, 1850)
Reuben Masey to Sarah Wheeler, Feb. 27, 1850.
  By J. D. Henley, J.P., McMinn Co. (Feb. 27, 1850)
Claiborne W. Bamay to Lucinda Foster, Feb. 27, 1850.
  (no returns)
John R. Foster to Malissa Buttram, Mar. 4, 1850.
  By E. E. Gillenwater, M.G. (Mar. 7, 1850)
Isham Hayes to Sarah Hayes, Mar. 4, 1850.
  (no returns)
William P. Rutherford to Elizabeth A. Loughmiller, Mar. 4,
  1850. By J. C. Carlock, J.P. (Mar. 5, 1850)
John Clerits to Caroline Emery, Mar. 6, 1850.
  By James Bonner, J.P. (Mar. 6, 1850)

Samuel Gilly to Catharine Brock, Mar. 13, 1850.
  By John Spears, J.P., McMinn Co. (Mar. 13, 1850)
William Henderson to Jane Cunningham, Mar. 23, 1850.
  By Wm. Burrus, J.P. (Mar. 24, 1850)
James M. Colier to Mary Douglas, Mar. 23, 1850.
  By J. C. Carlock, J.P. (Mar. 24, 1850)
Samuel H. Thompson to L. Brock, (no date given).
  By J. Jack, M.G. (Mar. 7, 1852(?)
Joseph R. Rutherford to Louisa E. Pearce, Apr. 17, 1850.
  By Thomas P. Russell, M.G. (Apr. 18, _____)
Hiram Webb to Susannah Roe, Apr. 22, 1850.
  By Thomas B. Waller, M.G. (Apr. 22, 1850)
Thomas Melton to Margaret Grady, Apr. __, 1855(?)
  By Ide Haney, J.P. (Apr. __, 1855(?)
Alexander F. Cox to Amelia V. Atlee, May 1, 1850.
  By J. W. Miller, M.G. (May 1, 1850)
D. F. Carson to Milly M. Barker, May 9, 1850.
  By H. C. Cooke, M.G. (May 9, 1850)
Morris O. Quinn to Nancy Malinda Secrest, May 15, 1850.
  (no returns)
Henry Rayburn to Martha Manery, May 18, 1850.
  By J. Jack, M.G. (May 20, 1850)
Onslow G. Crenell to Parthena Hickel, (no date given).
  By J. W. Miller, M.G.
E. W. Braden to Nancy Jane Smith, May 24, 1850.
  By John Key, M.G. (May 24, 1850)
John Hawks to Hetty Shook, May 29, 1850.
  (no returns)
John Philpots to Polly Little, June 6, 1850.
  By J. Jack, M.G. (June 6, 1850)
Caleb M. Ingram to Lurena E. Harless, June 12, 1850.
  By T. S. Rice, J.P. (June 13, 1850)
James Forrest to Nancy Jane Ellis, June 23, 1850.
  By J. C. Gaston, M.G. (June 23, 1850)
Alfred R. Byington to Elizabeth C. Guffey, June 25, 1850.
  (no returns)
Thomas Lewis to Catharine C. Lyle, June 30, 1850.
  By Reuben Faulkner, J.P. (June 30, 1850)
Jesse B. Caldwell to Martha J. Frizzell, July 4, 1850.
  By Robert Gregory, M.G. (July 4, 1850)
David Pearce, Jr. to Sarah Jane Hutson, July 4, 1850.
  By A. Barb, J.P. (July 4, 1850)
Silas H. Richey to Polly Cry, July 11, 1850.
  By S. D. Henly, J.P., McMinn Co. (July 11, 1850)
John B. Smith to Sarah Thompson, July 17, 1850.
  By Wilson Chapman, M.G. (July 25, 1850)
James L. Doss to Nancy Gage, July 23, 1850.
  By A. Swafford, J.P. (July 23, 1850)
Daniel Walker to Mary Jane McKenzie, July 30, 1850.
  By William Walker, J.P. (Aug. 4, 1850)
William G. Stone to P. Errickson, Aug. 7, 1850.
  (no returns)
John Cate to Harriet Errickson, Aug. 7, 1850.
  (no returns)

McMINN COUNTY MARRIAGES

Elijah Swinford to Caroline (or Selia Emley) Glass,
   Aug. 8, 1850. By M. G. Scarbrough. (Aug. 8, 1850)
Archibald Mairot to Sarah Lawson, Aug. 10, 1850.
   By Dan Carpenter, T.D.M.C.S. (Aug. 15, 1850)
Franklin C. Teague to Malinda L. Newton, Aug. 10, 1850.
   By J. M. Scarbrough, M.G. (Aug. 11, 1850)
Edward Lee to Esther S. Fitzgerald, Aug. 14, 1850.
   By E. A. Smith, V.D.M. (Aug. 15, 1850)
Jesse R. Grigg to Jane Prophet, Aug. 15, 1850.
   By C. R. Hoge, M.G. (Aug. 15, 1850)
David Teague to Emeline Orton, Aug. 18, 1850.
   (no returns)
William W. Hammond to Jane O. Patton, Aug. 15, 1850.
   By Thomas L. Russell, M.G. (Aug. 16, 1850)
James Hickey to Mary W. Paris, Aug. 15, 1850.
   By John Jenkins, J.P. (Aug. 16, 1850)
James Eaves to Mary Fowler, Aug. 17, 1850.
   By J. M. Scarbrough. (Aug. 18, 1850)
William P. Burk to Margaret A. Wilson, Aug. 20, 1850.
   By John G. Gaston, M.G. (Aug. 20, 1850)
Sterling Shipley to Lurana Buttram, Aug. 27, 1850.
   By Rev. D. Carpenter, L.D.M.E.C.S. (Sep. 1, 1850)
Thomas Hicks to Emely Lewis, Aug. 28, 1850.
   By C. R. Hoyl, M.G. (Aug. 29, 1850)
John C. George to Mary Womack, Aug. 28, 1850.
   (no returns)
Caleb R. Hoyl to Ataline Cantrell, Aug. 29, 1850.
   By James Carson, M.G. (Aug. 29, 1850)
John Jones to Margaret Mayabb, Aug. 29, 1850.
   By William Walker, J.P. (Aug. 29, 1850)
Andrew Foster to Sarah Buttram, Aug. 31, 1850.
   By E. E. Gillenwater, M.G. (Sep. 6, 1850)
Moses Buttram to Mary Ann Foster, Aug. 31, 1850.
   By E. E. Gillenwater, M.G. (Sep. 5, 1850)
William G. Martin to E. C. Liner, Sep. 3, 1850.
   By M. G. Scarbrough.
John A. Green to Margaret Henry, Sep. 6, 1850.
   By Moses Sweeney, J.P. (Sep. 6, 1850)
Jeremiah B. Ellis to Sarah Thompson, Sep. 10, 1850.
   By Robert Gregory, M.G. (Sep. 10, 1850)
Ezekiel Spriggs to Mary Ann Houston, Sep. 12, 1850.
   By Young L. McLemare, M.G. (Sep. 12, 1850)
J. M. McGougal to Mary Ann Shultz, Sep. 12, 1850.
   By Joseph Robertson, M.G. (Sep. 12, 1850)
John Felyeer to R. Coxey, Sep. 12, 1850.
   By Bje.(?) A. John, M.G. (Sep. 17, 1850)
Daniel Bledsoe to Peggy Cagle, (no date given).
   By John Gaston, M.G. (Sep. 17, 1850)
William Poe to Susannah Largent, Sep. 23, 1850.
   By William R. Walker, J.P.
Alcary McKanbe (or McNabb) to Rebecca Hunt, Sep. 26, 1850.
   By A. John, M.G. (Sep. 26, 1850)
Mordecai G. Blane to Mary A. Buttram, Sep. 27, 1850.
   By Hiel Buttram, M.G. (Sep. 28, 1850)

McMINN COUNTY MARRIAGES

Benton Reyton to Artemesy Bales, Sep. 28, 1850.
  By Hiel Buttram, M.G. (Sep. 26, 1850)
Jacob Buttram to Josephine Wilson, Sep. 30, 1850.
  By D. Carpenter, M.G. (Oct. 10, 1850)
Geo. W. Loughmiller to Fanny E. Rutherford, Sep. 30, 1850.
  By T. D. Hoyl, M.G. (Sep. 30, 1850)
Samuel R. Bain to Amanda E. Patty, Oct. 1, 1850.
  By Wilson Chapman, M.G. (Oct. 1, 1850)
W. T. Atkinson to Dorcus E. Loughmiller, Oct. 1, 1850.
  By T. L. Hoyl, M.G.
James Haggard to Isaphena M. McCrosky, Oct. 6, 1850.
  (no returns)
Henry Steed to Elizabeth Vanderpearl, Oct. 8, 1850.
  By Wm. Burns, J.P. (Oct. 8, 1850)
James P. Haynes to Margaret E. Elliott, Oct. 11, 1850.
  By J. W. Miller, Mst. Gsp. (Oct. 15, 1850)
Alexander Maxwell to Martha J. Norvell, Oct. 16, 1850.
  (no returns)
Jessie A. Hyden to Nancy M. Steed, Oct. 29, 1850.
  By T. S. Rice, J.P. (Oct. 31, 1850)
William B. Misemer to Mary Ann Torbett, Nov. 5, 1850.
  By Y. Cunningham, M.G. (Nov. 6, 1850)
Warren D. Moss to Elizabeth Cloud, Nov. 3, 1850.
  (Nov. 8, 1850)
Thomas Studdard to Armen(?) Jane Melton, Nov. 6, 1850.
  By John Jenkins, J.P. (Nov. 7, 1850)
Charles C. Barnett to Lucindy McGoss, Nov. 6, 1850.
  By Daniel McPhail, J.P. (Nov. 7, 1850)
William Richey to Margaret L. Cry, Nov. 7, 1850.
  By J. D. Henly, J.P. (Nov. 7, 1850)
Joseph Robertson to Elizabeth Ann Dodson, Nov. 14, 1850.
  (no returns)
Christifer Graves to Elizabeth Shelton, Nov. 25, 1850.
  (no returns)
Alfred W. Morris to Narcissa Trim, Nov. 28, 1850.
  By G. W. Wallis, J.P. (Nov. 28, 1850)
Rector Davis to Lien Anna Lemmons, Nov. 29, 1850.
  By J. Jenkins, J.P. (Nov. 29, 1850)
John Thompson to Martha Jones, Nov. 30, 1850.
  By Moses Sweeney, J.P. (Nov. 1, 1850(?)
I. R. Patty to Leah Smith, Dec. 2, 1850.
  (no returns)
Thomas B. Wright to Iraanah Cruse, Dec. 4, 1850.
  By Y. C. Bryant, J.P. (Dec. 5, 1850)
Samuel Hardy, Jr. to Elizabeth Copeland, Dec. 12, 1850.
  By M. Southard, M.G. (Dec. 13, 1850)
E. D. Atkins to Rebecca Melton, Dec. 13, 1850.
  (no returns)
Jackson Standifer to Mary Sweeney Ahl, Dec. 16, 1850.
  By L. B. Dodson, J.P. (Dec. 17, 1850)
William Langford to Lucy Hughes, Dec. 16, 1850.
  By Wm. Burns, J.P. (Dec. 17, 1850)
William Mayfield to Narcissa Hoyl, Dec. 17, 1850.
  (no returns)

David B. Cunningham to Mary Henderson, Dec. 25, 1850.
  By Wm. H. Ballew, J.P. (Dec. 25, 1850)
Porter B. Cate to Gemima Womack, Dec. 26, 1850.
  By William R. Walker. (Dec. 26, 1850)
Sonirom Judson Chamber to Eliza Thatch (or Thalch), Dec. 27,
  1850. By T. S. Rice, J.P. (Dec. 29, 1850)
William Howard to Mary Ann Hunt, Jan. 2, 1850(?).
  By Wm. H. Ballew, J.P. (Jan. 2, 1850(?)
George W. Morris to Mary C. Fitzgerald, Jan. 6, 1851.
  (no returns)
Samuel Farles to Polly Grisham, Jan. 6, 1851.
  By Bej.(?) A. John, M.G. (Jan. 6, 1851)
Wilbern Wilson to Louisa Thompson, Jan. 7, 1851.
  (no returns)
James O. Coffee to Eliza Ann Grady, Jan. 8, 1851.
  By Y. C. Bryan, J.P. (Jan. 8, 1851)
James Large to Lizer Monroe, Jan. 16, 1851.
  By Daniel McPhail, J.P. (Jan. 16, 1851)
Joseph Sharp to Eliza Richards, Jan. 16, 1851.
  By Wm. McKamy, J.P. (Jan. 16, 1851)
Richard Stuart to Elizabeth Nickels, Jan. 16, 1851.
  By Tapley Gregory, J.P. (Jan. 16, 1851)
John Corsey to Mary Orton, Jan. 21, 1851.
  By B. A. John, M.G. (Jan. 21, 1851)
David Weir to Margaret Stuart, Jan. 23, 1851.
  By William Walker. (Jan. 3, 1851(?)
John Dixon to Mary McCallie, Jan. 23, 1851.
  By A. Swafford. (Jan. 23, 1851)
Cornelius Vandyke to Louisa Jane Yount, Jan. 23, 1851.
  By Stephen Sharits, M.G. (Jan. 23, 1851)
Joseph W. McMillan to Sarah S. Ingram, Jan. 23, 1851.
  By Henry Price, M.G. (Jan. 23, 1851)
William T. Willis to Martha Hail, Jan. 24, 1851.
  By William Walker. (Jan. 26, 1851)
Daniel Kibble to Martha Only, Jan. 29, 1851.
  By William Walker. (Jan. 29, 1851)
William J. Green to Lidia Millsaps, Jan. 31, 1851.
  (no returns)
John Lewis to Nancy Gore, Feb. 7, 1851.
  (no returns)
James Branon to Susan Taylor, Feb. 8, 1851.
  By Jas. Douglass, M.G. (Dec. 13, 1851(?)
George Jones to Delila Morgan, Feb. 12, 1851.
  By William Walker. (Feb. 14, 1851)
Hugh M. Bales to Dorthula Hoback, Feb. 12, 1851.
  By Stephen Sharits, M.G. (Feb. 13, 1851)
W. W. McElden to Jane D. McCarty, Feb. 17, 1851.
  By James Scarbrough, M.G. (Feb. 2, 1851)
Patton L. Gamble to Nancy Ann Hounshell, Feb. 18, 1851.
  By Wm. H. Ballew, J.P. (Feb. 18, 1851)
William E. Gregory to Cinthia Ann Lillard, Feb. 20, 1851.
  By Rev. D. Carpenta(?), M.G. (Feb. 23, 1851)
Israel Beck to Christiam P. McKenzie, Feb. 26, 1851.
  By William Walker. (Feb. 27, 1851)

McMINN COUNTY MARRIAGES

Isaac Smart to Elizabeth Graves, Feb. 26, 1851.
    By Wm. Walker, J.P. (Feb. 27, 1851)
McKamy Shell to Mary Howard, Mar. 4, 1851.
    By D. D. Billingsby, M.G. (Mar. 4, 1851)
Madison McGinty to Martha Brock, Mar. 15, 1851.
    By Wm. McKamy, J.P. (Mar. 6, 1851(?)
Leonard W. Hutton to Milmer Frances Walker, (no date
    given) (no returns)
William R. Venable to Sarah Cornelia Hoyt, Mar. 10, 1851.
    By Rev. John Lyons, M.G. (Mar. 12, 1851)
Henry Price Ward to Mary McNabb, Mar. 19, 1851.
    By Nathaniel Barnes, M.G. (Mar. 20, 1851)
Wm. Smith to Rebecca Morgan, Mar. 29, 1851.
    By William Walker. (Apr. 1, 1851)
Richard S. Hickon to Mary Jane Millhight, Apr. 2, 1851.
    (no returns)
Andrew I. Bonine to Catharine Wyatt, Apr. 8, 1851.
    (no returns)
Samuel Lane to Nancy E. Wear, Apr. 16, 1851.
    By Robert Gregory, M.G. (Apr. 16, 1851)
John H. Worley to Virginia F. Thornton, Apr. 17, 1851.
    By Thomas T. Russell, M.G. (Apr. 17, 1851)
John J. Gee to Mary Grubb, Apr. 17, 1851.
    By Robert Gregory, M.G. (Apr. 17, 1851)
George H. McKeehan to Malinda Cunningham, Apr. 22, 1851.
    By Wm. Burns, J.P. (Apr. 22, 1851)
Martin Luther to Lourena Long, May 3, 1851.
    (no returns)
Joshua B. Wilson to Nancy Miller, May 5, 1851.
    By M. A. Cass, M.G. (May 6, 1851)
John Kiser to Elvira Casteel, May 10, 1851.
    By William C. Lee, M.G. (May 11, 1851)
H. J. Hirst to A. Sivels, May 10, 1851.
    By Wm. Burns, J.P. (June 8, 1851)
William B. Tipton to Phebe Hunt, June 19, 1851.
    By S. Sharits, M.G. (June 19, 1851)
Samuel B. Harris to Martha J. Yearwood, July 7, 1851.
    (no returns)
James Johnson to Rebecca Ann Kitcher, July 10, 1851.
    By Dan Carpenter, M.G. (July 12, 1851)
William M. Jones to M. E. Miller, July 11, 1851.
    By M. A. Cass, M.G. (July 13, 1851)
Charley T. Wilkens to Mary A. Kirkpatrick, July 21, 1851.
    (no returns)
Thomas Wattenbarger to Sarah Ann McWhen, July 25, 1851.
    By Heil Buttram, M.G. (July 31, 1851)
James Monroe to C. M. Hughes, Aug. 1, 1851.
    By G. W. Wallis, J.P. (Aug. 3, 1851)
William F. Alison to M. J. Scarborough(?), Aug. 5, 1851.
    (no returns)
Isaac M. Wilson to Eliza C. Newman, Aug. 6, 1851.
    By Robert Gregory, M.G. (Aug. 7, 1851)
John L. Poe to Nancy Bible, Aug. 21, 1851.
    By James Bonner, J.P. (Aug. 22, 1851)

McMINN COUNTY MARRIAGES

James Swinford to Sofira Davis, Aug. 23, 1851.
(no returns)
Edward England to Elizabeth S. Owens, Sep. 1, 1851.
(no returns)
Alexander Anderson to Nancy Ann Harris, Sep. __, 1851.
(no returns)
Wm. H. Neely to Elizabeth McPherson, Sep. 4, 1851.
(no returns)
James Y. Fitchgerald to Sarah E. Neel, Sep. 8, 1851.
By Jas. Douglass. (Sep. 8, 1851)
Samuel Gilbreath to Nancy Cobbs, Sep. 10, 1851.
By L. L. Hoyl. (Mar. 19, 1852)
William G. Harden to Margaret Mins, Sep. 11, 1851.
(no returns)
Josiah Johnson to Eliza Pearman, Sep. 16, 1851.
By T. S. Rice, J.P. (Sep. 16, 1851)
Jasper Newton to Percilia Crabtree, Sep. 7, 1851.
(no returns)
Annias Wattenbarger to Ameline McKeehan, Sep. 24, 1851.
By H. B. Brandon, M.G. (Sep. 25, 1851)
M. P. Martin to Ellen M. McElhaney, Sep. 25, 1851.
By Wm. H. Ballew, J.P. (Sep. 25, 1851)
Jacob P. Newman to L. M. Fetzel, Sep. 26, 1851.
By Netherland Barnet, M.G. (Sep. 26, 1851)
Joseph Eli Hughes to Elizabeth McKeehan, Sep. 29, 1851.
By Hiram H. Brandow, M.G. (Oct. 2, 1851)
James C. McCarty to Elizabeth Hanks, Oct. 1, 1851.
By J. M. Miller, M.G. (Oct. 2, 1851)
James F. Crittenden to Samantha Ellis, (no date given).
By Nathaniel Barnett, M.G. (Oct. 2, 1851)
William Buttram to Elizabeth Ann Foster, Oct. 6, 1851.
By Hiel Buttram, M.G. (Oct. 9, 1851)
John B. Fick to Jane Seertman, Oct. 7, 1851.
By Pat Lee, J.P. (Oct. 7, 1851)
John E. Feckers to Ansta Cox, Oct. 7, 1851.
By J. W. Miller, J.P. (Oct. 9, 1851)
James M. Patty to Mary Jane McCafery, Oct. 9, 1851.
By T. T. Russell, M.G. (Oct. 9, 1851)
David Cantrell to Rebecca Crocket, Oct. 17, 1851.
By C. R. Hoyl, M.G. (Oct. 19, 1851)
P. B. Stublefield to Catherine Martin, Oct. 17, 1851.
By Uriel Johnston, J.P. (Oct. 19, 1851)
John M. Minsey to Mary McElhaney, Oct. 21, 1851.
By Wm. H. Ballew, J.P. (Oct. 21, 1851)
W. S. Bell to Elizabeth D. Keith, Oct. 23, 1851.
By James Park, Jr., M.V.D. Chas. M. Clung, E. G. Pearl,
Wm. F. Keith, Witnesses. (Oct. 23, 1851)
Delaney Griffitts to Margaret Griffith, Oct. 25, 1851.
By Saml Wilson, J.P., McMinn Co. (Oct. 26, 1851)
Wm. McDaniel to Jemima Liles, Oct. 6, 1851.
By William C. Lee, M.G. (Oct. 28, 1851)
William W. Rickey to Elizabeth Couldwell, Oct. 30, 1851.
By Robert Gregory, M.G. (Oct. 30, 1851)
E. M. Flinn to R. E. Moore, Nov. 1, 1851.
(no returns)

McMINN COUNTY MARRIAGES

Armstead F. Wilson to Nancy Ann Shoerelt, (no date given).
   By Wm. C. Daily, M.G. (Nov. 6, 1851)
Jas. M. Oliver to Coraline (or Caroline) Rector, Nov. 10,
   1851. By Daniel McPhail, J.P. (Nov. 10, 1851)
Abraham L. Luck (or Slack) to Caroline True, Nov. 26, 1851.
   (no returns)
Josiah F. Crockett to Jwanona Derrick, Nov. 27, 1851.
   By C. R. Hoyl, M.G. (Nov. 27, 1851)
William Cantrell to Margaret Cooke, Nov. 29, 1851.
   By G. W. Kirksey, J.P. (Nov. 30, 1851)
John F. Robbinett to Rhoda T. McNabb, Dec. 3, 1851.
   By A. John, M.G. (Dec. 3, 1851)
Robert N. McEwin to Sarah C. Balfour, Dec. 11, 1851.
   By J. W. Miller, M.G. (Dec. 11, 1851)
Jas. Smith to Eglinetine Logan, Dec. 17, 1851.
   By Geo. W. Kirksey, J.P.
D. L. Campbell to Judith McAdoo, Dec. 16, 1851.
   By A. Barb, J.P. (Dec. 18, 1851)
Simeon Reed to Elizabeth Guthery, Dec. 17, 1851.
   (no returns)
James Long to Mary Jane Martin, Dec. 19, 1851.
   By Wm. McKamy, J.P. (Dec. 21, 1851)
Hesekiah Smith to Lucinda Swaford, Dec. 29, 1851.
   By J. Jenkins, J.P.
Matthew Thompson to Serbrenny Vandary Welch, Jan. 3, 1852.
   By Wm. McKamy, J.P. (Jan. 4, 1852)
Oliver Lewis to Sarah Emeline Rodden, Jan. 5, 1852.
   (no returns)
L. E. Cantrell to Sarah Firestone, Jan. 12, 1852.
   (no returns)
Berryman Wellem to Aroyan Allison, Jan. 16, 1852.
   By Wm. F. Forrest, M.G. (Jan. 21, 1852)
L. R. Vaughn to Caroline Emerson, Jan. 24, 1852.
   By Wm. G. Lee, M.G. (Jan. 28, 1852)
Geo. W. Handly to Mary Ann Stubblefield, Jan. 26, 1852.
   By James Douglass, M.G. (Jan. 27, 1852)
John Harris to Mary Howard, Jan. 21, 1852.
   By G. W. Kirksey.
Finley M. Malone to Martha Jane Ward, Feb. 4, 1852.
   By Nathaniel Barnett, M.G. (Feb. 5, 1852)
Lee Roy Kelly to Letty Elliott, Feb. 9, 1852.
   By J. Jack, M.G. (Feb. 9, 1852)
George W. Bogart to Nancy L. Barnett, Feb. 12, 1852.
   By Jona Lyons, M.G. (Feb. 12, 1852)
Jefferson Glaze to Mariah Dugan, Feb. 14, 1852.
   By Wm. C. Lee, M.G. (Feb. 17, 1852)
V. H. Jack to S. M. Dogherty, Feb. 14, 1852.
   By Benjamin Cass, J.P., McMinn Co. (Feb. 23, 1852)
George W. Wilson to Mary Glace, Feb. 16, 1852.
   (no returns)
Micajah Ford to Elizabeth C. Myers, Feb. 21, 1852.
   By William R. Walker, J.P. (Feb. 22, 1852)
David E. Gillespie to Sarah E. Cleage, Feb. 26, 1852.
   (no returns)

Joseph C. Reynolds to Rebecca Reynolds, Feb. 24, 1851.
  By Wm. McKamy, J.P. (Feb. 29, 1852)
Thomas Cauldwell to Lusey Long, Feb. 25, 1852.
  By Robert Gregory, M.G. (Feb. 26, 1852)
D. D. Stephenson to Mary Ann Anderson, Mar. 1, 1852.
  By W. C. Daily, M.G. (Mar. 2, 1852)
J. B. Cobb to L. C. Thompson, Mar. 1, 1852.
  By T. L. Hoyl. (Mar. 2, 1852)
Charles Hayden to Mary Ann Sivils, Mar. 5, 1852.
  (no returns)
John W. Brown to Sarah Jane Matlock, Mar. 11, 1852.
  (no returns)
J. B. Jenkins to Elvey Paris, Mar. 18, 1852.
  By T. L. Hoyl. (Mar. 19, 1852)
E. W. Williams to Elizabeth Ann Ellis, Mar. 20, 1852.
  By Robert Gregory, M.G. (Mar. 21, 1852)
Thomas M. McDonald to Lucindy March, Mar. 20, 1852.
  (no returns)
James Blackburn to Mary Carter, Mar. 25, 1852.
  (no returns)
John Hughs to Francis D. Isbell, Mar. 30, 1852.
  By D. Rose, R. M. Gospel. (Mar. 31, 1852)
Tubeller Zeigler to Francis J. Mansel, Mar. 31, 1852.
  By Nathaniel Barnett, M.G. (Mar. 31, 1852)
George Templeton to Eve Masongale, Apr. 5, 1852.
  By James Douglass, M.G. (Apr. 5, 1852)
Elisha Williams to Amanda L. Ellis, Apr. 5, 1852.
  By Robert Gregory, M.G. (Apr. 8, 1852)
Charles R. Basket to Susan Spearman, Apr. 8, 1852.
  By Wm. McKamy, J.P. (Apr. 8, 1852)
Pleasant Riddle to Kejiah Erwin, Apr. 8, 1852.
  By Daniel McPahil, J.P., McMinn Co. (Apr. 11, 1852)
Thomas W. Davis to Lorene Dethro, Apr. 10, 1852.
  By J. Jenkins, J.P.
Archibald West to Julia Swaffer, Apr. 13, 1852.
  By J. Jenkins, J.P.
James Brown to Susan Douglass, Apr. 19, 1852.
  By J. Jenkins, J.P.
Andrew J. Bonine to Eliza Kelly, Apr. 19, 1852.
  By J. Jack, M.G. (Apr. 21, 1852)
Perry G. Brock to Mary A. E. Lafferty, Apr. 21, 1852.
  (Apr. 22, 1852)
John Rudd to Jane Stansberry, Apr. 28, 1852.
  By A. Swaffer, J.P. (Apr. 29, 1852)
Peter Edwinten to Margaret Chavis, Apr. 29, 1852.
  By Jonathan Lewis, M.G. (Apr. 29, 1852)
William Duckworth to Nancy Versha, May 22, 1852.
  By Dan Carpenter, M.G. (May 23, 1852)
Hugh Roberts to Jane Green, May 24, 1852.
  By Daniel McPahil, J.P., McMinn Co. (May 26, 1852)
Philmer W. Green to Susan R. Cox, May 24, 1852.
  By Wm. W. Haymes, M.G. (May 25, 1852)
James M. Stephenson to Martha J. Wilson, Apr. 28, 1852.
  By Wm. R. Walker. (Apr. 29, 1852)

McMINN COUNTY MARRIAGES

James W. Davis to Sarah Spearman, Apr. 17, 1852.
(no returns)
J. T. Rowland to Louisa J. Keith, May 27, 1852.
By John Scruggs, M.G. (May 27, 1852)
John W. Clark to Amanda Rains, June 3, 1852.
(June 4, 1852)
S. Fenley Scheck to Huldah H. Hadin, June 19, 1852.
By T. L. Hoyl, M.G. (June 29, 1852)
Joseph H. Smith to Elizabeth C. Dixon, June 24, 1852.
By Samuel Wilson, J.P., McMinn Co. (June 24, 1852)
Mareda Paul to Orpha Wasson, July 2, 1852.
By Wm. R. Edler, M.G. (July 4, 1852)
F. E. Hacker to Virginia Fisher, July 6, 1852.
By Wm. C. Daily, M.G. (July 7, 1852)
John Gallant to Sarah Wilson, July 8, 1852.
By David W. Beaver, M.G. (July 8, 1852)
Roland Hudson to Mary J. Pearson, July 27, 1852.
By David W. Beaver, M.G. (July 27, 1852)
Allen Eakins to Susan Cash, July 21, 1852.
By David W. Beaver, M.G. (July 22, 1852)
O. P. Hall to Amanda J. Riggs, Aug. 11, 1852.
By John Hoyl, M.G. (Aug. 11, 1852)
Franklin A. Dixon to Elizabeth Studdard, Aug. 12, 1852.
By A. Swafford, J.P. (Aug. 12, 1852)
J. W. Davis to Sarah Spearman, Apr. 17, 1852.
By Wm. McKamy, J.P. (Apr. 20, 1852)
Thos. H. Gass to Rebeckah Croplin, Aug. 14, 1852.
By Wm. H. Ballew, J.P. (Aug. 14, 1852)
James D. Perkins to Eliza Hughs, Aug. 15, 1852.
By John Henkins, J.P.
Isaac Chrisman to Sarah Foster, Aug. 16, 1852.
By Wm. R. Elder, M.G. (Aug. 17, 1852)
Isaiah Garrison to Nancy Arnwine, Aug. 16, 1852.
By J. R. Fryar, M.G. (Aug. 17, 1852)
Felix Orrick to Dorcas Ann Decker, Aug. 19, 1852.
By G. W. Wallis, J.P. (Aug. 19, 1852)
George W. Moore to Rebeckah Jane Shields, Aug. 30, 1852.
By Heil Buttram, M.G. (Aug. 31, 1852)
Jacob Fisher to Frances E. Lowry, Sep. 1, 1852.
By W. C. Daily, M.G. (Sep. 1, 1852)
Robert McCramy to Elizabeth Grisham, Sep. 2, 1852.
By Wm. Burns, J.P. (Sep. 2, 1852)
Asberry Manis to Matilda J. Manis, Sep. 6, 1852.
By G. W. Wallis, J.P. (Sep. 9, 1852)
William Long to Nancy E. Liner, Sep. 6, 1852.
By O. M. Liner, J.P. (Sep. 12, 1852)
William B. Templeton to Elizabeth Ramy, Sep. 9, 1852.
By Stephen Sharits, M.G. (Sep. 9, 1852)
Edward Branum to Margaret Shook, Sep. 12, 1852.
(no returns)
Jacob Wasson to Sarah Jane Berry, Sep. 13, 1852.
By H. Small, J.P. (Sep. 16, 1852)
Thomas C. Scott to Emaline Burns, Sep. 23, 1852.
By J. W. Cox, J.P. (Sep. 24, 1852)

McMINN COUNTY MARRIAGES

Samuel Dennis to Mary Blankenship, Sep. 28, 1852.
  By A. Barb, J.P. (Sep. 28, 1852)
Miles Goforth to Mahala Vernom, Sep. 29, 1852.
  By Nathaniel Barnett, M.G.
Elbert S. McKeehan to Sarah M. Camron, Sep. 29, 1852.
  By H. Brandon, Local Deacon Decatur Circuit. (Sep. 30,
  1852)
Robert E. Chambers to Susan J. Meghee, Sep. 30, 1852.
  By Wm. Burns, J.P. (Sep. 30, 1852)
Silas W. Walker to Eliza Morgan, Oct. 4, 1852.
  By Wm. R. Walker, J.P. (Oct. 7, 1852)
William M. James to Martha J. Duckworth, Oct. 6, 1852.
  By Uriel Johnston, J.P. (Oct. 6, 1852)
William M. McKeown to Clarissa Wilson, Oct. 6, 1852.
  By Rev. D. Carpenter. (Oct. 6, 1852)
J. W. Prophet to Robert S. Newman, Oct. 7, 1852.
  By J. W. Cox, J.P. (Oct. 7, 1852)
John Willis to Elizabeth Hale, Oct. 9, 1852.
  By James Bonner, J.P. (Oct. 10, 1852)
Elbert McGinty to Emaline Baker, Oct. 18, 1852.
  By Samuel Wilson, J.P., McMinn Co. (Oct. 18, 1852)
James M. Jones to Sidney Jane Fry, Oct. 26, 1852.
  By Rev. H. Brandon, local Deacon. (Oct. 26, 1852)
William Hughes to Mahala Rhom, Oct. 30, 1852.
  By Wm. Burns, J.P. (Oct. 30, 1852)
Charles L. Matlock to Nancy L. Howard, Nov. 9, 1852.
  By W. C. Dailey, M.G. (Nov. 9, 1852)
William Bonine to Lucinda Raburn, Nov. 11, 1852.
  By Stephen Sharits, M.G. (Nov. 11, 1852)
Edom Dixon to Melissa E. Slaughter, Nov. 12, 1852.
  By Demmon Dorsey, Esq. (Nov. 14, 1852)
Andrew J. Kiker to Louisa J. Kennedy, Nov. 16, 1852.
  By Heil Buttram, M.G. (Nov. 16, 1852)
George W. Lewis to Adeline Maning, Mar. 18, 1852.
  By J. Jack, M.G. (Mar. 18, 1852)
William E. Gibbs to Melissa McCance, Nov. 23, 1852.
  By Benj. E. Cass, J.P., McMinn Co. (Nov. 25, 1852)
David Brock to Ann Stout, Nov. 27, 1852.
  By A. Swaffer, J.P. (Nov. 28, 1852)
Milton P. Jarnigan to Emily L. Murrell, Dec. 1, 1852.
  By George A. Caldwell, M.G. (Dec. 1, 1852)
Thomas Bishop to Nancy Wright, Dec. 1, 1852.
  By O. M. Liner, J.P. (Dec. 2, 1852)
G. W. Brown to Mary Ann Thompson, Dec. 9, 1852.
  By W. C. Daily, M.M.E.C.S.H.C. (Dec. 9, 1852)
William G. Nice to Elizabeth R. Balfour, Dec. 9, 1852.
  By Geo. A. Caldwell, M.G. (Dec. 9, 1852)
Berry M. Johnson to Phebe L. Tripnell, Dec. 16, 1852.
  By Reuben Faulkner, J.P. (Dec. 17, 1852)
Albert D. Long to Martha R. Davis, Dec. 22, 1852.
  By H. M. Dodson, M.G. (Dec. 23, 1852)
James M. Southard to Rachel A. Doan, Dec. 23, 1852.
  By M. Southard, M.G. (Dec. 23, 1852)
Isaac Lewis to Miram Buckner, Dec. 25, 1852.
  (no returns)

J. H. Walker to Lucy F. Franklin, Dec. 29, 1852.
By Wm. C. Dailey, M.G.M.E.C.S.H.C. (Dec. 29, 1852)
Wm. M. Heiskell to Virginia W. Netherland, Dec. 29, 1852.
By John Scruggs, M.G. (Dec. 30, 1852)
Richard Cannon to Delila Gilbert, Dec. 30, 1852.
By Wm. McKamy, J.P. (Dec. 30, 1852)
William H. Bridges to Rebeckah O. St. John, Dec. 30, 1852.
By J. Cunningham, M.G. (Dec. 30, 1852)
Alfred R. Byington to Mary J. Grisham, Jan. 4, 1853.
By Wm. R. Walker, J.P. (Jan. 6, 1853)
Francis M. Barb to Sarah Bedford, Jan. 6, 1853.
By S. Sharits, M.G. (Jan. 6, 1853)
Thomas J. Sherman to Sarah E. Cate, Jan. 8, 1853.
By J. H. Reagan, J.P. (Jan. 11, 1853)
Israel C. Smith to Elizabeth A. Pesterfield, Jan. 11, 1853.
By J. Cunningham, M.G. (Jan. 11, 1853)
William Harrel to Rinda Ford, Jan. 11, 1853.
By Samuel Wilson, J.P., McMinn Co. (Jan. 12, 1853)
William B. Clark to Abigail Humphrey, Jan. 12, 1853.
By O. M. Liney, J.P. (Jan. 13, 1853)
Joseph J. Hawkins to Elizabeth J. Parks, Jan. 13, 1853.
By A. Barb, J.P. (Jan. 13, 1853)
John G. Hale to Nancy Owens, Jan. 13, 1853.
(no returns)
William S. Ragan to Sarah J. Helums, Jan. 21, 1853.
By O. M. Liner, J.P. (Jan. 23, 1853)
Nelson Small to Mary Owen, Jan. 24, 1853.
By David W. Beaver, M.G. (Jan. 25, 1853)
George Large to Nancy Faulkner, Jan. 25, 1853.
By Daniel McPhail, J.P. (Jan. 26, 1853)
James Marler to Elizabeth Moon, Jan. 26, 1853.
By Nathaniel Barnett, M.G. (Jan. 27, 1853)
Abel Hix (or Hicks) to Mary Sliger, Jan. 27, 1853.
By Heil Buttram, M.G. (Jan. 27, 1853)
Joseph M. Cecill to Sarah Brazeal, Feb. 10, 1853.
By D. Carpenter, M.G. (Feb. 10, 1853)
J. F. Brummet to Letty Barnes, Feb. 15, 1853.
By O. M. Liner, J.P. (Feb. 20, 1853)
George W. McGehee to Nancy Jane Large, Feb. 16, 1853.
By Heil Buttram, M.G. (Feb. 17, 1853)
John Clementson to Mary Steed, Feb. 17, 1853.
By Wm. C. Daily, M.G. (Feb. 17, 1853)
Charles McKenzie to Stocia Murney, Feb. 21, 1853.
By J. Jenkins, J.P.
C. L. Owen to Mary A. Patton, Feb. 23, 1853.
By Thos. Brown, O.D.M. (Feb. 24, 1853)
Duke Ward to Susannah Moon, Feb. 23, 1853.
By A. John, M.G. (Feb. 24, 1853)
Solomon Gilbert to Polly Cannon, Mar. 9, 1853.
By J. Jenkins, J.P.
Francis Gallant to W. R. Ferryman, Mar. 17, 1853.
By D. W. Beaver, M.G. (Mar. 17, 1853)
James McKeehan to Mary A. Cunningham, Mar. 22, 1853.
By James W. Shelton, M.G. (Mar. 22, 1853)

John C. Carrigin to Minerva J. Harris, Mar. 23, 1853.
By Joseph Cobb, J.P. (Mar. 24, 1853)
Alfred Coppet to Mary Ann Shaw, Apr. 19, 1853.
By Wm. Walker, J.P. (Apr. 18, 1853)
D. P. McCroskey to Sarah Ann Detherow, Apr. 20, 1853.
By J. Jenkins, J.P.
Calvin Shoemaker to Lucinda N. Brewer, Apr. 21, 1853.
(no returns)
Abery Ward to Nancy Moore, Apr. 26, 1853.
By A. John, M.G. (Apr. 28, 1853)
George Marler to Sarah Moore, Apr. 26, 1853.
By A. John, M.G. (Apr. 28, 1853)
T. L. Farrell to Janette Borden, May 4, 1853.
By S. Sharrits, M.G. (May 4, 1853)
Wm. Bryan to Mary L. Cate, May 7, 1853.
By W. C. Daily, M. of M.E.C.S. (May 8, 1853)
Hiram J. Brown to Elizabeth J. Casteel, May 17, 1853.
By Wm. C. Daily, M.G. (May 19, 1853)
Wm. E. Roberts to Elizabeth J. Carter, May 18, 1853.
(no returns)
Richard Manry to Mary Jane Rice, May 28, 1853.
By J. Jack, M.G. (May 29, 1853)
David Watson to Delila Atkinson, May 29, 1853.
By J. W. Cox, J.P. (May 29, 1853)
Jefferson Hooser to Mary Brown, June 1, 1853.
By P. M. Lee, J.P., McMinn Co. (June 3, 1853)
Thomas Philips to Elizabeth Standefer, June 10, 1853.
By M. D. Anderson, J.P. (June 11, 1853)
Nathan Lowe to Gazilda Pearson, June 30, 1853.
By Reuben Faulkner, J.P. (June 30, 1853)
Alexander Everton to Caroline Jack, July 4, 1853.
By B. E. Cass, J.P., McMinn Co. (July 7, 1853)
Jonathan Gee to Margaret Grubb, July 25, 1853.
By W. C. Daily, M.G.M.E.C.S. (July 28, 1853)
Isaac Long to Diabah Wells, July 25, 1853.
By Robert Gregory, M.G.B.C. (July 25, 1853)
P. B. Nunn to Tabitha Breedin, July 26, 1853.
By Wm. Burris, J.P. (July 26, 1853)
William Anderson to Susan A. D. Hughes, July 28, 1853.
By Wm. A. Ballew, J.P. (July 25, 1853)
Benjamin Watson to Lydia Tallant, Aug. 1, 1853.
By G. W. Kirksey, J.P. (Aug. 1, 1853)
Joram R. Zeigler to Catharine Yount, Aug. 2, 1853.
By C. P. Vandyke. (Aug. 4, 1853)
Christopher Graves to Elizabeth Shelton, Aug. 5, 1853.
By William Walker, J.P. (Aug. 15, 1853)
John E. Shelton to Lucinda Perrin, Aug. 8, 1853.
By William Walker. (Aug. 12, 1853)
Henry M. Simpson to Hiley Carter, Aug. 10, 1853.
By J. H. Reagan, J.P. (Aug. 11, 1853)
Stephen J. Melton to Adaline Walker, Aug. 11, 1853.
(no returns)
Jesse M. Cobb to Mary V. Cooper, Aug. 23, 1853.
By C. R. Hoyl, M.G. (Sep. 8, 1853)

McMINN COUNTY MARRIAGES

Calvin Looper to Nancy Shoemaker, Aug. 24, 1853.
By Reuben Faulkner, J.P. (Aug. 25, 1853)
J. S. Buckner to Matilda Beaver, Aug. 31, 1853.
By A. John, M.G. (Aug. 31, 1853)
S. P. Henderson to S. B. Stephenson, Sep. 1, 1853.
By John Scruggs, M.G. (Sep. 1, 1853)
Simpson Marler to Olivia Hamreck, Sep. 3, 1853.
By Wm. R. Elder, M.G. (Sep. 4, 1853)
Andrew J. McCuiston to Sarah Jane Turk, Sep. 8, 1853.
By S. S. Sharrits, M. G.(Sep. 8, 1853)
James A. McBroom to Sarah M. (or N.) Patty, Sep. 8, 1853.
(no returns)
Robert A. Stephenson to Matilda C. Smith, Sep. 8, 1853.
By William W. Haymes, M.G. (Sep. 8, 1853)
H. C. P. Horton to Nancy M. Bryan, Sep. 8, 1853.
By M. A. Cass, M.G. (Sep. 8, 1853)
Douthet Hix to Marinda Whitten, Sep. 10, 1853.
By Morgan Miller, J.P. (May 7, 1854)
Wm. A. Dugan to Elmira Cooper, Sep. 14, 1853.
By H. C. Cook, M.G. (Sep. 15, 1853)
Wm. M. Morgan to Mary Ann Shumake, Sep. 16, 1853.
By J. Whiteside, M.G. (Sep. 17, 1853)
Andrew J. Clark to Sarah J. Swafford, Sep. 27, 1853.
(no returns)
John E. Wallis to Katharine J. Maxwell, Sep. 27, 1853.
By J. Cunningham, M.G. (Sep. 28, 1853)
B. H. Moss to E. G. Martin, Oct. 1, 1853.
By J. Jack, M.G. (Oct. 2, 1853)
William D. Waide to Louisa Wattenbarger, Oct. 4, 1853.
By Dan Carpenter, M.G. (Oct. 6, 1853)
John W. Cassada to Rebecca Davis, Oct. 4, 1853.
By Daniel McPhail, J.P., McMinn Co. (Oct. 6, 1853)
John Weir to Martha Bonner, Oct. 4, 1853.
(no returns)
Matthew L. McCaslin to Ellen H. Deaton, Oct. 6, 1853.
By James S. Russell, M.G. (Oct. 6, 1853)
John Vanzant to Nancy Hill, Oct. 10, 1853.
By William R. Walker, J.P. (Oct. 12, 1853)
A. J. Brock to Emeline Jack, Oct. 10, 1853.
By B. C. Cass, J.P. (Oct. 15, 1853)
Calvin Browder to Mary Ann Nance, Oct. 12, 1853.
By M. A. Cass, M.G. (Oct. 13, 1853)
Campbell Davis to Elizabeth Vaughan, Oct. 17, 1853.
By David W. Beavers, M.G. (Oct. 20, 1853)
James R. Owen to Catharine Hunt, Oct. 20, 1853.
By Dan Carpenter, M.G. (Oct. 20, 1853)
John B. Hix to Mariah Poe, Oct. 24, 1853.
By T. T. Russell, M.G. (Oct. 24, 1853)
Robert Coffey to Louisa Kinchelo, Oct. 27, 1853.
By James C. Bryan, J.P. (Oct. 28, 1853)
Isaac Janeway to Narcissa Moore, Nov. 1, 1853.
By A. John, M.G. (Nov. 3, 1853)
John L. Bridges to Eliza J. Gettys, Nov. 2, 1853.
By George A. Caldwell, M.G. (Nov. 2, 1853)

Peter Snider to Sarah E. Ensminger, Nov. 3, 1853.
By E. L. Miller, J.P. (Nov. 3, 1853)
James Massingale to Jane Watson, Nov. 5, 1853.
By J. M. Cass, J.P. (Nov. 6, 1853)
J. W. Howard to Mary Sowell, Nov. 9, 1853.
By Heil Buttram, M.G. (Nov. 10, 1853)
James McNabb to Levista Mynatt, Nov. 15, 1853.
By James C. Bryan, J.P. (Nov. 15, 1853)
George Stephens to Mary Cate, Nov. 16, 1853.
By William C. Lee, M.G. (Nov. 17, 1853)
Mordecai H. Morgan to Susan H. Elder, Nov. 16, 1853.
By J. Whiteside, M.G. (Nov. 17, 1853)
Michael D. Burger to Lotty Ann Clark, Nov. 19, 1853.
By J. Jack, M.G. (Nov. 19, 1853)
G. W. Loughmiller to Nancy A. C. Hester, Nov. 24, 1853.
By J. W. Cox, J.P. (Nov. 24, 1853)
J. T. Culpepper to Nancy J. Evans, Nov. 26, 1853.
By H. C. Cooke, M.G. (Nov. 27, 1853)
Elisha S. Gibson to Mary Ann Etter, Nov. 30, 1853.
By Moses A. Cass, M.G. (Dec. 1, 1853)
G. W. Melton to Eliza J. P. Rogers, Dec. 2, 1853.
By A. Swafford, J.P. (Dec. 14, 1853)
A. J. Chrisman to Elizabeth Foster, Dec. 10, 1853.
By E. L. Miller, J.P. (Dec. 10, 1853)
William Hughs to Amy A. McKehen, Dec. 20, 1853.
By Heil Buttram, M.G. (Dec. 22, 1853)
John G. Gibson to Sarah J. Anderson, Dec. 21, 1853.
By Robert Gregory, M.G. (Dec. 22, 1853)
Nathaniel Lawson to Mary L. Lillard, Dec. 23, 1853.
By Rev. D. Carpenter. (Dec. 25, 1853)
John W. Davis to Mary E. St. John, Dec. 15, 1853.
By George A. Caldwell, M.G. (Dec. 15, 1853)
William H. ODaniel to Mary Ann Burns, Dec. 28, 1853.
By S. W. Cox, J.P. (Dec. 28, 1853)
Larkin B. Rutherford to Julian W. Netherly, Jan. 2, 1854.
(no returns)
William Moore to Katharine Armstrong, Jan. 5, 1854.
By Robt. Gregory, M.G. (Jan. 5, 1854)
Moses Harrel to Martha J. Ford, Jan. 5, 1854.
(no returns)
James E. Wilson to Nancy Gallant, Jan. 5, 1854.
By D. W. Beaver, M.G. (Jan. 6, 1854)
L. B. Dodson to Mary Ann Anderson, Jan. 9, 1854.
(no returns)
James R. Lowry to Elizabeth M. McClatchey, Jan. 10, 1854.
By W. C. Daily, M.G. (Jan. 11, 1854)
Isaac Butter (or Bitter or Butler) to Martha Price, Jan. 11,
1854. By A. Barb, J.P. (Jan. 12, 1854)
John McGinty to Polly Whitten, Jan. 11, 1854.
By J. W. Cox, J.P. (Jan. 13, 1854)
Wright Melton to Nancy Crittenden, Jan. 24, 1854.
By James C. Bryan. (Jan. 24, 1854)
Wellford Dodson to Lusena J. Porter, Jan. 24, 1854.
By L. A. Spoffard, M.G. Presbyterian. (Jan. 24, 1854)

John Murphy to Mary Hahan, Jan. 25, 1854.
By A. Fitzgerald, M.G.
William Y. Davis to Elizabeth A. McCammon, Jan. 27 (or 28),
1854. (no returns)
Alfred T. Marler to Mary S. Coats, Jan. 31, 1854.
By A. John, M.G. (Feb. 2, 1854)
Joseph Reed to Margaret P. Dodson, Feb. 1, 1854.
(no returns)
H. J. Loughmiller to Jane Bolen, Feb. 4, 1854.
By G. W. Kirksey, J.P. (Feb. 9, 1854)
Harris Evans to Martha J. Gibbs, Feb. 4, 1854.
(no returns)
William Womack to Aelsay Mynatt, Feb. 6, 1854.
By A. John, M.G. (Feb. 7, 1854)
Jacob P. Jameson to Mary J. McCammon, Feb. 7, 1854.
By John Tate, M.G. (Feb. 7, 1854)
John G. Buttram to Sarah J. Foster, Feb. 14, 1854.
By Heil Buttram, M.G. (Feb. 15, 1854)
W. W. Peck to Dealtha R. Wilson, Feb. 21, 1854.
By W. Wetcher, M.G. (Feb. 21, 1854)
Jesse W. Smith to Dorothy Clark, Feb. 22, 1854.
(no returns)
Thomas N. McElhamy to Sarah J. Frank, Feb. 22, 1854.
By Hugh P. Wilson, J.P. (Feb. 22, 1854)
John E. Gore to Rachel A. C. Heck, Feb. 25, 1854.
By J. Jack, M.G. (Mar. 7, 1854)
Frances M. Cooper to Sarah Ann Manis, Feb. 27, 1854.
By G. W. Wallace, J.P. (Feb. 28, 1854)
James Shell to Laura Ann Turk, Mar. 4, 1854.
By S. Sharrits. (Mar. 5, 1854)
John W. D. Everett to Eliza Jane Brock, Mar. 6, 1854.
By Samuel W. Woods, M.G. (Mar. 7, 1854)
Alfred Loughmiller to Eveline Wetherly, Mar. 6, 1854.
(no returns)
Archibald R. Moon to Martha Cowden, Mar. 8, 1854.
By William H. Ballew, J.P. (Mar. 8, 1854)
E. S. Smith to Martha J. Morris, Mar. 12, 1854.
By Samuel Snoddy, J.P. (Mar. 12, 1854)
Robert M. Snider to Marha(?) Guthey, Mar. 16, 1854.
By E. L. Miller, J.P. (Mar. 16, 1854)
David Lawson to Jane Williams, Mar. 21, 1854.
By Rev. D. Carpenter. (Mar. 21, 1854)
James W. Buckner to Eliza Porter, Mar. 25, 1854.
By A. John, M.G. (Mar. 29, 1854)
Samuel Mezell to Lamera A. Barker, Mar. 26, 1854.
(no returns)
R. M. Hamrick to Martha Gregory, Apr. 6, 1854.
By E. M. Roberts, J.P. (Apr. 8, 1854)
Slark(?) D. P. Grills to Penelope Armstrong, Apr. 6, 1854.
By M. L. Phillips, J.P. (Apr. 6, 1854)
Alexander B. Harwell to Catharine L. Greene, Apr. 7, 1854.
(no returns)
Abraham Walker to Martha Jones, Apr. 12, 1854.
By J. A. Wilson, Esq. (May 24, 1854)

Houston Lemmons to Mary Blackwell, Aug. 13, 1854.
By Jas. Douglass, M.G. (Aug. 14, 1854)
William Rose to Mary Ann Wilson, Apr. 13, 1854.
By J. C. Carlock, J.P. (Apr. 20, 1854)
T. A. Cass to Susan A. Blackburn, Apr. 18, 1854.
By W. Whitcher, M.G. (Apr. 18, 1854)
Christopher Wattenbarger to Jane Buttram, May 3, 1854.
(no returns)
Samuel A. Berry to Sarah Ann Morrow, May 11, 1854.
By M. R. Ware, J.P. (May 11, 1854)
Frastus L. Derrick to Louisa Stansberry, May 17, 1854.
By J. J. Elliott, J.P. (May 28, 1854)
Samuel B. Hughes to Eliza A. Collins, May 17, 1854.
By James Baker, J.P. (May 18, 1854)
John W. Sims to Mary E. Moon, May 23, 1854.
By T. J. Russell, M.G. (May 23, 1854)
Charles L. Reynolds to Frances E. Regan, May 30, 1854.
By O. M. Liner, J.P. (June 1, 1854)
Elias Lawson to Martha J. Williams, June 13, 1854.
By D. Carpenter, M.G. (June 18, 1854)
Henry Rice to Mary E. Hawks, June 15, 1854.
By Robt. Gregory, M.G. (June 15, 1854)
I. B. Kimbrough to M. A. E. Thompson, July 1, 1854.
By H. C. Cooke, M.G. (July 4, 1854)
Duke W. Kimbrough to Julia Ann Parkinson, July 1, 1854.
By H. C. Cooke, M.G. (July 6, 1854)
Russell Dean to Louisa Minerva Gamble, July 7, 1854.
By M. Southard, M.G. (July 7, 1854)
John Gordon to Jane Shamblin, July 15, 1854.
By Joel Culpepper, J.P. (July 16, 1854)
Samuel D. Creasman to Mary E. Dugger, July 25, 1854.
By J. A. Wilson, J.P. (July 27, 1854)
Gamaliel Bryant to Rebecca Dobkins, Aug. 1, 1854.
By Reuben Deavers, M.G. (Aug. 1, 1854)
William Shelton to _____ Becker, Aug. 2, 1854.
By Robt. Gregory, M.G. (Aug. 3, 1854)
Ezekiel Sherrell to Mrs. Morgans Burk, Aug. 2, 1854.
By Robert Gregory, M.G. (Aug. 2, 1854)
Houston Lemmons to Mary Blackwell, Aug. 13, 1854.
By Jas. Douglass, M.G. (Aug. 14, 1854)
John W. Paris to Margaret Wheeler, Aug. 15, 1854.
By J. C. Carlock, J.P. (Aug. 17, 1854)
Leroy Tucker to Caroline Newton, Aug. 16, 1854.
By Jas. Parkinson, J.P. (Aug. 17, 1854)
T. F. Gibson to E. F. Mayfield, Aug. 17, 1854.
(no returns)
George W. Weaver to Julia Ann W. Walker, Aug. 25, 1854.
By Jas. Parkinson, J.P. (Aug. 28, 1854)
John L. Epperson to Melinda J. Borlison, Aug. 29, 1854.
By Jas. Parkison, J.P. (Aug. 29, 1854)
Wm. L. Lawson to M. C. Snider, Sep. 4, 1854.
By E. L. Miller, J.P. (Sep. 7, 1854)
Peter Thurman to Eliza Shipley, Sep. 6, 1854.
(no returns)

McMINN COUNTY MARRIAGES

Geo. Snoddy to Sarah A. Armstrong, Sep. 18, 1854.
  By P. W. Cox, J.P. (Sep. 18, 1854)
G. W. Haynie to Sarah J. Newman, Sep. 20, 1854.
  By Robert Gregory, M.G. (Sep. 24, 1854)
Mark Dennis to Rachel Matthews, Sep. 23, 1854.
  By J. A. Zeigler, J.P. (Sep. 24, 1854)
H. H. Bower to Ann Honery, Sep. 25, 1854.
  By David W. Beaver, M.G. (Sep. 25, 1854)
James Cretendon to Nancy I. Colvell, Sep. 27, 1854.
  By Robert Gregory, M.G. (Sep. 28, 1854)
Wm. H. Rudd to C. M. Zeigler, Sep. 27, 1854.
  By M. A. Cass, M.G. (Sep. 27, 1854)
J. N. Smith to Nancy Snoddy, Sep. 29, 1854.
  By J. B. Cobb, J.P. (Sep. 29, 1854)
David F. Roberts to Elizabeth Madden, Oct. 4, 1854.
  By H. M. Roberts, J.P. (Oct. 5, 1854)
Jas. M. Rucker to _____ Wassom, Oct. 4, 1854.
  By A. John, M.G. (Oct. 4, 1854)
John C. Newman to Sydney Ann Myers, Oct. 5, 1854.
  (no returns)
Nathaniel Jones to Jane McSpadden, Oct. 9, 1854.
  By George A. Caldwell, M.G. (Oct. 9, 1854)
James Hannah to Eliza A. Gilly, Oct. 13, 1854.
  By Morgan Miller, J.P. (Oct. 14, 1854)
Silas Jones to Elizabeth Hunt, Oct. 18, 1854.
  (no returns)
Marshall C. Owen to Caroline Thomas, Oct. 19, 1854.
  By T. B. Waller, M.G. (Oct. 19, 1854)
T. L. Benton to Mary Shipley, Oct. 20, 1854.
  (no returns)
Geo. Decker to Jane McMillan, Nov. 12, 1854.
  By A. D. Bryant, J.P. (Nov. 12, 1854)
H. H. Burk to Sarah C. Rucker, Nov. 18, 1854.
  By Joseph A. Zeigler, J.P. (Nov. 18, 1854)
Robert Y. Vaughan to Martha A. Triplett, Nov. 15, 1854.
  By George A. Caldwell, M.G. (Nov. 15, 1854)
John T. McCarty to M. A. H. Ball, Nov. 20, 1854.
  By W. C. Reynolds, M.G. (Nov. 21, 1854)
Joseph Couing to E. S. West, Nov. 20, 1854.
  By D. Carpenter, M.G. (Nov. 24, 1854)
Wm. H. Stubblefield to Elizabeth Studdart, Nov. 25, 1854.
  By J. W. Cox, J.P. (Nov. 26, 1854)
David Hunt to Darcus McKenzie, Dec. 2, 1854.
  (no returns)
E. W. Roberts to Mary Wommack, Dec. 4, 1854.
  By W. H. H. Duggan, M.G. (Dec. 5, 1854)
John McMillan to Pharibe Wasson, Dec. 6, 1854.
  By J. S. Garrison, J.P. (Dec. 6, 1854)
George W. Martin to Mary Ann Brummut, Dec. 7, 1854.
  (no returns)
John H. Murray to Rebecca Grigsby, Dec. 8, 1854.
  By Hugh P. Holland, M.G. (Dec. 8, 1855(?))
Hamilton Neill to Nancy Ann Burnet, Dec. 11, 1854.
  By Wm. R. Elder, M.G. (Dec. 11, 1854)

McMINN COUNTY MARRIAGES

John Gilly to Martha Parks, Dec. 11, 1854.
  By James Baker, J.P. (Dec. 11, 1854)
Alexander Michael to Martha J. Strain, Dec. 14, 1854.
  By J. N. Blackburn, M.G. (Dec. 17, 1854)
A. A. Lowry to Clarissa E. Guffey, Dec. 15, 1854.
  (no returns)
Marshall Smith to Nancy Dyer, Dec. 16, 1854.
  By David W. Beaver, M.G. (Dec. 17, 1854)
Chas. A. Proctor to Sarah A. Martin, Dec. 18, 1854.
  (no returns)
E. W. King to Velince W. Atkinson, Dec. 19, 1854.
  By W. H. H. Duggan, M.G. (Dec. 20, 1854)
Wm. M. Prather to Roselvim(?) Kemp, Dec. 20, 1854.
  By Geo. A. Caldwell, M.G. (Dec. 20, 1854)
John Reynolds to Mary M. M. Smith, Dec. 21, 1854.
  (no returns)
Noah Cate to Mahala Isham, Dec. 21, 1854.
  By J. Thomas, J.P. (Dec. 21, 1854)
Francis M. West to Susan Kitchen, Dec. 27, 1854.
  (no returns)
Drury Goforth to Evaline Pugh, Dec. 27, 1854.
  By M. R. Ware, J.P. (Dec. 28, 1854)
F. S. Ray to Eliza T. C. Ware, Dec. 30, 1854.
  By M. A. Cass, M.G. (Dec. 31, 1854)
Wm. C. Peake to Nancy P. Matlock, Jan. 1, 1855.
  By Geo. A. Caldwell, M.G. (Jan. 4, 1855)
John P. Love to Elizabeth N. Barker, Jan. 2, 1855.
  By J. B. Cobbs, J.P. (Jan. 2, 1855)
John T. Bayless to Ann A. Haynie, Jan. 3, 1855.
  By T. T. Russell, M.G. (Jan. 3, 1855)
John Ginow to Carrutt Lawson, Jan. 3, 1855.
  By Rev. D. Carpenter. (Jan. 4, 1855)
John Kirby to Martha McCrary, Jan. 7, 1855.
  By James Baker, J.P. (Jan. 7, 1855)
James V. Walker to Susan Hunk, Jan. 8, 1855.
  By M. R. Ware, J.P. (Jan. 16, 1855)
Wm. H. Simpson to Angeline Triplett, Jan. 11, 1855.
  By J. Douglass, J.P. (Jan. 14, 1855)
John G. Mayfield to Mary Elizabeth Cobbs, Jan. 17, 1855.
  By T. L. Hoyl, M.G. (Dec. 18, 1855(?)
John Price to Catharine Baker, Jan. 18, 1855.
  By Jonathan Thomas, J.P. (Jan. 18, 1855)
Frances N. Million to Elizabeth Hart, Jan. 24, 1855.
  By T. B. Waller, M.G. (Jan. 25, 1855)
James D. Green to Sarah Lewis, Jan. 24, 1855.
  By H. J. Brock, J.P. (Jan. 24, 1855)
Jacob Vickers to Martha Wolffe, Jan. 24, 1855.
  By Wm. McKamy, J.P. (Jan. 25, 1855)
Henry Pearman to Martha J. Standifer, Jan. 25, 1855.
  (no returns)
A. M. Duggan to Margaret L. Burnett, Jan. 27, 1855.
  By Wm. R. Elder, M.G. (Jan. 28, 1855)
John Orten to Elizabeth McNabb, Jan. 30, 1855.
  By M. R. Ware, J.P. (Jan. 31, 1855)

McMINN COUNTY MARRIAGES

Abraham Booker to N. C. Nelson, Feb. 12, 1855.
 (no returns)
C. H. Ward to Jerusha Paris, Feb. 14, 1855.
 By James C. Carlock, J.P. (Feb. 14, 1855)
Joseph H. Creasman to Francis J. Guffy, Feb. 17, 1855.
 (no returns)
Wm. Raburn to Zilpha Breden, Feb. 18, 1855.
 By Robert Cockran, J.P. (Feb. 19, 1855)
Edmund White to Lucy Ellen Rothwell, Feb. 24, 1855.
 By H. N. Roberts, J.P. (Mar. 1, 1855)
Silas Witt to Emaline Blankenship, Feb. 24, 1855.
 By John Douglass, M.G. (Feb. 25, 1855)
Nelson M. Crockett to Edith Patty, Mar. 1, 1855.
 By Robert Gregory, M.G. (Mar. 1, 1855)
Martin M. Sweeney to Mary Moore, Mar. 4, 1855.
 By James Baker, J.P. (Mar. 4, 1855)
Albert Bracket to Elizabeth Neill, Mar. 5, 1855.
 By James Baker, J.P. (Mar. 5, 1855)
Joseph Bunch to Judith Massey, Mar. 6, 1855.
 By M. R. Wear, Esq. (Mar. 8, 1855)
Eli D. Baker to Louisa Rose, Mar. 7, 1855.
 By J. B. Waller, M.G. (Mar. 8, 1855)
Riley R. Long to Catharine Zeigler, Mar. 7, 1855.
 By C. P. VanDyke, M.G. (Mar. 7, 1855)
S. A. Wallace to Harriet Maxwell, Mar. 12, 1855.
 (no returns)
Thomas Coats to Caroline Rose, Mar. 14, 1855.
 By Jonathan Thomas, J.P. (Mar. 14, 1859(?))
J. O. Pennington to Esther C. Bryant, Mar. 17, 1855.
 By Robert Sneed, M.G. (Mar. 20, 1855)
James Billingsly to Sarah McCollum, Mar. 26, 1855.
 By D. W. Beaver, M.G. (Mar. 27, 1855)
G. W. Butler to Elizabeth Catharine Porter, Apr. 3, 1855.
 By A. Vance, M.G. (Apr. 5, 1855)
Christopher Sliger to Mary Ann Gibson, Apr. 3, 1855.
 By Robert Gregory, M.G. (Apr. 5, 1855)
Lewis W. Pickle to Nancy L. Lowry, Apr. 5, 1855.
 By John Tate, M.G. (Apr. 5, 1855)
I. J. Gibson to Elizabeth Braden, Apr. 19, 1855.
 By Robert Cochran, J.P. (Apr. 19, 1855)
M. Nelson to Rebecca A. McGaughey, Apr. 25, 1855.
 By George A. Caldwell, M.G. (Apr. 25, 1855)
Worden C. P. E. Heddington to Sarah Ball, Apr. 25, 1855.
 By W. H. H. Dugan, M.G. (Apr. 27, 1855)
Arthur Burus (or Burrus) to Eliza Cooke, Apr. 27, 1855.
 By B. A. Prophet, M.G. (Apr. 27, 1855)
Robert A. Rutherford to Mary Jane Loughmiller, May 3, 1855.
 By J. C. Carlock, J.P. (May 3, 1855)
Andrew J. Snider to Mary T. Conner, May 5, 1855.
 By E. M. King, M.G. (May 6, 1855)
S. M. Bogges to Martha M. McKeehan, May 11, 1855.
 By Hiel Buttram, Rve Mnts(?) (May 13, 1855)
Joseph Tuck to Louisa Goodwin, May 14, 1855.
 (no returns)

McMINN COUNTY MARRIAGES

W. R. Crittenden to Sarah Ann Miller, May 21, 1855.
  By H. M. Roberts, J.P. (May 22, 1855)
John W. Fry to Jane Garrison, May 22, 1855.
  By Isah Garrison, J.P. (May 23, 1855)
James Henderson to Eliza Jane Norville, June 6, 1855.
  By Robert Cochran, J.P. (June 7, 1855)
Wm. Hudgins to Winney Reneau, June 7, 1855.
  By Robert Cochran, J.P. (June 7, 1855)
Samuel Powers to Margaret Ann Smith, June 9, 1855.
  By Isah Garrison, J.P. (Nov. 9, 1855)
N. B. Stephens to Elizabeth Joines, June 13, 1855.
  By John Scruggs, M.G. (June 14, 1855)
Wm. Long to Isabella McNeilly, June 21, 1855.
  By Jack Culpepper, J.P. (June 24, 1855)
John Kimbrough to Melisa Jane Cate, June 23, 1855.
  (no returns)
Wm. Scarbrough to Elizabeth Rogers, June 28, 1855.
  By Wm. McAmy, M.G. (June 28, 1855)
Saml. P. Gibson to Nancy Studdard, June 29, 1855.
  By J. G. Swisher, M.G. (June 30, 1855)
Thos. J. Thompson to Mary A. Knight, June 30, 1855.
  By Wm. McAmy, M.G. (July 1, 1855)
Richard F. Jenkins to Arminda Rather, July 3, 1855.
  By A. P. Early, M.G. (July 3, 1855)
Mathew Thompson to A. R. Walsh, July 2, 1855.
  By Wm. McAmy, J.P. (July 2, 1855)
George Monroe to Margaret Simpson, July 2, 1855.
  By Robert Gregory, M.G. (July 15, 1855)
R. A. McMillaon (or McMillion) to L. M. Isbell, July 9, 1855.
  By S. M. Ham, M.G. (July 9, 1855)
Wm. T. Long to Mary B. Bechel, July 14, 1855.
  (no returns)
John Wasom to Margaret Twiner, July 30, 1855.
  By Robert Gregory, M.G. (July 15, 1855)
James Gibbs to Caroline Patterson, Aug. 4, 1855.
  By H. M. Sloop, M.G. (Aug. __, 1859(?)
James H. Dixon to Sarah E. Newman, Aug. 4, 1855.
  By Robert Gregory, M.G. (July 9, 1855)
Silas G. Latham to Elmy Green, Aug. 9, 1855.
  By D. Mephart, J.P. (Aug. 9, 1855)
Wm. W. W. James to Harriet M. Crewes, Aug. 15, 1855.
  By J. Cunningham, M.G. (Aug. 14, 1855(?)
David Grogan to N. J. Roddair, Aug. 14, 1855.
  By H. J. Brock, J.P. (Aug. 19, 1855)
James F. Roberts to Esther C. Tunnell, Aug. 15, 1855.
  By J. Swisher, M.G. (Sep. 16, 1855)
Wm. C. Varnell to Mary M. C. Yount, Aug. 16, 1855.
  By C. P. Vandike, M.G. (Aug. 16, 1855)
John A. Thompson to Manervy Z. Burk, Aug. 18, 1855.
  By M. A. Cass, M.G. (Aug. 18, 1855)
Francis M. Sliger to Hester E. Brock, Aug. 20, 1855.
  By James Parkison, J.P. (Aug. 21, 1855)
James Calhoun to Mary E. George, Aug. 23, 1855.
  By George A. Caldwell, M.G. (Aug. 23, 1855)

78

J. N. Stansberry to E. R. Erreton, Aug. 28, 1855.
By J. Jack, M.G. (Aug. 30, 1855)
Frederick Patterson to Mary E. Williams, Aug. 30, 1855.
By B. A. Prophet, J.P. (Aug. 30, 1855)
Luk (or Luke) Landers to Mary C. Marr, Sep. 8, 1855.
By B. A. Prophet, J.P. (Sep. 8, 1855)
Michael Malone to Quincy Meredith, Sep. 15, 1855.
By Wm. F. Ballew. (Sep. 16, 1855)
Wm. C. Witte to Mary J. Heron, Sep. 20, 1855.
By Geo. A. Caldwell, M.G. (Sep. 20, 1855)
Henry P. Walker to Mary T. Smith, Sep. 21, 1855.
By Joseph McSpadden, M.G. (Oct. 3, 1855)
N. L. Ansborn to Harriet C. Godard, Sep. 27, 1855.
By J. Cunningham, M.G. (Sep. 27, 1855)
S. W. Dixon to Nancy A. E. Howell, Sep. 27, 1855.
By J. Cunningham, M.G. (Sep. 27, 1855)
James Sanders to Rody Beck, Sep. 28, 1855.
By Jacob Whitsides, M.G. (Sep. 29, 1855)
John Cate to Sarah J. Witt, Oct. 4, 1855.
By James A. Zegler, J.P. (Oct. 4, 1855)
W. H. Staples to Martha S. Franklin, Oct. 6, 1855.
By M. A. Cass, J.P. (Oct. 10, 1855)
Wm. Cavill to Elizabeth Renfrow, Oct. 6, 1855.
By James Forrest, J.P. (Oct. 7, 1855)
James M. Biggs to Sarah M. Hambright, Oct. 8, 1855.
By J. M. Blackburn, M.G. (Oct. 10, 1855)
Lang R. Dodd to Virginia A. Ensminger, Oct. 11, 1855.
By S. Sharits, M.G. (Oct. 11, 1855)
Wm. J. Varnell to Mary E. Roberts, Oct. 11, 1855.
(no returns)
James Eatons to Celia Hambrick, Oct. 12, 1855.
By James A. Zegler, J.P. (Oct. 12, 1855)
Jourdan Harrod to Lucianah Coats, Oct. 12, 1855.
By T. B. Waller, M.G. (Oct. 13, 1855)
James M. Combs to Sarah Shell, Oct. 12, 1855.
(no returns)
Wm. Bassell to Amanda A. Sallee, Oct. 16, 1855.
By C. Gregory, M.G. (Oct. 16, 1855)
John Miller to Lydia Morgan, Oct. 19, 1855.
(no returns)
John Pry to Rebecca E. Adare, Oct. 20, 1855.
By H. M. Sloop, M.G. (Oct. 21, 1855)
John Alexander to Eialpha Turner, Oct. 24, 1855.
By A. D. Bryant, J.P. (Oct. 24, 1855)
John Cunningham to Margaret Sallee, Oct. 27, 1855.
By C. Godley, M.G. (Oct. 28, 1855)
M. D. Cantrell to Nanny E. Vaughan, Oct. 27, 1855.
By T. T. Russell, M.G. (Nov. 1, 1855)
John White to Mary Loyd, July 22, 1855.
By L. R. Hurst, J.P. (July 19, 1855)
Samuel Workman to Arrena Wolf, Nov. 12, 1855.
By A. M. Liner, J.P. (Nov. 13, 1855)
Columbano Cass to Mary E. Beaver, Nov. 15, 1855.
By Hill Buttram, M.G. (Nov. 12, 1856(?)

McMINN COUNTY MARRIAGES

James M. Reynolds to Mary B. Hansy, Nov. 15, 1855.
  By T. T. Russell, M.G. (Nov. 15, 1855)
James M. Yearwood to Susan R. Lowry, Nov. 20, 1855.
  By Thomas R. Bradshaw, M.G. (Nov. 20, 1855)
John A. Prather to Matilda Steed, Nov. 29, 1855.
  By Wm. C. Dailey, M.G. (Nov. 29, 1855)
Mark Dennis to Mary W. Elder, Nov. 29, 1855.
  By H. M. Roberts, J.P. (Dec. 2, 1855)
Thomas H. Smith to Jemima Wommack, Dec. 2, 1855.
  By H. M. Roberts, J.P. (Dec. 6, 1855)
Gabriel Clark to Elizabeth M. Swaffer, Dec. 5, 1855.
  By Jack Culpper(?), J.P. (Dec. 6, 1855)
Wm. P. Mahoney to Elizabeth Hicks, Dec. 10, 1855.
  By Morgan Miller, J.P. (Dec. 10, 1855)
Joseph D. Erwin to Allemarmda Erkerson, Dec. 17, 1855.
  By M. A. Cass, M.G. (Dec. 18, 1855)
Eli Hellenns to Elizabeth E. Bryan, Dec. 17, 1855.
  By O. M. Liner, J.P. (Dec. 18, 1855)
John Pinda to Judieth A. Guthery, Dec. 20, 1855.
  By E. G. Miller, M.G. (Dec. 20, 1855)
Jesse A. Hunt to Salina J. Smith, (no date given).
  By M. R. Wear, J.P. (Dec. 20, 1855)
A. J. Kirksey to Mary A. Brock, Dec. 24, 1855.
  By C. R. Hoyl, M.G. (Dec. 25, 1855)
Israel Stansfield to Susanah Pearman, Dec. 25, 1855.
  (no returns)
John Newman to Martha A. Keiker, Jan. 3, 1856.
  By Daniel McPhail, J.P. (Jan. 3, 1856)
S. S. Rhohdes (or Rhoades) to Margaret E. Hamby, Jan. 5,
  1856. By R. A. Gidins, M.G. (Jan. 7, 1856)
Martin J. Shipley to Barbary Goodwin, Jan. 5, 1856.
  By A. S. Bryant, J.P. (Jan. 6, 1856)
Samuel Patterson to Malvina Johnson, Jan. 5, 1856.
  By H. M. Sloop, M.G. (Jan. 6, 1856)
S. Bogart to Margaret Baker, Jan. 7, 1856.
  By Wm. Newman, J.P. (Jan. 10, 1856)
Ransom Hellan to Sarah Carright, Jan. 10, 1856.
  By Robert Cochran, J.P. (Jan. 10, 1856)
Thos. Densom to Margaret Collins, Jan. 11, 1856.
  (no returns)
John D. Lowry to Sarah C. Forest, Jan. 7, 1856.
  By John Scruggs, M.G. (Jan. 6, 1856)
Alfred _____ to Salena Dodson, Jan. 13, 1856.
  By R. A. Giddins, M.G. (Jan. 13, 1856)
John H. Madden to Lois Roberts, Jan. 15, 1856.
  By M. B. Wear, J.P. (Jan. 16, 1856)
J. N. Stephens to M. W. Rice, Jan. 15, 1856.
  By T. J. Russell, M.G. (Jan. 17, 1856)
John Densan to Martha Ivans, Jan. 19, 1856.
  (no returns)
Charles Wolf to Nancy E. Madden, Jan. 19, 1856.
  By H. W. Roberts, J.P. (Jan. 20, 1856)
Thos. R. Backet to Jane C. Wingo, Jan. 22, 1856.
  (no returns)

John H. White to Jane Madden, Jan. 29, 1856.
By M. R. Wear, J.P. (Feb. 2, 1856)
James I. Cash to Elizabeth J. Eakin, Feb. 4, 1856.
By David M. Beaver, M.G. (Feb. 4, 1856)
James Ratledge to Malinda Barlow, Feb. 7, 1856.
By Robert Reynolds, J.P. (Feb. 7, 1856)
G. C. Davis to Ataline Dotherroe, Feb. 12, 1856.
By J. H. Melton, J.P. (Feb. 14, 1856)
Andrew Jackson Brown to Rebecca Jane Mize, Feb. 15, 1856.
By Robert Reynolds, J.P. (Feb. 18, 1856)
John Neil to Harriet Cate, Feb. 22, 1856.
By Wm. R. Elder, M.G. (Feb. 22, 1856)
W. H. Weaterby to Eliza Jane Cook, Feb. 23, 1856.
By Morgan Miller, J.P. (Feb. 24, 1856)
Aaron Mathews to Margaret Edgmon, Feb. 27, 1856.
By James Baker, J.P. (Feb. 27, 1856)
Wm. C. Adare to Martha Reed, Mar. 4, 1856.
By H. M. Sloop, M.G. (Mar. 6, 1856)
Wm. S. Robison to Sarah E. Smith, Mar. 15, 1856.
By T. J. Rusell, M.G. (Mar. 16, 1856)
Samuel B. Rucker to Eliza Jane Ivans, Mar. 17, 1856.
By O. M. Liner, J.P. (Mar. 20, 1856)
Wm. B. Erwin to Sarah Gregory, Mar. 22, 1856.
By H. M. Roberts, J.P. (Mar. 29, 1856)
Wm. Rentfro to Melvina Ray, Mar. 27, 1856.
By James Baker, J.P. (Mar. 27, 1856)
George Whitten to Louiza J. Lasiter, Mar. 28, 1856.
By J. Zeigler, J.P. (Mar. 28, 1856)
George Brown to Susan Barker, Apr. 3, 1856.
By R. Reynolds, J.P. (Apr. 3, 1856)
P. K. Wheselle to N. F. Swinney, Apr. 4, 1856.
By M. A. Cass, M.G. (Apr. 4, 1856)
R. R. Thompson to M. A. Gandd, Apr. 7, 1856.
By H. J. Brock, J.P. (Apr. 8, 1856)
Edmond Golbert to Nancy Swafford, Apr. 26, 1856.
By Wm. M. Camy, J.P. (Apr. 27, 1856)
J. B. Houston to Mahala Cate, May 13, 1856.
By R. A. Prophet, J.P. (May 13, 1856)
W. W. Kelley to L. A. McKnight, May 13, 1856.
By J. M. Miller, M.G. (May 14, 1856)
J. N. Wear to E. Cate, May 15, 1856.
By Robert Gregory, M.G. (May 15, 1856)
Larkin Shelton to Martha A. Melton, May 15, 1856.
By A. F. Cox, M.G. (May 15, 1856)
John L. Atlee to Sarah Humphries, May 22, 1856.
By S. Philips, M.G. (May 22, 1856)
Wm. Emerson to Josephine Haggard, May 26, 1856.
By Robert Gregory, M.G. (May 26, 1856)
Wm. Young to Sidney Swinford, May 29, 1856.
(no returns)
George I. Walker to Martha E. Mabs, May 30, 1856.
By M. R. Wear, J.P. (June 1, 1856)
W. B. Ash to Mary M. Culpepper, June 10, 1856.
By Wm. R. Long, M.G. (Sep. 13, 1856)

Samuel U. P. Gipson to A. C. Edington, June 12, 1856.
By J. M. Miller, M.G. (June 13, 1856)
Larkin F. Swafford to Effee N. Wilson, June 14, 1856.
By Joel Culpepper, J.P. (June 15, 1856)
W. C. Fulton to Mary Ann Ashley, June 14, 1856.
By A. F. Cox, M.G. (June 24, 1856)
H. Webb to P. A. Beasley, June 17, 1856.
By Joseph Neil, J.P. (June 19, 1856)
J. James to M. J. Gipson, June 29, 1856.
By H. C. Cook, M.G. (June 29, 1856)
Ira Whaley to Sarah A. Rogers, June 28, 1856.
By H. C. Cook, M.G. (June 29, 1856)
Wm. Webb to Caroline Beasley, July 10, 1856.
By Joseph Neil, J.P. (July 10, 1856)
Wm. Rinker to Mary A. Burk, July 10, 1856.
By Jas. Zeigler, J.P. (July 10, 1856)
Joseph Yadle to Sarah A. Sharits, July 22, 1856.
By Geo. A. Caldwell, M.G. (July 22, 1856)
Daniel Holback to Mary Sharits, July 22, 1856.
By Geo. A. Caldwell, M.G. (July 22, 1856)
Daniel W. Mize to Sarah J. Bean, July 29, 1856.
By Joseph Peeler, M.G. (Aug. 5, 1856)
Robert H. Griffin to Margaret Chancy, Aug. 2, 1856.
By D. W. Beaver, M.G. (Aug. 3, 1856)
S. C. Brumit to Leona A. Rogers, Aug. 2, 1856.
By Jas. Parkison, J.P. (Aug. 5, 1856)
B. A. Gipson to Rebecca Wallin, July 5, 1856.
By H. C. Cook, M.G. (Aug. 7, 1856)
John Walton to Auma Iewin(?), Aug. 22, 1856.
By R. A. Giddins, M.G.
B. G. Glaze to Lucy J. Reynolds, Aug. 19, 1856.
(no returns)
David M. Wilson to Nancy L. Underdown, Aug. 19, 1856.
By M. A. Cass, M.G. (Aug. 21, 1856)
Marshall Arwine to Angeline Thomas, Aug. 21, 1856.
By T. B. Waller, M.G. (Aug. 22, 1856)
Samuel H. Hailly to Julia A. Fisher, Aug. 24, 1856.
By Wm. H. Ballew, J.P. (Aug. 24, 1856)
Robert Bryant to Ann Eliza Brown, Sep. 1, 1856.
By Joseph Neil, J.P. (Sep. 1, 1856)
Noah Shoemaker to Melvina Forester, Sep. 3, 1856.
By E. L. Miller, M.G. (Sep. 4, 1856)
Wm. S. Morgan to Mary J. James, Sep. 3, 1856.
By M. R. Wear, J.P. (Sep. 7, 1857(?))
T. J. McDaniel to Sarah J. Turner, Sep. 11, 1856.
By I. S. Garrison, J.P. (Sep. 11, 1856)
Wm. Johnson to Polly Patterson, Sep. 13, 1856.
By Hiel Buttram, M.G. (Sep. 13, 1856)
Thos. A. Cleage to Penelope S. Vandyke, Sep. 15, 1856.
By George A. Caldwell, M.G. (Sep. 15, 1856)
Mailstill Duckworth to Abigail S. Stanton, Sep. 13, 1856.
By G. W. Rentfro, M.G. (Sep. 14, 1856)
R. A. Lowery to Lydia C. Wassan, Sep. 16, 1856.
By George Caldwell, M.G. (Sep. 16, 1856)

McMINN COUNTY MARRIAGES

Uriah E. Poller to Delila E. Jones, Sep. 20, 1856.
(no returns)
A. M. Collins to Sarah Burns, Sep. 21, 1856.
By J. C. Swisher, M.G. (Sep. 25, 1856)
Robert A. Carter to Catharine Gilley, Sep. 24, 1856.
By Wm. McCamy, J.P. (Sep. 28, 1856)
Stokeley Bean to Mira Brandon, Sep. 24, 1856.
By Robert Reynolds, J.P. (Sep. 25, 1856)
Isham Dennis to Rebecca Thompson, Sep. 25, 1856.
By H. M. Roberts, J.P. (Sep. 25, 1856)
John L. Hamilton to Susan Senter, Sep. 30, 1856.
By J. A. Rowles, J.P. (Sep. 30, 1856)
John Hart to Nancy A. Wommack, Oct. 3, 1856.
By T. B. Waller, M.G. (Oct. 4, 1856)
James A. Smith to Malinda J. Armstrong, Oct. 4, 1856.
By Robert Cochran, J.P. (Oct. 5, 1856)
David Lewis to Margaret Cline, Oct. 6, 1856.
By Robert Cochran, J.P. (Oct. 18, 1856)
John Burk to Rebecca Pew, Oct. 7, 1856.
(no returns)
Cornelius Geffey to Mary J. Combs, Oct. 7, 1856.
By R. A. Giddins, M.G. (Oct. 8, 1856)
Wm. B. Sampley to Caroline Rider, Oct. 11, 1856.
By A. John, M.G. (Oct. 12, 1856)
Benjamin Casteel to Martha Madison, Oct. 12, 1856.
By G. W. Rentfro, M.G. (Oct. 12, 1856)
John R. Erwin to Debora A. Dely, Oct. 14, 1856.
By Jas. Parkison, J.P. (Oct. 15, 1856)
Henry M. C. Kinzy to Arvetzena Wells, Oct. 15, 1856.
By James Parkison, J.P. (Oct. 15, 1856)
Wyatt Sliger to Nearva Hampton, Oct. 25, 1856.
By James Parkison, J.P. (Oct. 28, 1856)
Alfred Melton to Jane Barker, Oct. 25, 1856.
By J. M. Melton, J.P. (Nov. 2, 1856)
Asa Sliger to Matilda N. Frank, Oct. 25, 1856.
By A. D. Briant, J.P. (Nov. 6, 1856)
Henry Vinsant to Celia Murphy, Oct. 25, 1856.
(no returns)
Hugh Robinett to Celia Murphy, Oct. 25, 1856.
By M. R. Wear, J.P. (Oct. 25, 1856)
Samuel Rose to Nancy Elliott, Oct. 31, 1856.
By Wm. Newman, J.P. (Nov. 2, 1856)
John C. Shipley to Theby Fitch, Oct. 31, 1856.
By D. W. Beaver, M.G. (Oct. 2, 1856)
J. A. Culpepper to Elizabeth A. Benton, Nov. 4, 1856.
By T. L. Hoyl, M.G. (Nov. 6, 1856)
T. B. Sample to C. R. Campbell, Nov. 4, 1856.
By Geo. A. Caldwell, M.G. (Nov. 4, 1856)
Granville Williams to Margaret Hamilton, Nov. 5, 1856.
By Hiel Buttram, M.G. (Nov. 5, 1856)
Andrew Woods to Harriet Fuguway, Nov. 6, 1856.
By Wm. H. Ballew, J.P. (Nov. 6, 1856)
David Bowman to Sarah Shamblain, Nov. 9, 1856.
By Jacob Culpepper, J.P. (Nov. 9, 1856)

Thos. A. Jones to Susan N. Maslin, Nov. 11, 1856.
(no returns)
Harvy Fry to Mary J. Adare, Nov. 13, 1856.
By C. W. Renfro, M.G. (Oct. 13, 1856(?)
Robert Ritchey to Sarah Cry, Nov. 15, 1856.
By Robert Gregory, M.G. (Nov. 16, 1856)
Andrew Stephenson to Elmira Kinzalow, Nov. 18, 1856.
(no returns)
Valentine Etter to Cintha P. Willhite, Nov. 19, 1856.
By M. A. Cass, M.G. (Nov. 20, 1856)
Wm. M. Beane to Sarah E. Beard, Nov. 20, 1856.
By James Parkison, J.P. (Nov. 20, 1856)
A. J. Cottharp to Harriet M. Lowery, Nov. 5, 1856.
By George A. Caldwell, M.G. (Nov. 6, 1856)
Isaac Rowland to Eliza Shook, Nov. 26, 1856.
By A. M. Liner, J.P. (Nov. 26, 1856)
Talton B. Tuck to Mary A. Pierce, Nov. 26, 1856.
By David W. Beaver, M.G. (Nov. 27, 1856)
J. G. Parshall to M. M. Rowan, Nov. 27, 1856.
By Geo. A. Caldwell, M.G. (Nov. 2, 1856(?)
Moses Tuck to Nancy A. Rabay, Dec. 3, 1856.
By David W. Beaver, M.G. (Dec. 3, 1856)
Wm. A. Stephens to Sarah S. Jourdin, Dec. 4, 1856.
By Thos. J. Rusell, M.G.
John Denton to Narcissa Womack, Dec. 4, 1856.
By H. M. Roberts, J.P. (Dec. 4, 1856)
J. S. Barker to Mahala H. Caldwell, Dec. 4, 1856.
By Robert Reynolds, J.P. (Dec. 4, 1856)
J. F. Wilson to Francis J. Barnette, Dec. 6, 1856.
(no returns)
George S. Sewell to Margaret E. Wilson, Dec. 8, 1856.
By Stephen Sharitts, M.G. (Dec. 11, 1857(?)
Charles A. Barnette to Louisa Armstrong, Dec. 9, 1856.
By Geo. A. Caldwell, M.G. (Dec. 9, 1856)
John L. Bridges to Margaretta Amanda Deadrick, Dec. 9, 1856.
By Geo. A. Caldwell, M.G. (Dec. 9, 1856)
Ezekiel Johns to Adaline Richard, Dec. 11, 1856.
By James Forest, J.P. (Dec. 11, 1856)
Scloa Wade to Adaline McGhehan, Dec. 15, 1856.
By Daniel Carpenter, M.G. (Dec. 18, 1856)
George Fitch to Nancy B. Jimerson, Dec. 17, 1856.
By D. W. Beaver, M.G. (Dec. 10, 1856)
Patton Denton to Sarah Womack, Dec. 22, 1856.
By H. W. Roberts, J.P. (Dec. 23, 1856)
John W. Lowery to Louisa E. C. Anderson, Dec. 22, 1856.
By Geo. A. Caldwell, M.G. (Jan. 6, 1857)
M. E. Rogers to Sarah J. Thompson, Dec. 30, 1856.
By C. R. Hoyl, M.G. (Jan. 6, 1857)
Andew (or Andrew) Burk to Emily Gibbs, Dec. 30, 1856.
By George A. Caldwell, M.G. (Jan. 7, 1857)
Wm. M. Cass to Julia A. Douglass, Dec. 31, 1856.
By C. Long, M.G. (Jan. 1, 1857)
James H. Lawson to Elizabeth G. Cass, Jan. 1, 1857.
By Joel Culpepper, J.P. (Jan. 2, 1857)

McMINN COUNTY MARRIAGES

A. J. Graves to Lolona Carter, Jan. 7, 1857.
  By I. S. Garrison, J.P. (Jan. 8, 1857)
Isaac Benson to Angeline Cobb, Jan. 12, 1857.
  By J. Atkins, M.G. (Jan. 13, 1857)
Wm. Moore to Margaret Eadens, Jan. 15, 1857.
  (no returns)
Joseph Johnson to Martha A. Green, Jan. 16, 1857.
  By Joseph Neil, J.P. (Jan. 20, 1857)
George L. Ratledge (or Rutledge) to Nancy E. Dooley,
  Jan. 17, 1857. By Jas. Parkison, J.P. (Jan. 18, 1857)
John P. Griffin to Francis J. Howard, Jan. 22, 1857.
  By J. W. Gibson, J.P. (Jan. 22, 1857)
James Moore to Julia A. Mitchell, Jan. 27, 1857.
  By Jas. Baker, J.P. (Jan. 27, 1857)
Robert Rucker to Lavesta Mitchell, Feb. 4, 1857.
  By M. R. Wear, J.P. (Feb. 7, 1858(?)
Isaac Dennis to Mary Dennis, Feb. 9, 1857.
  (no returns)
John J. Mason to Amanda Pierce, Feb. 9, 1857.
  By M. R. Ware, J.P. (Feb. 12, 1857)
Samuel Gregg to Jane Dolan, Feb. 17, 1857.
  By T. L. Hoyl, M.G. (Feb. 18, 1857)
E. T. Wason to Matta Lowery, Feb. 25, 1857.
  By Geo. A. Caldwell, M.G. (Feb. 26, 1857)
John M. Riddle to Nancy M. Kennedy, Feb. 6, 1957.
  By Daniel McPhail, J.P. (Feb. 8, 1857)
L. L. Ball to Lucinda Pearce, Mar. 12, 1857.
  By S. V. Philips, M.G. (Mar. 12, 1857)
Henry Moore to Mary Haze, Mar. 14, 1857.
  By J. A. Rolls, J.P. (Mar. 17, 1857)
Thos. N. Duckworth to Mary Simons, Mar. 16, 1857.
  By Geo. W. Rentfro, M.G. (Mar. 17, 1857)
Thos. B. Matlock to Miram Dixon, Mar. 18, 1857.
  By John Scruggs, M.G. (Mar. 24, 1857)
Wm. Liles to Emaline Hambrick, Mar. 19, 1857.
  By I. S. Garrison, J.P. (Mar. 20, 1857)
David Cate to Serelsey McCrary, Mar. 21, 1857.
  By Jas. Baker, J.P. (Mar. 22, 1857)
Jas. Marler to Malinda Fields, Mar. 25, 1857.
  By H. Roberts, J.P. (Mar. 26, 1857)
Wm. H. Haze to Nancy Collins, Apr. 7, 1857.
  By J. A. Rowles, J.P. (Apr. 7, 1857)
Wm. Paris to Patsy Weathery, Apr. 15, 1857.
  By T. L. Hoyl, M.G. (Sep. 19, 1857)
Ritchard (or Richard) Brown to Mary Presley, Apr. 17, 1857.
  By James Bonner, J.P. (Apr. 16, 1857(?)
Abner Chambers to Rachel M. Thornhill, Apr. 23, 1857.
  By J. A. Zeigler, J.P. (Apr. 23, 1857)
E. D. Cartright to Jane Haggard, Apr. 30, 1857.
  By Wm. Newman, J.P. (Apr. 30, 1857)
George W. Green to Mary Jane West, May 6, 1857.
  By David W. Beaver, M.G. (May 7, 1857)
Hardy Moss to Adaline Reatherford, May 9, 1857.
  By H. J. Brock, J.P. (May 10, 1857)

Wm. W. Cross to Nancy C. Miller, May 13, 1857.
  By H. M. Roberts, J.P. (May 24, 1857)
Thos. Smithers to Sarah F. Wells, May 27, 1857.
  By R. Reynolds, J.P. (May 30, 1857)
Riley Strullin to Leathy Jones, June 4, 1857.
  By M. A. Cass, M.G. (June 5, 1857)
George E. Burger to Hannah R. Everton, June 11, 1857.
  By J. Jack, J.P. (June 11, 1857)
Frances A. Taff to Manerva Gaut, June 17, 1857.
  By S. Philips, M.G. (June 17, 1857)
M. J. Borden to Eliza J. Pierce, July 2, 1857.
  By J. M. Gibson, J.P. (July 2, 1857)
John Brandon to Tilathea T. Firestone, July 9, 1857.
  By R. Reynolds, J.P. (Aug. 23, 1857)
L. C. Ferguson to S. H. Ferguson, July 10, 1857.
  By S. M. Haun, M.G. (July 12, 1857)
Wm. H. Cook to Mary A. Kantz, July 22, 1857.
  By J. M. Miller, M.G. (July 23, 1857)
Philip Rowland to Sarah A. McCroskey, July 23, 1857.
  By W. W. Haymes, M.G. (July 23, 1857)
Jas. D. Smith to Nancy A. Winters, July 29, 1857.
  By I. S. Garrison, J.P. (July 29, 1857)
G. W. Stephens to Sarah J. Kimbrough, July 29, 1857.
  By John Jack, M.G. (Aug. 30, 1857)
T. M. Long to Louisa Jane Crittenden, July 30, 1857.
  By H. C. Cooke, M.G. (July 30, 1857)
Robert Cate to Mary J. Hardin, Aug. 3, 1857.
  By C. Long, M.G. (Aug. 4, 1857)
J. A. Tewell to Lucy Shook, Aug. 4, 1857.
  By S. Phillips, M.G. (Aug. 4, 1857)
John W. Shoemaker to Sarah Bowerman, Aug. 17, 1857.
  By Stephen Sharits, M.G. (Aug. 19, 1857)
Holoway T. Winston to Sarah Rabourn, Aug. 19, 1857.
  By Stephen Sharits, M.G. (Aug. 19, 1857)
Robert R. Haze to Elizabeth J. Woods, Aug. 31, 1857.
  By S. Phillips, M.G. (Sep. 1, 1857)
Joshua Long to Mary Emmerson, Sep. 2, 1857.
  By H. C. Cooke, M.G. (Sep. 3, 1857)
Wm. T. _____ to Nancy Cooper, Sep. 8, 1857.
  By C. R. Hoyl, M.G. (Sep. 15, 1857)
R. W. Shipley to Catharine Shelton, Sep. 8, 1857.
  By James Bonner, J.P. (Sep. 17, 1857)
R. M. Evans to Eliza J. Lowry, Sep. 9, 1857.
  By John Scrugg, M.G. (Sep. 10, 1857)
Lewis S. Erwin to Sarah A. Casteel, Sep. 10, 1857.
  By T. Sullins, M.G. (Sep. 10, 1857)
John Sparks to Zelpha Helms, Sep. 12, 1857.
  By O. M. Liner, J.P. (Sep. 17, 1857)
Wm. D. McPhail to Margaret A. Wattenbarger, Sep. 24, 1857.
  By Hiel Buttram, M.G. (Sep. 24, 1857)
John F. Miller to Mary A. Miller, Sep. 26, 1857.
  By H. M. Roberts, J.P. (Sep. 27, 1857)
John Goolsby to Elizabeth Stansberry, Sep. 29, 1857.
  By Robert Reynolds, J.P. (Sep. 30, 1857)

James Green to Margaret MCollum (or McCollum), Sep. 6, 1857.
By D. W. Beaver, M.G. (Sep. 6, 1857)
James B. Kennedy to Rebecca J. Newman, Oct. 15, 1857.
By Daniel McPhail, J.P. (Oct. 15, 1857)
Chrisley Foster to Degenira Buttram, Oct. 20, 1857.
By Hiel Buttram, M.G. (Oct. 20, 1857)
W. J. McDaniel to Sarah C. McDaniel, Oct. 22, 1857.
By A. D. Brient, J.P. (Oct. 22, 1857)
Robert E. Cate to Rachel E. Dennis, Oct. 29, 1857.
By H. M. Roberts, J.P. (Oct. 29, 1857)
Allen Moore to Leantine Dugan, Nov. 5, 1857.
By Joseph Niel, J.P. (Nov. 5, 1857)
Samuel N. Howell to Ruth J. Blevins, Nov. 9, 1857.
(no returns)
Duke H. Kimbrough to Mary E. Cook, Nov. 10, 1857.
By C. R. Hoyl, M.G. (Nov. 11, 1857)
Charles Shell to Manerva Ellis, Nov. 11, 1857.
By Wm. H. Newman, M.G. (Nov. 12, 1857)
John Swafford to Elizabeth Hampton, Nov. 21, 1857.
By Wm. McAmy, J.P. (Nov. 26, 1857)
Miles H. McCuiston to Elizabeth Tuck, Nov. 25, 1857.
By E. L. Miller, J.P. (Dec. 25, 1857)
Wm. Burk to Elmer Gregory, Nov. 30, 1857.
By Joseph Gibson, J.P. (Nov. 21 or 31, 1857)
S. H. Mayfield to Martha Rice, Nov. 30, 1857.
By J. Atkins, M.G. (Dec. 3, 1857)
J. H. Williams to Darcus Murry, Dec. 1, 1857.
By Joseph Gibson, J.P. (Dec. 2, 1857)
Martin Riggs to Elizabeth A. Elliott, Dec. 4, 1857.
By H. J. Brock, J.P. (Dec. 6, 1857)
John McInturf to Nancy Graves, Dec. 4, 1857.
(no returns)
Jas. G. Gibson to Mary T. Hurst, Dec. 9, 1857.
By Robert Sneed, M.G. (Dec. 10, 1857)
Jas. Pritchard to Nancy A. Wilson, Dec. 16, 1857.
By M. L. Philips, J.P. (Dec. 18, 1857)
Wm. S. Chisnut to Martha E. Furgerson, Dec. 9, 1857.
By C. R. Hoyl, M.G. (Dec. 24, 1857)
George Deavenport to Salie H. Mitchell, Dec. 22, 1857.
By George A. Caldwell, M.G. (Dec. 22, 1857)
Jas. T. Whit(?) to Margaret C. Harles, Dec. 24, 1857.
By Joseph Neil, J.P. (Dec. 24, 1857)
A. J. Owens to Susan Chambers, Dec. 24, 1857.
By S_____(?), M.G. (Oct. 13, 1837(?)
Joseph M. Horton to Margaret J. McGaughey, Dec. 24, 1857.
By S. Sharits, M.G. (Dec. 24, 1857)
William P. Smith to Eliza J. Huggins, Dec. 25, 1857.
By Wm. Newman, J.P. (Dec. 27, 1857)
Levy Deaton to Elizabeth Maetheny, Jan. 2, 1858.
By Wm. H. Ballew, J.P. (Jan. 2, 1858)
Jas. B. Rudd to Mary A. Brown, Jan. 6, 1858.
By S. Philips, M.G. (Jan. 6, 1858)
John A. Cazy to Mary J. Filio, Jan. 6, 1858.
By Joseph Gibson, J.P. (Jan. 7, 1858)

McMINN COUNTY MARRIAGES

Benjmain Gregory to Mary Wilson, Jan. 7, 1858.
    By H. M. Roberts, J.P. (Jan. 7, 1858)
Wm. Malone to Hannah Hicks, Jan. 7, 1858.
    By James Baker, J.P. (Jan. 7, 1858)
Francis Reavely to Mariah J. Culpepper, Jan. 9, 1858.
    By Wm. R. Long, M.G. (Jan. 12, 1858)
Jas. R. Haze to Louiza C. Parker, Jan. 11, 1858.
    By Joel Culpepper, J.P. (Jan. 12, 1858)
Andrew Couson to MArgaret Fisher, Jan. 11, 1858.
    By Jonathan Thomas, J.P. (Jan. 12, 1859(?)
G. H. Powers to Martha J. Hamilton, Jan. 12, 1858.
    By E. L. Miller, J.P. (Jan. 14, 1858)
W. J. Ballington to Sarah Bevan, Jan. 13, 1858.
    By Thos. Russell, M.G. (Jan. 13, 1858)
John D. Daugherty to Harriet E. Randolph, Jan. 13, 1858.
    By J. J. Elliott, J.P. (Jan. 12, 1858(?)
John Banner to Caroline Rue, Jan. 13, 1858.
    By J. J. Elliott, J.P. (Jan. 3, 1858(?)
Jas. M. Daugherty to Martha E. Riggs, Jan. 19, 1858.
    By J. J. Elliott, J.P. (Jan. 21, 1858)
Wm. H. Hicks to Martha Bullryton, Jan. 21, 1858.
    By Thos. Russell, M.G. (Jan. 21, 1858)
F. J. Lemons to Elizabeth M. Lusk, Jan. 21, 1858.
    By H. C. Cook, M.G. (Jan. 21, 1858)
John Liles to Dacus E. Strutten, Jan. 25, 1858.
    By H. M. Roberts, J.P. (Jan. 28, 1858)
John H. McGrew to Josephine Crittenden, Jan. 26, 1858.
    By Neddy Newton, M.G. (Jan. 26, 1858)
Oston Sewell to Nancy E. Runnion, Feb. 3, 1858.
    By E. L. Miller, J.P. (Feb. 4, 1858)
Wm. Decker to Emaline Turner, Feb. 11, 1858.
    By Joseph Neil, J.P. (Feb. 11, 1858)
John Fitch to Mary M. C. Nath, Feb. 13, 1858.
    By A. D. Brient, J.P. (Feb. 17, 1858)
Lucus Ludbetter (or Ledbetter) to Sarah Whaley, Feb. 15,
    1858. (no returns)
Chrisley A. Foster to Mary C. Buttran, Feb. 17, 1858.
    (no returns)
Robert Boyd to Juduth C. Coffee, Feb. 19, 1858.
    By E. L. Miller, J.P. (Feb. 19, 1858)
Miles H. Riddle to Mary A. Bishop, Mar. 2, 1858.
    By Dan McPhail, J.P. (Mar. 4, 1858)
David J. Hamelton to Sarah Williams, Mar. 2, 1858.
    By J. H. Gibson, J.P. (Mar. 2, 1858)
Anderson Bunch to Louisa Kinsor, Mar. 5, 1858.
    By Wm. H. Newman, M.G. (Mar. 6, 1858)
J. H. Graves to Martha M. Carter, Mar. 11, 1858.
    By A. D. Brient, J.P. (Mar. 14, 1858)
A. J. Clark to Mary Ann Shook, Mar. 25, 1858.
    By Thos. Rogers, J.P. (Mar. 28, 1858)
James M. Rodden to Cathrin Lambert, Mar. 27, 1858.
    By H. P. Wilson, J.P. (Apr. 1, 1858)
Raphael Wilson to Rebecca Lirret, Mar. 29, 1858.
    By D. W. Beaver, M.G. (Apr. 1, 1858)

Thos. R. White to Mary Lamar, Apr. 1, 1858.
  By H. M. Roberts, J.P. (Apr. 1, 1858)
Philip Neal to Eliza J. Marcuan, Apr. 13, 1858.
  By Geo. A. Caldwell, M.G. (Apr. 13, 1858)
McKamy W. Dorsey to Laura S. Newman, Apr. 14, 1858.
  By George A. Caldwell, M.G. (Apr. 15, 1858)
Willie Lowery to Arlie E. Power, Apr. 20, 1858.
  By Geo. A. Caldwell, M.G. (Apr. 21, 1858)
James P. Senter to Nancy Jane Matlock, Apr. 21, 1858.
  By Henry Rice, M.G. (Apr. 21, 1858)
Mike Pearman to Louisa C. Renue, Apr. 2, 1858.
  By L. R. Hust, J.P. (Apr. 2, 1858)
Wm. Hampton to Sarah Woody, Apr. 22, 1858.
  By Jonathan Thomas, J.P. (Apr. 22, 1858)
Samuel B. Hughes to Martha A. Stansberry, Apr. 22, 1858.
  By H. P. Wilson, J.P. (Apr. 22, 1858)
Gilber (or Gilbert) Vandergriff to Eve Templeton, Apr. 22,
  1858. By Wm. R. Long, M.G. (Apr. 22, 1858)
James H. Rucker to E. C. Douglas, Apr. 23, 1858.
  (no returns)
G. C. Randolph to H. M. Mashburn, Apr. 24, 1858.
  By G. Randolph, M.G. (Apr. 27, 1858)
James Monroe to Miller M. Discon, Apr. 29, 1858.
  By J. W. Gibson, J.P. (Apr. 29, 1858)
T. S. M. Hawk to R. J. Wilson, May 3, 1858.
  By J. W. Gibson, J.P. (May 5, 1858)
Elijah Williams to Mary E. Cooper, May 28, 1858.
  By C. B. Hoyl, M.G. (June 3, 1858)
John Russell to Sarah Weatherby, June 1, 1858.
  By R. Reynolds, J.P. (June 10, 1858)
Felix Orick to Eliza Newcum, June 7, 1858.
  By C. L. Owen, J.P. (July 8, 1858)
C. C. Cate to L. C. Russell, June 12, 1858.
  By John Scuggs (or Scruggs), M.G. (June 13, 1858)
John Baker to Pamelia Davis, June 12, 1858.
  (no returns)
Aman Lamar to Martha Cooley, June 26, 1858.
  By Wm. H. Ballew, J.P. (June 26, 1858)
T. L. Toomey to Juliann Tira, June 26, 1858.
  By J. J. Eliot, J.P. (June 30, 1858)
Francis E. Marney to C. C. Brock, July 3, 1858.
  By John Jack, M.G. (July 4, 1858)
John P. McPhail to Mary J. Sharits, July 3, 1858.
  By D. Carpenter, M.G. (July 4, 1858)
P. C. Lowery to Rhue H. Dillean, July 3, 1858.
  By Joel Culpepper, J.C.(?) (July 4, 1858)
John R. Veears to Martha Crawford, July 6, 1858.
  By J. A. Zeglar, J.P. (July 14, 1858)
J. F. J. Lewis to Laura A. Mitchell, July 8, 1858.
  (no returns)
H. M. Brown to Elizabeth Tomson, July 10, 1858.
  By C. Long, M.S.(?) (July 13, 1858)
Jas. T. Smith to Nancy Wallen, July 20, 1858.
  (no returns)

McMINN COUNTY MARRIAGES

John Woodey to Nancy Shelton, July 22, 1858.
  By D. W. Beaver, M.G. (July 22, 1858)
John Boobbher to Catharine McCann, July 31, 1858.
  (no returns)
George Kirklin to Mary Rollins, 1st____, 1858(?).
  By Joseph Zigler, J.P. (July 1, 1858)
M. B. Godard to U. V. Hutsell, Aug. 5, 1858.
  (no returns)
John M. Leatherwood to Elizabeth C. Garland, Aug. 11, 1858.
  (no returns)
Miles H. McCuistian to Harriet A. Delea Smith, Aug. 12,
  1858.
Wm. M. Brock to Eliza J. Reabourn, Aug. 13, 1858.
  By J. J. Elliot, J.P. (Aug. 12, 1858(?)
John H. Scarbrough to Sarah A. Wallen, Aug. 19, 1858.
  By Joel Culpepper, J.P. (Aug. 22, 1858)
J. F. McAfer to M. J. Collier, Aug. 25, 1858.
  By Thos. Rogers, J.P. (Aug. 26, 1858)
A. H. Barker to Elizabeth Melton, Aug. 25, 1858.
  By C. Long, M.G. (Aug. 25, 1858)
Wm. Whitlock to Eliza Smith, Aug. 26, 1858.
  (no returns)
Amos Hardin to Sarah Creasman, Aug. 28, 1858.
  (no returns)
G. W. D. Buckner to S. E. Owens, Aug. 30, 1858.
  By G. W. Rentfro, M.G. (Sep. 1, 1858)
Jas. Ratledge (or Rutledge) to Elizabeth A. Goins, Sep. 1,
  1858. (no returns)
Thos. Fleming to Jane Gibany, Sep. 2, 1858.
  By J. N. S. Huffaker, M.G. (Sep. 2, 1858)
E. G. Brown to Lucy Whitsell, Sep. 12, 1858.
  By George A. Caldwell, M.G. (Sep. 12, 1858)
Ovrille (or Orville) Rice to Molly Reynolds, Sep. 13, 1858.
  By John Scruggs, M.G. (Sep. 14, 1858)
Hueston Daves to Elizabeth Davis, Sep. 13, 1858.
  By Joseph Neil, J.P. (Sep. 13, 1858)
F. M. Elliot to Eliza J. Crocket, Sep. 13, 1858.
  By H. M. Sloop, M.G. (Sep. 16, 1858)
J. L. Haney to Sarah Maloon, Sep. 18, 1858.
  By Edward Atlee, M.G. (Sep. 19, 1858)
Thos. F. Guffey to Narcissa Porter, Sep. 21, 1858.
  By H. M. Roberts, J.P. (Sep. 22, 1858)
Wm. M. Harrod to Sarah L. Lamar, Sep. 23, 1858.
  (no returns)
Ezekiel Sherel to Luzany F. Staples, Sep. 23, 1858.
  By Wm. H. Ballew, J.P. (Sep. 23, 1858)
W. A. Buckner to Mary J. Owen, Sep. 23, 1858.
  By H. Rice, M.G. (Sep. 24, 1861(?)
Uriah L. York to Mary M. Deadrick, Sep. 27, 1858.
  By George A. Caldwell, M.G. (Sep. 28, 1858)
B. A. Riggs to Mary Daugherty, Sep. 29, 1858.
  By M. A. Cooper, M.G. (Oct. 3, 1858)
E. M. Carlock to Mary J. Wells, Oct. 12, 1858.
  By S. J. Philips, M.G. (Oct. 14, 1858)

McMINN COUNTY MARRIAGES

James Magill to A. E. Lowery, Oct. 14, 1858.
By Geo. A. Caldwell, M.G. (Oct. 14, 1858)
L. W. Crouch to Mary E. Varnell, Oct. 15, 1858.
By J. Atkins, M.G. (Oct. 19, 1858)
L. J. Duckworth to Nancy A. Bracket, Oct. 16, 1858.
By M. A. Cass, M.G. (Oct. 16, 1858)
E. F. King to Mary J. Sugart, Oct. 18, 1858.
By C. Long, M.G. (Oct. 19, 1858)
George M. McCully to Jame (or Jane) M. Godard, Oct. 27,
1858. By J. M. Miller, M.G. (Oct. 27, 1858)
R. J. Faugevar to Margaret M. Roberts, Oct. 28, 1858.
By J. S. Russell, J.P. (Oct. 28, 1858)
Jackson Swagerty to Sally Henry, Oct. 29, 1858.
By D. W. Beaver, M.G. (Oct. 31, 1858)
James Thompson to Elvira Branum, Nov. 1, 1858.
By E. Reynolds, J.P. (Nov. 3, 1858)
W. H. Anderson to Sarah M. Crow, Nov. 2, 1858.
By T. Sullins, M.G.
H. J. Morrow to Lydiann Forister, Nov. _(?), 1858.
By H. M. Roberts, J.P. (Nov. _(?), 1858)
E. S. Shipley to Mary E. Love, Nov. 8, 1858.
By Joseph Neil, J.P. (Nov. 8, 1858)
F. W. Martin to S. G. Liece (or Rice), Nov. 10, 1858.
By J. A. Hyden, M.G. (Nov. 11, 1858)
Wm. F. Kiker to Emily C. Newman, Nov. 10, 1858.
(no returns)
Jas. C. Bains to Louiza E. McAffey, Nov. 13, 1858.
By Robert Cochran, J.P. (Nov. 14, 1858)
Wm. A. Cartright to Mary Ann Jones, Nov. 13, 1858.
(no returns)
R. E. Cate to Arminda Stephenson, Nov. 15, 1858.
By J. S. Rusell, M.G. (Nov. 16, 1858)
James F. H. Gregory to Adarcus Fisher, Nov. 16, 1858.
By Dan Carpenter, M.G.M.E.C. (Nov. 16, 1858)
W. P. Cate to Mary Wolf, Nov. 17, 1858.
By F. M. Hauer, M.G. (Nov. 20, 1858)
J. H. Hale to Margaret L. Campbell, Nov. 23, 1858.
By Geo. A. Caldwell, M.G. (Dec. 23, 1858)
Wm. Power to Elizabeth White, Nov. 29, 1858.
By M. B. Manelle, M.G. (Dec. 3, 1858)
C. L. Norvill to Mary M. Smith, Nov. 30, 1858.
By John H. Brener, M.G. (Dec. 2, 1858)
T. M. Stephenson to Sarah C. Melton, Dec. 2, 1858.
By M. L. Philips, J.P. (Dec. 2, 1858)
John Fitch to Catharine MCollum (or McCollum), Dec. 4, 1858.
By M. Parin, M.G. (Dec. 5, 1858)
S. W. Rice to Catharine Guthrey, Dec. 7, 1858.
By M. Love, M.G. (Dec. 7, 1858)
Joseph H. Sellers to Margaret Tummire, Dec. 12, 1858.
By Joel Culpepper, J.P. (Dec. 13, 1858)
C. D. Hoyl to Susan C. Hoyl, Dec. 13, 1858.
By Rufus M. Hecky, M.G. (Dec. 16, 1858)
Wm. M. Simpson to E. A. Metcalf, Dec. 20, 1858.
By J. A. Caldwell, M.G. (Dec. 20, 1858)

John M. Masham to Mary C. Grayson, Dec. 11, 1858.
By R. Reynolds, J.P. (Dec. 12, 1858)
Abram Befarner to Matilda A. Crawford, Dec. 22, 1858.
By Joseph Neil, J.P. (Dec. 22, 1858)
L. L. Stansberry to Margaret A. Hance, Dec. 23, 1858.
By Jas. Baker, J.P. (Dec. 23, 1858)
Samuel MCamis (or McCamis) to Elizabeth Underwood, Dec. 24,
1858. By A. D. Briant, J.P. (Dec. 24, 1858)
John H. Wood to Sarrah E. Stacecy (or Stacey), Dec. 27,
1858. By S. M. Haun, M.G. (Dec. 30, 1858)
John W. Large to Melvina Cooke, Jan. 1, 1859.
(no returns)
Jasper Coats to Elizabeth Grigsby, Jan. 3, 1859.
By Jonathan Thomas, J.P. (Jan. 3, 1859)
Jacob Zeigler to C. McMillian, Jan. 3, 1859.
By J. B. Harvey, J.P. (Jan. 3, 1859)
Jedson Lockmiller to I. R. Stanton, Jan. 3, 1859.
By Jonathan Thomas, J.P. (Jan. 4, 1859)
Moses Long to Currinda Mitchell, Jan. 10, 1859.
(no returns)
Jas. Cartright to Martha C. E. Smith, Jan. 13, 1859.
By Robert Cochran, J.P. (Jan. 16, 1859)
H. S. Amans to Nancy Thompson, Jan. 13, 1859.
By James Henderson, J.P. (Jan. 16, 1859)
Edward Philips to Nancy Haney, Jan. 17, 1859.
By I. B. Haney, J.P. (Jan. 20, 1859)
W. C. Logan to Judy F. Weatherly, Jan. 22, 1859.
By H. J. Brock, J.P. (Jan. 22, 1859)
Wm. Brown to Mary Weatherly, Jan. 27, 1859.
By R. Reynolds, J.P. (Jan. 27, 1859)
J. H. Crockett to Caroline Martin, Feb. 3, 1859.
By Robert Cochran, J.P. (Feb. 6, 1859)
Nathanl Lawson to Jane Cate, Feb. 5, 1859.
By Jonathan Thomas, J.P. (Feb. 6, 1859)
John Manze to Lydia Herrell, Feb. 7, 1859.
(no returns)
John Rayborn to Rebecca Ann Rice, Feb. 9, 1859.
By Robert Cochran, J.P. (Feb. 9, 1859)
Thos. Martin to Prusila Firestone, Feb. 10, 1859.
By Robert Cochran, J.P. (Feb. 15, 1859)
John J. Dixon to Lucinda Hampton, Feb. 16, 1859.
By Joel Culpepper, J.P. (Feb. 17, 1859)
J. T. Stephens to Elmira Harmon, Feb. 17, 1859.
(no returns)
Z. T. Lambert to Martha Hardin, Feb. 24, 1859.
By Joseph Gibson, J.P. (Feb. 24, 1859)
Samuel Newman to Malinda Bain, Feb. 25, 1859.
By Wm. Newman, J.P. (Feb. 27, 1859)
John Rue to Silday M. Reatherford, Feb. 27, 1859.
By James Baker, J.P. (Feb. 27, 1859)
G. E. Burgar to Mary Hamilton, Mar. 2, 1859.
(no returns)
Wm. Shoemaker to Mary J. Morrow, Mar. 3, 1859.
By Jas. Parkison, J.P. (Mar. 3, 1859)

McMINN COUNTY MARRIAGES

J. D. Coleman to Amy Williams, Mar. 3, 1859.
By Wm. Newman, J.P. (Mar. 9, 1859)
James W. Pike to Polly Ann Scivils, Mar. 7, 1859.
By Jas. M. Henderson, J.P. (Mar. 7, 1859)
Stephen Liles to Malinda Powers, Mar. 5, 1859.
By M. B. Manselle, M.G. (Mar. 6, 1859)
Isaac W. Fyffe to Elizabeth Fleming, Mar. 8, 1859.
By Joseph A. Dellar, J.P. (Apr. 7, 1859)
Rece Crabtree to Celia Ward, Mar. 9, 1859.
By Jas. A. Melton, J.P. (Mar. 10, 1859)
John P. Fifer to Susan E. Smith, MAr. 15, 1859.
By Geo. A. Caldwell, M.G. (Mar. 18, 1859)
John L. Pearce to Lucy Harrod, Mar. 23, 1859.
By Jonathan Thomas, J.P. (Mar. 23, 1859)
James C. King to Orlenia Lattimore, Mar. 29, 1859.
By Uriah Payne, J.P. (Mar. 30, 1859)
A. M. Benton to Mary A. Firestone, (no date given).
By Robert Reynolds, J.P. (Mar. 30, 1859)
Wm. MConnelly (or McConnelly) to Isabella Millsaps,
Apr. 4, 1859. By Jas. H. Melton, J.P. (Apr. 6, 1859)
Duke Warde to Martha Ware, Apr. 5, 1859.
By J. Whitesides, M.G. (Apr. 7, 1859)

Book "E" 1859-1864 (not in sequence)

Henry Rogers to C. S. Thompson, July 26, 1863.
  By W. H. C. Thompson, J.P. (July 27, 1863)
Emanuel Griffitts to Sarah McCluen, Aug. 8, 1859.
  By Morgan Miller, J.P. (Aug. 14, 1859)
John Underwood to Harreitt (or Harriett) L. Sellers,
  Mar. 20, 1860. By Joel Culpepper, J.P. (Mar. 21, 1860)
J. V. Bain to Rebecca Newman, June 10, 1859.
  By W. M. Newman, J.P. (June 12, 1859)
Robert Long to Sarah Leamon, June 5, 1863.
  By J. M. Miller, M.G. (June 7, 1863)
John Woolsey to Margaret Ellis, Aug. 13, 1859.
  By J. W. Gibson, J.P. (Aug. 15, 1859)
Edward Newton to Mary D. Rogers, Oct. 10, 1863.
  By Calvin Denton, M.G. (Oct. 15, 1863)
J. G. Purdy to Sarah A. Firestone, Sep. 7, 1859.
  By Robert Cochran, J.P. (Sep. 8, 1859)
Bernhart Gilbert to Louisa M. Kelly, Feb. 23, 1860.
  By E. Rowley, M.G. (Feb. 23, 1860)
N. C. Jones to S. M. McCaslin, June 14, 1860.
  By Geo. A. Caldwell, M.G. (June 14, 1860)
James Johnson to Sarah E. Dillon, Sep. 10, 1860.
  By C. J. Wright, M.G. (Sep. 11, 1860)
Wm. L. Fore to Nancy Thurman, Aug. 21, 1860.
  By Stephen Sharitts, M.G. (Aug. 22, 1860)
J. V. Bainn to Rebecca Newman, June 10, 1859.
  By W. M. Newman, J.P. (June 12, 1859)
Emanuel Griffitts to Sarah McCluen, Aug. 8, 1859.
  By Morgan Miller, J.P. (Aug. 14, 1859)
John L. Smedley to Mary E. Trout, Sep. 22, 1860.
  By C. R. Hoyl, M.G. (Sep. 27, 1860)
Jas. Kelly to Martha E. Landers, Nov. 17, 1863.
  By C. R. Hoyl, M.G. (Nov. 19, 1863)
James Land to Fanny Aily, July 4, 1859.
  By Robert Cochran, J.P. (July 4, 1859)
Wm. Brown to Mary Weatherby, Dec. 27, 1859.
  (no returns)
H. M. Thompson to Malinda Melton, June 20, 1859.
  By J. C. Masingale, J.P. (June 30, 1859)
Elijah Petitt to Malinda Deaton, Aug. 6, 1859.
  By Thomas Rogers, J.P. (Aug. 7, 1859)
F. M. Pennington to Virginia M. Lowery, Nov. 30, 1859.
  By Geo. A. Caldwell, M.G. (Dec. 1, 1859)
Wm. S. Ball to Sarah J. Ball, May 5, 1859.
  By D. A. Beaver, M.G. (May 14, 1859)
James M. Carroll to Mahala Kelly, Oct. 6, 1859.
  By J. Jack, M.G. (Oct. 7, 1859)
J. N. Yearwood to E. V. Netherland, Nov. 3, 1859.
  By James Forrest, J.P. (Nov. 3, 1859)
Josiah Sampson to Hannah E. Smith, July 22, 1859.
  By A. D. Brient, J.P. (July 24, 1859)
John Key to Martha J. Wattenbarger, Oct. 18, 1859.
  (no returns)

McMINN COUNTY MARRIAGES

Wm. Shoemaker to Mary J. Morrow, Mar. 3, 1859.
By James Parkison, J.P. (Mar. 3, 1859)
Jesse C. Rice to Martha Benson, Dec. 7, 1862.
By Geo. A. Caldwell, M.G. (Dec. 7, 1862)
M. V. Grisham to Mary C. Eaton, Jan. 12, 1860.
By J. A. Zeigler, J.P. (Jan. 12, 1860)
James Land to Fanny Aily, July 4, 1859.
By Robert Cochran, J.P. (July 4, 1859)
F. W. Waugh to T. S. M. Dixon, Feb. 23, 1862.
By A. D. Brient, J.P. (Feb. 23, 1862)
Wm. Knox to Tennessee Smith, Mar. 11, 1861.
By J. M. Miller, M.G. (Mar. 14, 1861)
Silas N. Rucker to Martha Zeigler, May 23, 1861.
By D. L. Miler, M.G. (May 23, 1861)
Martin Brook to Nancy Johnson, Jan. 16, 1860.
By C. R. Hoyl, M.G. (Jan. 17, 1860)
John Underwood to Harriet L. Seller, Mar. 20, 1860.
(see also John Underwood, page 94)
Tempee Kindrick to Thena Hambrick, Sep. 22, 1860.
By John McGaughey, J.P. (Sep. 22, 1860)
John Crawford to Libbie J. Tompkins, Mar. 6, 1860.
By Geo. A. Caldwell, M.G. (Mar. 6, 1860)
Joseph A. Guffy to May C. Robinett, Jan. 5, 1860.
By H. M. Roberts, J.P. (Jan. 5, 1860)
Francis B. Jack to Sue Kelly, Aug. 27, 1862.
By John Jack, J.P. (Aug. 28, 1862)
Benjamin Brock to Mary Baker, Nov. 16, 1862.
By John Jack, M.G. (Nov. 17, 1862)
G. H. Colthorp to Martha A. Denton, June 27, 1860.
By C. R. Hoyl, M.G. (June 28, 1860)
Wm. Brown to Mary Weatherby, Dec. 27, 1859.
(no returns)
Elijah Pettitt to Malinda Deaton, Aug. 6, 1859.
By Thomas Rogers, J.P. (Aug. 7, 1859)
Matthews Roberts to Margaret A. Witt, Jan. 27, 1860.
By Rev. D. Carpenter. (Jan. 29, 1860)
T. J. Lowery to Clarissa Jackson, June 18, 1860.
By Geo. A. Caldwell, M.G. (June 21, 1860)
J. M. Thompson to Nancy J. Carlock, Aug. 15, 1860.
By C. R. Hoyl, M.G. (Aug. 15, 1860)
John E. Hutsell to Margaret Bonner, Oct. 3, 1860.
By A. W. Crouch, M.G. (Oct. 4, 1860)
H. M. Thompson to Malinda Melton, June 20, 1859.
By J. C. Masingale, J.P. (June 30, 1859)
F. M. Pennington to Virginia M. Lowery, Nov. 30, 1859.
By Geo. A. Caldwell, M.G. (Dec. 1, 1859)
H. C. P. Horton to Bettie Steed, May 30, 1860.
By T. J. Pope, M.G. (May 31, 1860)
Harrison Kitchen to Martha Ball, Mar. 14, 1860.
By D. Carpenter, M.G. (Mar. 15, 1860)
Alex F. C. Alexander to Martha A. Pearce, Aug. 11, 1860.
By L. W. Crouch, M.G. (Aug. 13, 1860)
F. M. Culpepper to P. M. Lemmons, Aug. 20, 1860.
By Calvin Denton, M.G. (Aug. 23, 1860)

McMINN COUNTY MARRIAGES

James M. Carroll to Mahala Kelly, Oct. 6, 1859.
By J. Jack, M.G. (Oct. 7, 1859)
Wm. S. Ball to Sarah J. Ball, May 5, 1859.
By D. A. Beaver, M.G. (May 14, 1859)
Prior Dobbs to Jane Dotson, Jan. 29, 1864.
By Z. Rose, M.G. (Jan. 29, 1864)
John W. Teague to Sarah A. Brock, Jan. 2, 1861.
By J. Jack, M.G. (Jan. 2, 1861)
Wm. Brandon to M. A. F. Landers, Dec. 8, 1863.
By W. B. Long. (Dec. 17, 1863)
John F. Lane to Caroline Walker, Mar. 21, 1860.
By L. W. Crouch, M.G. (Mar. 22, 1860)
J. M. Yearwood to E. V. Netherland, Nov. 3, 1859.
By James Forrest, J.P. (Nov. 3, 1859)
Josiah Sampson to Hannah E. Smith, July 22, 1859.
By A. D. Brient, J.P. (July 24, 1859)
Henry H. Knox to Nancy J. Baughan, Dec. 29, 1863.
By C. Long, M.G. (Dec. 30, 1863)
Wm. T. Atkinson to Manerva Smith, Feb. 11, 1864.
By A. H. Wilson. (Feb. 11, 1864)
R. P. Crowder to H. M. Magill, June 23, 1860.
By A. H. Barkly, M.G. (June 28, 1860)
Wm. Randolph to Mary Murray, May 8, 1860.
By John Scarbrough, J.P. (May 8, 1860)
Robert Patton to Mary L. Ward, Mar. 5, 1861.
By Geo. A. Caldwell, M.G. (Mar. 5, 1861)
Wm. P. Burnett to Sarah S. Shults, Feb. 20, 1861.
By Joseph Neil, J.P. (Feb. 20, 1851)
Wm. Holden to Sarah A. Fry, Nov. 28, 1861.
By H. M. Sloop. (Nov. 28, 1861)
Wm. M. Dixon to Margaret C. Kahill, June 16, 1860.
By Morgan Miller, J.P. (July 1, 1860)
J. P. Peters to H. H. Basinger, Jan. 18, 1864.
By W. H. Stephenson, J.P. (Jan. 19, 1864)
Alfred C. Aytse to Loretta Reed, Mar. 10, 1864.
By Rev. D. Carpenter. (Mar. 17, 1864)
John Griffey to Sarah A. Walker, Nov. 2, 1863.
(no returns)
A. J. Sligar to Sarah Cole, Mar. 2, 1864.
By Wm. G. Wilson, M.G. (Mar. 9, 1864)
Joseph Fitch to Rody A. Fitch, July 28, 1863.
By D. W. Beavers, M.G. (Aug. 2, 1863)
Robt. H. Wells to Sally L. Carlock, Mar. 3, 1864.
By C. Long, M.G. (Mar. 4, 1864)
James M. Clark to Susan Hoback, Mar. 30, 1864.
By Rev. D. Carpenter. (Apr. 8, 1864)
Benjamin Jenkins to C. Haney, Jan. 20, 1861.
By J. F. Pugh, J.P. (Jan. 20, 1861)
Wm. H. Loughmer to Tebitha Logan, Mar. 2, 1864.
By C. R. Hoyl, M.G. (Mar. 3, 1864)
Bennett Cooper to Mary Robinson, Oct. 10, 1860.
By John McGaughey, J.P. (Oct. 10, 1860)
J. W. Axley to M. A. Smith, Aug. 6, 1860.
By John H. Bruner, M.G. (Aug. 7, 1860)

McMINN COUNTY MARRIAGES

Samuel Burk to Elizabeth J. Biggins, Oct. 4, 1860.
By Thos. Grisham, J.P. (Oct. 4, 1860)
Jacob Zeigler to Annabelle Gibbony, May 23, 1860.
By T. J. Pope, M.G. (May 23, 1860)
John R. Moss to Nancy E. Forgey, Jan. 29, 1860.
By O. M. Liner, J.P. (Jan. 29, 1860)
W. L. Rice to Jeniva Wattenbarger, Sep. 10, 1861.
By D. Carpenter, M.G. (Sep. 11, 1861)
Wm. Shoemaker to Mary J. Morrow, Mar. 3, 1859.
By Jas. Parkison, J.P. (Mar. 3, 1859)
John Kez to Martha J. Wattenbarger, Oct. 18, 1859.
By Rev. D. Carpenter. (Oct. 20, 1859)
Thos. P. West to Margaret McClelan, Mar. 23, 1864.
By N. B. McNabb. (Mar. 24, 1864)
Hiram Crutchfield to Martha Witt, Feb. 25, 1864.
By Rev. D. Carpenter. (Feb. 25, 1864)
Thomas Grigsby to Rebecca Davis, July 11, 1860.
By J. F. Pugh, J.P. (July 13, 1860)
Thomas J. Cook to Sarah M. Moss, Feb. 17, 1864.
By C. R. Hoyl, M.G. (Feb. 18, 1864)

INDEX

Barnett, Charles C. 61
E. J. 33
Eliza Jane 33
Joseph R. 54
Mary C. 58
Mary E. 28
Nancy A. 34
Nancy L. 65
Nathaniel 6
Saml. 4
Sarah M. 35
Thunay 9
Barnette, Charles A. 84
Francis J. 84
Barrett, Barbara 24
Mary O. 34
Basalm, Gottlick 35
Basinger, H. C. 52
H. H. 96
L. P. 35
Basket, Charles R. 66
Bassell, Wm. 79
Bates, Ezekiel 46
Batson, Betsey 2
Battles, Margaret 17
Baughan, Nancy J. 96
Baulding, John R. 34
Bayles, Donnie M. 45
Bayless, John P. 39
John T. 76
Louisa 21
Sarah Jane 48
Beam, Ezekiel 26
Bean, Sarah J. 82
Stokeley 83
Wm. R. 53
Beane, Wm. M. 84
Beard, Sarah E. 84
Beasley, Caroline 82
P. A. 82
Beaver, David W. 10
Mary E. 79
Matilda 71
Beavers, Ann Eliza 25
Catherine 54
Mary 17
Spencer 19
Sterling C. 25
Bebibim, Nancy 14
Bechel, Mary B. 78
Beck, Israel 62
Rody 79
Beckett, Saprina 1
Bedford, Catherine 45
Elisabeth 40
Jane 40
Mary 23
Sarah 69
Susan 9
Befarner, Abram 92
Belcher, Elizabeth 56
Bell, W. S. 64
Bellew, George W. 3
Bellows, Mathias R. 9
Bench, Avy E. 40
James H. 40
Bennett, Rachel 56
Wm. J. Y. 55
Benoutt, Sarah Jane 58
Benson, Isaac 24, 85
Martha 95
Mary 41
Tabitha 37
Benton, A. M. 93
Abigale 53
Elijah 14, 15
Elizabeth A. 13
Hannah 45

Benton (cont.)
James 15
James F. 31
John 39, 45
Mary E. 32
Olevia 14
Rebecca 1
T. L. 75
Berry, Samuel A. 74
Sarah Jane 67
Bevan, Sarah 88
Bible, Nancy 63
Bicknele, Winney 38
Bicknels, Sarah 43
Biggins, Elizabeth J. 97
Biggs, James M. 79
Bigham, Nancy Ann Lurena 39
Billingsly, James 77
Emelia 3
Bingham, Isaac M. (see Brigham)
Bingman, Celia 36
Bird, Elvira 36
Bishop, Hannah 24
Mary A. 88
Ruth 27
Sarah 24
Thomas 68
Bitter, Isaac (see Butter)
Black, Betsey 3
Betsy 4
Elizabeth Ann 51
Blackburn, James 66
Susan A. 74
Blackwell, Angeline 20
Anna 48
C. R. 12
Caroline 53
Hellen E. 20
Mary 74, 74
Blain, M. V. 40
Blair, A. T. 42
Blane, Mordecai G. 60
Blankenship, Elizabeth Jane 51
Emaline 77
Mary 68
Blanton, Hezekiah 51
John 2
Rosanah 46
Bledsoe, Amy 27
Daniel 60
Mahala 28
Blevins, Ruth J. 87
Sarah 57
Boands, Mahaley 49
Boeils, James K. 41
Bogart, George W. 65
S. 80 ·
Solomon 5
Bogges, S. M. 77
Bolden, Sidna 3
Bolding, Amanda 14
Biddy 8
Matilda C. 45
William 37
Bolen, Jane 73
Boling, Tabitha 15
Bollen, Samuel 56
Bolton, Nancy Ann 46
Bond, Elisabeth 45
Elizabeth 15, 25
Nancy 11
Polly 16, 16
Rachel 39
Rosanna 13

Bonine, Andrew I. 63
Andrew J. 66
William 68
Bonner, Margaret 95
Martha 71
Mary 58
Sarah 53
Bonnis, Elizabeth 41
Boobbher, John 90
Boofer, John 34
Booker, Abraham 77
Bookout, John 15
Boon, Allen 9
Sarah 32
Vashtie 43
Borden, Janette 70
M. J. 86
Boren, Russel 33
Boring, Caroline 42
Borlison, Melinda J. 74
Bottoms, Elizabeth 44
Bower, H. H. 75
Bowerman, Michael 23
Nancy L. C. 36
Sarah 86
Bowman, David 83
R. P. 4
Bowsen, Long 11
Boyd, Andrew 48
Daniel L. 37
John K. 18
Robert 88
Brabson, R. B. 34
Bracket, Albert 77
Nancy A. 91
Brad, Elizabeth 33
Bradack, Ashael 2
Braden, E. W. 59
Elizabeth 77
James 25
Bradford, David 26
Mary G. 2
Bradley, Nancy Ann 47
Brandon, Ann E. 32
H. B. 39
John 86
Mira 83
Wm. 96
Branham, Jane 8
Parmer 27
Patsey 2
Brannock, Emily J. 22
Branon, James 62
Branum, Edward 67
Elvira 91
Brazeal, Sarah 69
Breadwell, Washington 12
Breck, Malinda 23
Breden, Zilpha 77
Breeden, George 3
Breedin, Tabitha 70
Breeds, P. W. 18
Brewer, Lucinda N. 70
Briant, Hannah 13
James A. 50
Martha 8
Brickson, Williamson 26
Bridges, Frances E. 42
Geo. W. 50
Isabella 29
James H. 55
John L. 20, 71, 84
Lois A. 28
Martha D. H. 55
Mary M. 20
William H. 69
Brigham, Isaac M. (Bingham) 54

100

Brigham (cont.)
Matilda 14
Brittain, W. C. 35
Britton, William C. 48
Brock, A. J. 71
Anna 43
Artilessa 53
Benjamin 95
Benjamin Y. 48
C. C. 89
Caroline 56
Catharine 59
David 68
Eliza Jane 73
Elmore 58
Henry J. 8
Hester E. 78
Isaac 50
Joel 2
L. 59
Lawrence R. 8
Martha 63
Mary A. 80
Perry G. 66
Sarah A. 96
Susan 31
Wm. M. 90
Brook, Martin 95
Brookshire, Ann 1
Katharine 48
Mary 16, 57
Rebecca C. 55
Vardra 57
William 55
Browder, Calvin 71
Celia 8
Lewann 25
Martha 26
Robert F. 40
Samuel D. 43
Tabitha 37
Brown, A. B. 21
Andrew I. 11
Andrew Jackson 81
Ann Eliza 82
Columbus 55
David 9, 57
E. G. 90
Elizabeth 31
Elizabeth A. 16
G. W. 38, 68
George 81
H. M. 89
Henry 19
Hester Ann 17
Hiram J. 70
James 50, 51, 66
James R. 9
Joel K. 17
John W. 66
Joseph 52
Joseph H. 3
Martha 55
Mary 70
Mary A. 87
Nancy 1
Nancy Ann 12
Richard 85
Ritchard 85
Sarah C. 56
Sarah L. 27
William F. 8
Wm. 23, 92, 94, 95
Bruer, Nasamond 35
Brumit, S. C. 82
Brummet, J. F. 69
Brummut, Mary Ann 75
Brussell, William B. 57

Bryan, Elizabeth E. 80
Mary J. 37
Nancy A. 1
Nancy M. 71
Robert 36
Wm. 70
Bryant, Elizabeth Jane 51
Esther C. 77
Gamaliel 74
James 9, 15
Pleasant 22
Robert 82
Buchanan, Joseph 52
Buchannon, Elias 32
Buck, Blasengame 29
Matilda 26
Tessy 30
Buckner, G. W. D. 90
J. S. 71
James 7
James W. 73
Miram 68
W. A. 90
Bullard, Patsy 5
Bullryton, Martha 88
Bunch, Anderson 88
Daniel 56
Jenny 44
Joseph 77
Lamber 20
Burch, Eliza 4
Burgar, G. E. 92
Burger, Adam 6
George E. 86
John M. 42
Lidia 8
Michael D. 72
Burk, Amanda M. 43
Andew 84
Andrew 84
H. H. 75
John 83
Manervy Z. 78
Marthee 1
Mary A. 82
Morgans (Mrs.) 74
Samuel 97
William P. 60
William T. 7
Wm. 87
Burke, Rosevell P. 32
Burks, Allen 5
Burnet, John M. 47
Nancy Ann 75
Burnett, Elizabeth 30
John W. 51
Lewis 12
Margaret L. 76
Martha J. 34
Mary P. 51
Sarah 36
Wm. P. 96
Burns, Emaline 67
Mary Ann 72
Sarah 83
Burris, William 57
Burrus, Arthur (see Burus)
Burus, Arthur (Burrus) 77
Bush, George 41
Butler, Amanda 15
Elizabeth 13, 15
G. W. 77
Isaac (see Butter)
Nancy M. 38
Butram, Nancy 36
Butter, Isaac (Bitter)
(Butler) 72
John 42

Buttram, Degenira 87
Embre 43
Jacob 61
James 34
Jane 9, 74
John G. 73
Julia 53
Lurana 60
Malissa 58
Margaret 41
Mary A. 60
Moses 60
Pamelia 9
Saphronia 27
Sarah 60
Viney 22
William 64
Buttran, Mary C. 88
Byington, Alfred R. 59,
69
Byran, Peter L. 42
Cagle, Ignatious W. 52
Matthew 24
Peggy 60
Cain, Jacob 23
Calahan, William 26
Caldwell, Elizabeth 53
Jesse B. 59
Lucinda 28
Mahala H. 84
Oliver P. N. 31
R. P. 2
Thomas 25
Calhoun, Frances 24
James 78
Jordan 37
Callahan, Phany 12
Cambright, Deniz 31
Camp, John 4
Campbell, C. R. 83
Catherine 31
Charlotte R. 11
D. L. 65
Elizabeth 50
Louisa J. 29
Malchiah 49
Margaret L. 91
Mary E. 17
Mary S. 29
Richard B. 29
T. J. 42
Thomas 3
William 44
Camron, Henry 26
Sarah M. 68
Cannon, Edward D. 13
Elizabeth 58
Isaac 10
Jane 53
Nancy 17
Polly 69
Richard 69
W. 40
William 33
Canseller, Israel 45
Cansler, Martha 48
N. H. 23
Cantrell, Ataline 60
Clementine 44
David 19, 64
F. M. 57
Gabriel 26
L. E. 65
Lucinda 29
M. D. 79
Malinda 7
Mary 12, 16
Mary Ann 16

Cantrell (cont.)
Nancy 29
Nancy M. 21
Noah C. 42
Reynolds 54
Robert C. 35
Terrell 38
Thomas C. 28
Thomas K. 41
William 65
Card, Eveline 19
Cardwell, James H. 18
Carlock, Asahel 23
E. M. 90
Nancy J. 95
Sally L. 96
Carmel, Galloway 27
Carmichael, J. L. 32
Carney, Edward H. 23
Joshua 8
Madison 46
Sarah 28
Carny, Frances 33
Carr, William 9
Willias B. 44
Carrigan, Charles H. 32
John C. 70
Carright, Sarah 80
Carrol, James A. 56
Carroll, Alfred 22
C. C. 54
Elizabeth 23
Evaline 18
James M. 94, 96
Mary 51
Carson, Alfred 50
D. F. 59
Edmund C. 56
James 37
Thos. C. 49
Carter, Adaline Amanda 7
Eliza 13
Elizabeth J. 70
Elender 37
Hiley 70
John 9
Lolona 85
Martha M. 88
Mary 66
Peter 24
Robert A. 83
Susan A. 52
William 27
Wm. M. 38
Cartright, E. D. 85
Elizabeth Jane 57
Jas. 92
Wm. A. 91
Casad, John C. 25
Casada, Calesta 19
James M. 25
Rhoda 5
Wesley 17
William 41
Cadady, Rachel 19
Casey, Moses 4, 5
Susanah 15
Cash, Bogan 23
James I. 81
Louisa 13, 15
Lucinda 21
Susan 67
Caslowe, James 44
Cass, Columbano 79
Elizabeth G. 84
T. A. 74
Wm. M. 84
Cassada, Andrew 1

Cassada (cont.)
John W. 71
Casst, Louize 2
Casteel, Benjamin 83
Edmond 3
Elijah 2
Elizabeth 19
Elizabeth J. 70
Elvira 63
M. H. 58
Sarah 14
Sarah A. 86
William 14
Caster, Susan 55
Cate, Alfred W. 44
C. C. 89
Charles 3, 13
David 85
E. 8
Elizabeth Ann 32
Elize 32
Francis 5
Greenberry 30
Harriet 81
Jane 30, 92
John 59, 79
Jonathan N. 56
Magdalena 30
Mahala 81
Maldonetty 26
Mary 72
Mary Ann 27, 40
Mary L. 70
Melisa Jane 78
Noah 76
Porter B. 62
R. E. 91
Rebecca 50
Rebecca M. 47
Robert 31, 86
Robert E. 87
Sarah 48
Sarah E. 69
Soloman 44
W. P. 91
Cates, Menada 2
Cauldwell, Anna 56
Stalin 49
Thomas 66
Caves, Manda 42
Wm. 4
Cavet, Malinda 8
Cavill, Wm. 79
Caywood, Mary Ann 3
Cazy, John A. 87
Cearl, Edy 1
Cecil, Sarah 43
Cecill, Joseph M. 69
Center, Calvin H. 53
Douisan 1
Partina 16
Cesil, Elizabeth 43
Chamber, Sonirom Judson
62
Chambers, Abner 85
Edmond 4
John 33
John J. 57
Robert E. 68
Susan 87
Chamlee, William 31
Chamley, Mary Emaline 8
Champlin, Mary 39
Chancy, Margaret 82
Chapman, Coleman W. 10
Madison 36
Maiden 7
Nancy 27

Charles, James M. 55
Chattin, J. D. 46
Chavis, Margaret 66
Chesnut, Mary Ann 45
Childers, George W.
(Childress) 42
Childres, Josiah 8
Childress, George W. (see
Childers)
Sarah Matilda 51
Chisnut, Wm. S. 87
Choate, Emery 44
Chrisman, A. J. 72
Isaac 67
Christian, Allen 46
Eliza 4
James 4
Churn, Sarah A. 18
Cicils, Mary 57
Clam, Polly 8
Clark, A. J. 88
Andrew J. 71
Dorothy 73
Gabriel 80
Isabel 44
James M. 96
John 33
Jdhn F. 4
John W. 67
Lotty Ann 72
Mary E. 29
Nancy 7
Peter 3
Sarah 49
William B. 69
Cleage, Sarah E. 65
Thos. A. 82
Clementson, John 69
Clemmons, Sarah 2
Clemonson, Mary Ann 17
Clemontson, Sarah Jane 9
Clerits, John 58
Cline, Margaret 83
Cloud, Elizabeth 61
Patsy 32
Sarah 8
Usly 16
Coats, Aby 2
Albia 3
Jasper 92
Lucianah 79
Mary S. 73
Thomas 77
Cobb, Angeline 85
C. W. 42
George 5
J. B. 66
Jesse M. 70
Joseph 35
Julia C. 32
Martha Ann 42
R. B. 34
Cobbs, Mary 19
Mary Elizabeth 76
Nancy 64
Cochran, Robert E. 22
Coe, Elizabeth 4, 5
Coffee, James O. 62
Juduth C. 88
Cofer, Elizabeth 27
Nancy 16
Coffey, Asbury M. 2
Robert 71
Coffman, Abner L. 29
Albert 38
Anderson 29
David H. 43
G. P. L. 20

Cofman, A. N. 39
Lucy 49
Cogghill, Mary L. 55
Cold, Philip 31
Cole, John 51
Joseph 24
Sarah 96
Solomon 29
Coleman, Ann E. 24
Charles F. 26
Harriet C. 57
J. D. 93
James U. 18
Colier, Eliza 16
James M. 59
Colin, Banister 7
Collier, Jane 24
M. J. 90
Mary Ann 9
Sarah 38
Susan 10
Collins, A. M. 83
Alfred M. 44
Eliza A. 74
J. B. 57
Jacob M. 45
Larkin 41
Margaret 80
Nancy 85
William 8
Colthorp, G. H. 95
Colvill, Katherine 17
Colville, John 21
John H. 29
Sally 40
Colwell, Marthy 2
Colvell, Nancy I. 75
Combs, Gideon 21
James M. 79
Mary J. 83
Conner, Mary T. 77
Peggy 9
Cook, Elisabeth 39
Eliza Jane 81
Elizabeth 20, 51
Jane 20
Martin 47
Mary 21
Mary E. 87
Samuel 49
Thomas J. 97
Wm. H. 86
Cooke, Attaline 37
Eliza 77
George W. 18
Margaret 65
Melvina 92
S. M. 21
Susan 46
Cooley, Andrew 40
Lidia 40
Martha 89
Cooper, Bennett 96
E. J. 18
Elmira 71
Frances M. 73
Hiram 2
Lucinda 23
Mary E. 89
Mary V. 70
Nancy 86
Copeland, Charles P. 17
Elizabeth 61
Elizabeth Ann 57
Emily 41
John J. 45
Wm. P. 19
Coppet, Alfred 70

Corey, John 55
Correy, Almina 53
Corrigan, James M. 45
Corsey, John 62
Cotter, Eliza White 12
Cottharp, A. J. 84
Couch, Elizabeth 38
Joseph 20
Mary 26
Sarah 29
Couldwell, Elizabeth 64
Courtney, Charlotte R. 44
John M. 19
Couson, Andrew 88
Couing, Joseph 75
Cowan, David 3
Wm. S. 3
Cowden, Martha 73
Cox, Alexander F. 59
Ansta 64
Benjamin 3
Elisha 19
Eliza 8
Hiram 34
Susan R. 66
Coxey, R. 60
Crabtree, Anis 51
Percilia 64
Rece 93
Thomas 19
Cracy, John N. 30
Craige, Milly 47
Crawford, Amanda 37
James 52
John 95
John C. 46
Malissa B. 41
Martha 89
Matilda 33
Matilda A. 92
S. K. 15
Susan 52
Thomas 13
Crawley, Elisha 50
Creasman, James M. 54
Joseph H. 77
Samuel D. 74
Sarah 90
Creevs, Elizabeth 27
Cregg, Anna 12
Crenell, Onslow G. 59
Cretendon, James 75
Crewes, Harriet M. 78
Crewse, Johnson 28
Crisman, Elizabeth 40
Wilbert 48
Crisp, Elvira 25
John 16
Nancy Manerva 41
Susannah 26
Crittenden, George W. 28
James F. 64
Josephine 88
Louisa Jane 86
Nancy 72
Nathaniel 1
Sarah Ann 51
W. R. 78
Crocket Eliza J. 90
Rebecca 64
Crockett, J. H. 92
Josiah F. 65
Nelson M. 77
William H. 17
Cromwell, James S. 3
John B. 3
Criplin, Rebeckah 67
Cross, Mahala 15

Cross (cont.)
Wm. W. 86
Crossland, John 1
Crouch, L. W. 91
Sarah 17
Crow, Adolphus H. 32
Benjamin S. 5
Catharine 4
Sarah M. 91
Susan 58
Crowder, R. P. 96
Crowell, Izerael E. 3
Crows, Nancy 28
Cruse, Iraanah 61
John 32
Crutchfield, Hiram 97
Mary Jane 16
Cry, Margaret L. 61
Polly 59
Sarah 84
Crysock, Frederick 3
Culpepper, F. M. 95
G. W. 12
J. A. 83
J. T. 72
Joseph I. 41
Mariah J. 88
Mary M. 81
W. 52
Culton, Alexander 21
Ursula 24
Cunningham, Amanda 36
Charity 32
David B. 62
Ellen Levina 45
Jane 59
John 79
Malinda 63
Mary A. 69
Moses 58
Nancy 7
Sarah D. 50
Thos. W. 26
Cusp, John 16
Dake, Henry J. 51
Jackson G. 18
Joseph M. 1
Sarah C. 21
Daniel, Mary O. 28
Darr, Vina 43
Daugherty, Eliza Jane 39
Jas. M. 88
John D. 88
Mary 90
William 44
Daves, Hueston 90
David, Henry B. 10
Davis, Ann L. 4
Benjamin C. 18
Campbell 71
Cassa 2
Eliza 13
Elizabeth 90
G. C. 81
H. M. 37
I. T. 40
J. W. 67
James W. 67
John W. 19, 72
Jucilla 20
Martha R. 68
Mary 10
Mary C. 33
Pamelia 89
Rachel 18
Rebecca 8, 71, 97
Rector 61
Sarah 39

103

Davis (cont.)
Safira 64
Thomas W. 66
William 53
William Y. 73
Dawson, James M. 12
Day, Hiram 24
Deadrick, Margaretta
Amanda 84
Mary M. 90
Deam, James A. 56
Dean, Aaron 53
Charlotte Craven 1
Polly Ann 74
Russell 74
Dearin, Lorinda 46
Dearman, Thos. B. 49
Dearmon, Easter 24
William B. 21
Deaton, Ellen H. 71
Levy 87
Malinda 94, 95
Sarah O. 36
William 44
Deavenport, George 87
Decker, Dorcas Ann 67
Geo. 75
Wm. 88
Delay, Anna Caroline 7
Dellon, Emily 29
Dely, Debora A. 83
Delzell, John N. 21
Dennis, Charles 31
Isaac 85
Isham 83
James D. 17
Joel 52
Mark 75, 80
Mary 85
Mary A. 30
Nancy 31
Rachel E. 87
Samuel 68
Telmon 7
William 44
Densan, John 80
Densom, Thos. 80
Denton, John 84
Martha A. 95
Patton 84
Deputy, James 5
Derrick, A. G. 35
Elizabeth M. 36
Frastus L. 74
Jwanona 65
Mary 42
Sarah 19
Susan 25
Desham, Margarette 1
Detherage, Rebecca 7
Detherow, Nancy 48
Sarah 48
Sarah Ann 70
Dethro, Amanda C. 54
Lorene 66
Dethroe, Mary Elizabeth
39
Detmore, Eliza 14
John 14
Devault, William 14
Dickard, Emily E. 16
Dicks, Polly Ann 6
Dickson, Isabella 19
Dill, Harrison 54
Dillard, John 11
Dillean, Rhue H. 89
Dillon, Sarah E. 94
Discon, Miller M. 89

Ditmore, John 4
Mary 4
Vincent G. 7
Divine, Jemima 51
Dixon, Edom 68
Eli 26, 45
Elizabeth 1
Elizabeth C. 67
Franklin A. 67
James H. 78
John 45, 62
John J. 92
John T. 36
Mary 16
Miram 85
Nancy L. 54
S. M. 95
S. W. 79
Thomas 49
William 17
Wm. M. 96
Doan, Absolom H. 27
Rachel A. 68
Dobbins, Sarah 48
Dobbs, Daniel 45
Eva 30
Jarusha 24
Lide W. 31
Pamela 22
Parris L. 43
Polly Jenny 10
Prior 96
William W. 44
Dobkins, Rebecca 74
Dobson, Margaret 52
Dockery, Sarah 51
William 16
Dodd, Berry 16
Lang R. 79
William 43
Dodson, C. A. 38
Elijah 1
Elisabeth 40
Eliza Jane 55
Elizabeth 2
Elizabeth Ann 61
Francis 35
Jefferson 4
Jesse 2
Jesse B. 26
Jesse W. 58
Jessie 52
John 4, 5
L. B. 72
Lazarus 55
Marcellus M. 28
Margaret P. 73
Martha 31
Mary Jane 42
McMillan 50
Nancy W. 28
Nimrod 29
Rebecca K. 25
Salena 80
Sarah W. 22
Wellford 72
Dogherty, S. M. 65
Dolan, Jane 85
Donahoo, Irvan 2
Dooley, Nancy E. 85
Dorcy, McCamy N. 28
Dorherty, Nancy 55
Serene 57
Dorsey, Demmon 9
Jonathan 56
Martha 11
McKany W. 89
Mecayah 11

Dorsey (cont.)
Nancy 54
Nancy W. 8
Sarah D. 50
Doss, Charlotte Temple 54
Frances 46
James L. 59
John 45
Mary 40
William 53
Dotherroe, Ataline 81
Dotson, Alfred 15
Allen 18
Edmund 15
George 11
Jane 96
Dougherty, Charlotte 25
Julia 23
Sarah 26
Douglas, E. C. 89
Elizabeth J. 46
John 40
Mary 59
Sarah 50
Douglass, Julia A. 84
Mary 23
Susan 66
Douthil, Samuel 37
Drake, John 23
Duckworth, Hopy 52
L. J. 91
Mailstill 82
Martha A. 68
Thos. N. 85
William 66
Duff, Mahala 51
Dugan, James H. 28
Leantine 87
Mariah 65
Robert 3, 3
Wilson 9
Wm. A. 71
Duggan, A. M. 76
Dugger, James 18
Mary E. 74
Duglass, James 3
Duke, Juliet 5
William 24
Dunn, Joseph 2
Durham, William D. 25
Dy, Artimelia 58
Dye, Judy 46
Robert 54
Thos. 46
Dyer, Cealy Ann 16
Eveline 34
James 7
Nancy 76
Sarah Elizabeth 50
Eadens, Margaret 85
Eakin, Elizabeth J. 81
Eakins, Allen 67
Eaten, Matilda 11
Eaton, C. H. 50
Eli A. 40
Henry J. 49
James T. 32
Jane 44
Mary C. 95
William 27
Eatons, James 79
Eaves, James 60
Eddington, Eliza Jane 47
Eden, Clarinda 28
Edens, F. M. 40
James 45
Jane 20
Edgemon, Samuel 29

Edgmon, Margaret 81
Edington, A. C. 82
Edmissons, Saml 4
Edmondson, Samuel 7
Edwards, Eliza 13
  Fletcher 3, 4
  John 2
  Nancy 2
  William 13, 16
Edwinten, Peter 66
Effert, J. H. 50
Elbert, Mary N. 58
Elder, Mary W. 80
  Nancy 48
  Robert 19, 53
  Susan H. 72
Eldredge, Joseph 43
Eldridge, Benjamin 47
  James F. 35
Eldridge, Susan 41
Eliott, Elisabeth 48
Elliot, Elizabeth 14
  F. M. 90
  Jemima 17
  Jessie 50
Elliott, Elizabeth A. 87
  John 28
  Letty 65
  M. R. 52
  Margaret E. 61
  Nancy 41, 83
  P. B. 33
  Thomas 45
  Thomas W. 45
Ellis, A. B. 16
  Allen 51
  Amanda L. 66
  Angeline 19
  Benjamin A. 51
  Dicy 18
  Elizabeth Ann 66
  James 43
  Jeremiah B. 60
  John M. 27
  Manada 53
  Manerva 87
  Margaret 94, 94
  Nancy Jane 59
  Philip 11
  Samantha 64
Ellison, Barbay 38
  James 5
  Jane 10
Elmore, William 54
Embree, Jonathan H. 53
Emerson, Caroline 65
  Henry 28
  J. W. 48
  Nancy 19
  William 55
  Wm. 81
Emery, Caroline 58
  Elizabeth 56
  James 53
  Silas 24
Emmerson, Debby 11
  Delila 46
  Mary 86
Emory, Harriet 29
England, Edward 64
Engledow, Richard T. 25
Ensminger, Sarah E. 72
  Virginia A. 79
Epperson, John L. 74
Erkerson, Allemarmda 80
Erreton, E. R. 79
Errickson, Harriet 59
  Jacob K. 20

Errickson (cont.)
  Johnson 57
  P. 59
Erskin, Eliza 24
  Nancy 22
Ervin, Isaac N. 14
Erwin, Benjamin 1
  Catharine 1
  John 3
  John R. 83
  Joseph D. 80
  Kejiah 66
  Lewis 38
  Lewis S. 86
  Mary Jane 56
  Wm. B. 81
Esmon, Margaret 9
Etter, Mary Ann 72
  Valentine 84
Evans, Elizabeth 2
  Harris 73
  Lucinda 58
  Nancy J. 72
  R. M. 86
Everett, John W. D. 73
Everton, Alexander 70
  Ann 26
  Hannah R. 86
Ewing, Saml. A. 5
Fagan, William S. 10
Fair, Edny 30
  Elizabeth 31
Fairbanks, Mary 30
Faire, Martin 45
Fairell, Elizabeth J. 44
Falkner, James 58
  Nancy 36
Fannon, Nathaniel 8
Fantz, Mary A. 86
Farles, Samuel 62
Farmer, Isham W. 23
  Jesse 1
Farner, Coonrod 1
  Sarah 2
Farrell, T. L. 70
Farris, Isbell 30
  Jeremiah 10
  Pleasant M. 7
Faugevar, R. J. 91
Faulkner, Ann 25
  Nancy 69
Feckers, John E. 64
Fellaynor, Fourris 21
Felyeer, John 60
Fennell, George W. 13
Ferguson, Ann 10
  Ede 31
  John 17
  John P. 47
  L. C. 86
  S. H. 86
Ferrell, Martha C. 42
Ferryman, W. R. 69
Fetzel, L. M. 64
Fick, John B. 64
Fields, Dudley 23
  Elizabeth 5
  Lucinda 43
  Malinda 85
  Mary 3, 40
  Nancy 2
Fifer, John P. 93
Filio, Mary J. 87
Finney, James 52
Firestone, David 3
  Elizabeth 3
  Mary 49
  Mary A. 93

Firestone (cont.)
  Prusila 92
  Sarah 65
  Sarah A. 94, 94
  Tilathea T. 86
Fisher, Adarcus 91
  Ann T. 30
  Jacob 67
  John A. S. 55
  Julia A. 82
  Margaret 88
  Rebecca 44
  Richard M. 28
  Ruhanny 27
  Virginia 67
Fitch, George 84
  John 88, 91
  Joseph 96
  Rody A. 96
  Theby 83
Fitchgerald, James Y. 64
Fite, Peter 5
Fitzgerald, Esther S. 60
  Jabez 27
  John R. 34
  Mary C. 62
  Sarah E. 27
Flatford, Elizabeth 47
Fleming, Elizabeth 93
  Thos. 90
Flinn, E. M. 64
  Eliza 40
  Jesse W. 45
Floyd, Lucy Ann 39
Ford, Martha J. 72
  Mary Ann 25
  Micajah 65
  Nimrod 41
  Rinda 69
  Sarah 21
  William 28
Fore, Wm. L. 94
Foreman, Bark 1
Forest, Sarah C. 80
Forester, Melvina 82
Forgey, Nancy E. 97
Forgg, Sarah 12
Forgy, John T. 25
  Mary (Mrs.) 52
Forister, Lydiann 91
Forrest, James 59
  Rachel C. 38
Fort, Augustine P. 4
  Mary 56
Foster, Andrew 34, 60
  Catherine 41
  Chrisley 87
  Chrisley A. 88
  Elizabeth 7, 48, 72
  Elizabeth Ann 64
  John R. 58
  Lucinda 54
  Malinda 51
  Mary Ann 60
  Nancy Jane 55
  Oliver P. 23
  Sarah 67
  Sarah J. 73
  Wm. 51
  Wm. S. 35
Fowler, Mary 60
  Rebecca 23
Fox, Daniel 40
  Maranda 36
  Mary 12
  Nancy 5
  Rebecca 22
Frank, Matilda N. 83

Frank (cont.)
  Sarah J. 73
Franklin, Catherine 45
  Esom 10
  John S. 9
  Jonathan F. 38
  Lewey Ann 12
  Lucy F. 69
  Martha Jane 39
  Martha S. 79
Frazer, Lorenzo D. 13
Frazier, Nancy 14
  Permelia 36
  Philip 36
  Rebeckah 21
Freeman, William H. 27
Frizzell, Martha J. 59
Frost, John 14
Fry, Anna Jane 41
  David G. 34
  Eliza Ann 43
  G. W. 41
  Harvy 84
  Harvey 46
  John W. 78
  Joseph M. 57
  Sarah A. 96
  Sarah K. 49
  Sidney Jane 68
Fuguway, Harriet 83
Fulgam, Becksey 42
Fulton, W. C. 82
Furgerson, Martha E. 87
Fyffe, Elizabeth J. 3
  Isaac W. 93
Fyke, Ann 16
Gage, Nancy 59
  Sarah 53
Gallahan, Robert 22
Gallaher, Gainey M. 55
  James M. 19
  John 20
  Mary Ann 30
Gallahon, George W. 21
Gallant, Francis 69
  John 67
  Mary 18
  Nancy 72
Galleon, Elizabeth 37
Galloway, Sely 5
  Thomas 49
Gamble, Louisa Minerva 74
  Patton L. 62
  Rebecca A. 31
Gammon, Rebecca W. 37
Gandd, M. A. 81
Gant, I. Hamilton 57
Garland, Eliza 21
  Elizabeth C. 90
  John R. 18
Garreson, Mary 25
Garrison, Isaiah 54, 67
  Jane 78
Gass, Thos. H. 67
Gaston, Elizabeth 17
Gaut, George W. 8
  John C. 14
  Manerva 86
Gee, John 1
  John J. 63
  Jonathan 70
Geffey, Cornelius 83
Gentry, Nancy 26
  Samuel 25
  William J. 45
George, John C. 60
  Mary E. 78
  Nancy 50

Gerald, Elijah F. 18
Gettys, Ann M. 28
  Eliza J. 71
  Margaret D. 50
Ghaston, Wesley 50
Gibany, Jane 90
Gibbony, Annabelle 97
Gibbs, A. S. 34
  C. B. 34
  Emily 84
  Flemmings G. 44
  James 78
  Martha J. 73
  William E. 68
  William H. 29
Gibson, Elisabeth 48
  Elisha S. 72
  I. J. 77
  Jas. G. 87
  John G. 72
  Joseph W. 34
  Malinda C. 23
  Mary Ann 77
  Naomy 34
  Pleasant B. 52
  Saml. P. 78
  T. F. 74
  William 6
  William Y. 48
Gilbert, Bernhart 94
  Delila 69
  Marcus 51
  Maryann 35
  Solomon 69
Gilbreath, Joseph 57
  Samuel 64
  Sarah J. 18
Giles, Calvin 37
  Houston 52
  Luramy S. 56
Gillespie, David E. 65
Gilley, Catharine 83
  James 29
Gillian, Lorenzo Dow 16
Gillingwaters, Elijah 3
Gilly, Eliza A. 75
  John 76
  Samuel 59
Gilton, Eliza C. 35
Ginon, James 34
Ginow, John 76
Gipson, B. A. 82
  M. J. 82
  Samuel U. P. 82
Givins, Jesse 49
Glace, Mary 65
Glaize, Elizabeth 55
Glase, Henry 15
Glass, Caroline 60
  John 37
  Selia Emley 60
Glaze, B. G. 82
  Emeline 32
  Jefferson 65
  William 13
Godard, Harriet C. 79
  Jame M. 91
  Jane M. 91
  M. B. 90
  Mary Ann 40
Goddard, Elizabeth C. 22
Goforth, Drury 76
  Henry 16
  Miles 68
Goins, Elizabeth A. 90
  N. A. 35
Golbert, Edmond 81
Gold, Martin 22

Golden, Abraham 2
  Caswell 18
Gollahon, Frishy(?) J. 48
Gonce, Abraham 2
Good, Richard T. 11
Goode, Eliza 11
  Lucinda 8
Goodner, John 38
Goodwin, Barbary 80
  John S. 23
  Louisa 77
Goolsby, John 86
Gordan, Thomas W. 15
Gorden, Nancy 9
Gordon, John 74
  William 53
Gore, Anna R. 46
  John E. 73
  Nancy 62
Gorman, David H. 16
Goss, Elizabeth 34
  Marg 27
Grady, Eliza Ann 62
  Margaret 59
Graham, Elijah 25
Grant, William 15
Graves, A. J. 85
  Christifer 61
  Christopher 70
  Elizabeth 63
  J. H. 88
  Lucinda 18
  Margaret A. 58
  Nancy 87
  Sarah 53
  Vilana 47
  William 12, 15
Gray, Elizabeth 27
  Milly 28
Gray N(?), Amanda 30
Grayson, Mary C. 92
  Sarah Ann 38
Green, David 46
  Delila 10
  Easter 19
  Elmy 78
  Frederick 24
  George W. 85
  Jacob 26
  James 87
  James D. 76
  Jane 66
  John 28
  John A. 60
  Letitia 18
  Malinda 3, 17
  Martha 24
  Martha A. 85
  Philmer W. 66
  Rufus 16, 27
  William B. 5
  William J. 62
Greene, Catharine L. 73
Greenway, Harriet E. 46
  Sarahann 41
Greenwood, Beverly 8
  Lucy 7
Gregg, Mable 31
  Robert W. 55
  Samuel 85
  Sarah 22
Gregory, Benjamin 88
  Charlotte A. 22
  Elizabeth 7
  Elmer 87
  James 41
  James F. H. 91
  John 23

Gregory (cont.)
Jothan 7
Martha 73
Mary 44
Matilda 46
Minnda 35
Sarah 81
Tapley 31
William E. 62
Gresham, James 5
Jesse 5
William T. 2
Griffey, John 96
Griffin, John P. 85
Robert H. 82
William 4
Griffith, Clarissa 56
John W. 39
Margaret 64
William 39
Griffitts, Delaney 64
Emanuel 94, 94
Grigg, Eunice 54
Jesse R. 60
Nelson 47
Grigsby, Elizabeth 92
James 1
Margaret Ann 29
Rebecca 75
Thomas 97
Grills, Slark D. P.(?)
73
Grisham, Elizabeth 8, 67
Ellen 32
James 46
Jane 33
Jessie, Sr. 56
John 14, 38, 47, 50
Looney 29
M. V. 95
Marion 14
Mary J. 69
Polly 62
Grogan, David 78
Grubb, John 47
Margaret 70
Mary 63
Guffey, Clarissa E. 76
Elizabeth C. 59
Thos. F. 90
Guffy, Clive 30
Francis J. 77
John 39
Joseph A. 95
Gulleage, Sarah Ann 9
Gulliage, Sarah Ann 15
Gulls, Mary E. 40
Gunter, Susannah 54
Guthery, Elizabeth 65
Judieth A. 80
Guthey, C. H. 40
Marha(?) 73
Guthrey, Catharine 91
Guthrie, Elizabeth 44
Thomas 4
Gwinn, Matthew 36
Gyerris, John 13
Hacker, F. E. 67
Hackler, Katherine 7
Susanah 15
Hackrider, Mary 54
Hadin, Huldah H. 67
Hafely, William 29
Hafly, Frankford W. 31
Haggard, James 61
Jane 85
Josephine 81
Hahan, Mary 73

Hail, Martha 62
Hailly, Samuel H. 82
Hale, Caleb G. 48
Churchwell 22
Elizabeth 20, 68
J. H. 91
John G. 69
M. J. 51
Mark 37
Haley, Charles 43
John 22
Hall, Catherine 42
James 25, 53
Leremiah 53
Louisa Jane 48
O. P. 67
Samuel 46
Hambrick, Celia 79
Emaline 85
James 50
Lucinda 2
Narcissa 36
Thena 95
Hambright, Malissa 35
Sarah M. 79
William S. 10
Hamby, Margaret E. 80
Hame, Joseph 43
Hamelton, David J. 88
Hamilton, John L. 83
Margaret 83
Martha J. 88
Mary 92
Robt. K. 6
Hammer, Elizabeth 21
Hammond, William W. 60
Hammontree, Mary 20
Hampton, Elizabeth 87
Jane 53
Lucinda 92
Nancy 33
Nearva 83
R. F. 35
Rebecca 54
Wm. 89
Hannah, James 75
Hamreck, Olivia 71
Hamrick, R. M. 73
Hance, Margaret A. 92
Handly, Geo. W. 65
Mary P. 35
Haney, C. 96
Eliza Jane 38
Emanuel 54
G. W. 30
George W. 30
J. L. 90
John J. 39
Manervia 45
Nancy 43, 92
Thomas 43
Hank, Elizabeth 20
Hankins, Andrew M. 18
Hanks, Alfred 19
Elizabeth 64
Jonathan 13
Hannah, Jane 23
Hansy, Mary B. 80
Harden, Louisa 11
Tabitha 53
William G. 64
Hardin, Anios 90
Josiah R. 51
Martha 92
Mary J. 86
Peggy 5
Hardy, Anna 9
Martha 56

Hardy (cont.)
Mary 56
Samuel, Jr. 61
Susan 28
Harkrider, Reece 20
Sarrah 4
Harles, Margaret C. 87
Harless, Eliza T. 36
Lurena E. 59
Harmon, Elmira 92
Orinda 18
Rebecca 8
Harrel, Enoch 32
Moses 72
William 69
Harris, Andrew 17
Charles 10
David L. 43
Elizabeth 12
Henry 47
John 46, 65
John B. 22
Lucinda 34
Minerva J. 70
Nancy Ann 64
Samuel B. 63
Zeporah 34
Harrod, Jourdan 79
Lucy 93
William 15
Wm. M. 90
Hart, Elizabeth 76
John 83
Maredeth 33
Polly 9
Wm. M. 58
Hartly, Marinda 21
Harwell, Alexander B. 73
Hass, Montgomery (Hess)
43
Hauce, Samuel 55
Hawk, J. H. 37
M. A. W. 50
T. W. M. 89
Hawkins, Jane 3
Joseph J. 69
Mary 6
Hawks, John 59
Mary E. 74
Hay, James 43
Hayden, Charles 66
Hayes, Absalem C. 11
Absolem C. 2
Emily 11
Isham 58
L. L. 35
Martha 11
Sarah 58
Hayl, Moses 43
Hayley, Allen 8
Haymes, Elizabeth 13
Nancy 54
Pamelia 9
William W. 13
Haynes, James P. 61
John E. 10
Vincent 39
Haynie, Ann A. 76
G. W. 75
Hessol P. 10
Susan 10
Hays, James 25
Margora 41
Mary Ann 30
William 17
Haze, Jas. R. 88
Mary 85
Robert R. 86

Haze (cont.)
Wm. H. 85
Head, Martha Ann 45
Heard, Glaphrey 24
Minerva 4
Heath, John S. 2
Heck, Elizabeth 22
James 56
Rachel A. C. 73
Heddington, Worden C. P.
E. 77
Heddleston, Wm. W. 30
Hedrick, Lidy 1
Heenysheys, Mira 39
Hegdon, Amanda 13
Heiskell, Wm. M. 69
Hellan, Ransom 80
Hellenns, Eli 80
Hellum, Ann 10
Hellums, Rebecca 10
Helms, Martha Jane 46
Nancy Ann 46
Zelpha 86
Helums, Sarah J. 69
Helvey, Daniel M. 6
Helvy, Ann 27
Daniel M. 7
Hemphill, Thomas 29
William A. 56
Henderson, Alexander 49
Benjamin F. 24
Elias 32
Elizabeth 29
Emaline 11
F. S. 22
James 78
Margaret 46
Martha 1
Mary 15, 62
S. P. 71
William 59
Henley, Thomas C. 42
Henly, Frances 46
W. C. 32
Henry, Margaret 60
Sally 91
Henson, Elizabeth 44
Herald, Elizabeth 38
Patsy 10
Herd, Eliza 32
Herdin, Joseph 4
Heron, Mary J. 79
Herrell, Lydia 92
Hess, Margaret C. 37
Montgomery (see Hass)
Phillip 37
Hester, James 33
Nancy A. C. 72
Hetterbrand, Eliza 43
Hickel, Parthena 59
Hickey, James 60
Nancy E. 39
R. H. 38
Hickman, Elizabeth Jane
49
P. M. M. 38
Hickon, Richard S. 63
Hicks, Abel (see Hix)
Arsley 4
Elizabeth 80
Hannah 88
Jas. M. 47
Joseph 12
Matilda 52
Thomas 60
William 43
William (Hix) 55
Wm. H. 88

Hickson, Lemira Jane 54
Higdon, John 47
Nancy 44
Noah 40
Higgins, Mary A. 20
Hill, Elisabeth 41
James F. 7
Lucinda 7
Nancy 71
Stephen 54
Sterling 54
Hillard, Jane 29
Hinkle, John 20
Hinkler, Catherine 40
Hirst, H. J. 63
Hitchcock, William 8
Hix, Abel (Hicks) 69
Douthet 71
John 36
John B. 71
Leonard 40
Margaret 28
Merady 1
William (see Hicks)
Hoback, Dorthula 62
Susan 96
Hogan, Thomas M. 35
William 5
Hogs, Mary C. 53
Holback, Daniel 82
Holcomb, Daniel D. 80
Holden, Wm. 96
Holland, John 11
Holman, Buttean 11
Holmes, Margaret 18
Holt, Francis A. 39
Serena J. 12
Honery, Ann 75
Hood, Hathorn 24
Margaret 15
Margaret A. 12, 15
Hooser, Jefferson 28, 70
Hoozier, Amanda 48
Hornsby, James A. 57
Horton, Anna 42
Ecana D. 55
H. C. P. 71, 95
Joseph M. 87
Mahala 20
Wm. G. 51
Hotchkisson, Geo. 54
Hounsell, Susan 56
Hounshell, Nancy Ann 62
Housley, Anne 17
Hously, Mary 20
Tabitha 21
Houston, J. B. 81
Mary Ann 60
Howard, C. W. B. 37
Francis J. 85
J. W. 23, 72
Mary 63, 65
Nancy 19
Nancy L. 68
Susannah 27
Walter 45
William 29, 62
William H. 26
Wm. 16
Howel, Mary A. 54
Howell, James M. 3
Nancy A. E. 79
Samuel N. 87
Sipe 4
Hoyl, C. D. 91
C. R. 21
Caleb R. 60
John 4

Hoyl (cont.)
Narcissa 61
Susan C. 91
Susan O. 37
Sarah Cornelia 63
Huckaby, Anna 16
Huddleston, Sarah L. 42
Hudgens, Elizabeth 57
Hudgins, Eli 20
Wm. 78
Hudson, Roland 67
William C. 43
Huggins, Eliza J. 87
Hughes, C. M. 63
Geo. W. 51
James 55
Joseph 38
Joseph Eli 64
Lucy 61
Malisa Jane 38
Margaret 15
Samuel 32
Samuel B. 74, 89
Susan A. D. 70
William 68, 72
Hughs, Eliza 67
G. W. 32
John 66
Mary 29
Hull, Daniel 3
Wm. 47
Humphrey, Abigail 69
Crate 3
Norris 19
Thomas 2
Humphries, Sarah 81
Hunk, Susan 76
Hunnycut, John 7
Hunt, Catharine 71
David 75
Elizabeth 47, 75
Jesse A. 80
John M. 32
Judith 53
Mary Ann 62
Phebe 63
Sarah 43
Hunter, Mary J. 35
Hurst, Mary T. 87
Huse, Katherine 18
Hutsell, George M. 56
John E. 95
U. V. 90
Hutson, Sarah Jane 59
Hutton, Leonard W. 63
Hyden, Jessie A. 61
Iewin, Auma 82
Ingals, Peter 36
Ingram, Caleb M. 59
Sarah S. 62
Inman, John 34
Ireland, Roady 5
Irwin, Amanda 54
Isbell, Francis D. 66
L. M. 78
M. A. 34
Mary I. 35
Nancy M. 12
Sarah Elizabeth 57
Thomas M. 31
Isham, Mahala 76
Ruby 14
Ivans, Eliza Jane 81
Martha 80
Jack, V. H. 65
Wm. H. 20
Jacks, John 4
Jackson, Clarissa 95

Jackson (cont.)
Mary 3, 4
Peggyann 56
Washington 11
Jamerson, Evaline T. 25
James, Hiram 47
J. 82
Malinda 48
Mary J. 82
William G. 10
William M. 68
Wm. W. W. 78
Jameson, Jacob P. 73
Mary J. 34
Jamison, Eliza 44
Janeway, Isaac 71
Juna 52
Jarnagan, Sarah L. 49
Jarnagin, Amanda M. 31
Hamilton 19
Martha 21
Sarah J. 24
Jarnigan, Milton P. 68
Jenkins, Adison 40
Benjamin 96
J. B. 66
Mary Jane 57
Richard F. 78
Jimerson, Nancy B. 84
Jimmison, Rebecca E. 47
John, Benjamin 29
Rebecca R. M. 26
Robert 4
Sam'l 21
William 7, 15
Johnes, Jonathan 8
Johns, Ezekiel 84
Lydia 28
William 13
Johnson, Berry M. 68
Hutson 6
Jackson 7
James 63, 94
Jane 53
Jarrett 37
John C. 14
Joseph 85
Josiah 64
Lindley M. 33
Lucinda J. 31
Lycander N. 33
Madison 21
Malvina 80
Marcellis B. 37
Mary Ann I. F. 36
Mitchell 33
Nancy 95
Robert L. 8
Rubin 1
Susan 16, 37
Wm. 37, 82
Johnston, Andrew Jackson 50
Elizabeth J. 25
Elmadoras R. 58
William 50
Joines, Elizabeth 78
Jones, Delila E. 83
George 62
Hugh 52
James M. 22, 68
John 60
John T. 41
Joshua B. 25
Leathy 86
Martha 61, 73
Martha C. 91
Mary Ann 91

Jones (cont.)
N. C. 94
Nathaniel 75
R. D. 15
Sarah E. 35
Silas 75
T. W. 38
Thomas 14, 15
Thos. A. 84
Thomas H. 37
William M 63
Jordan, Columbus A. W. 50
Marena L. 5
Jourdin, Sarah S. 84
Joy, Edwin S. 27
Julian, Margaret 24
Robert P. 13
Samuel 14
Kahill, Margaret C. 96
Keaton, Matilda 15
Keelin, William 3
Keeling, Margaret 52
Keeton, Allen 17
Matilda 14
Keiker, Martha A. 80
Keith, Alexander 21
Elizabeth D. 64
Louisa J. 67
Sarah M. 34
Kelley, W. W. 81
Kelly, Daniel 5
Eliza 66
Emeline 33
James 28
Jas. 94
Lee Roy 65
Lina 53
Louisa M. 94
Mahala 94, 96
Malinda 45
Nathan 9
Richard 3
Richd. 4
Sue 95
Terry 11
Wm. 4
Kemp, Roselvim(?) 76
Kenman, Wesley 5
Kennedy, James B. 87
Louisa J. 68
Nancy M. 85
Ketron, Sally 33
Key, John 94
Kez, John 97
Kibble, Daniel 62
Elias 38
James 58
Rupey 10
Kigby, Absolom D. 18
Kiker, Andrew J. 68
Wm. F. 91
Kile, Hugh 16
Mary 42
Killingsworth, Elizabeth A. 21
Nancy 24
William 10
Kimbrough, Duke H. 87
Duke W. 74
Elisha (Kimbrow) 54
I. B. 74
John 78
Plisha (Kimbrow) 54
Sarah J. 86
Kimbrow, Elisha (see Kimbrough)
Plisha (see Kimbrough)

Kinchelo, Louisa 71
Pheoby 26
Polly 38
Julia A. 57
Mahala 22
Nancy 52
Kinchlow, Gemima 38
Kindrick, Tempee 95
King, E. F. 91
E. W. 76
Elizabeth 5
Elizabeth A. 23
George 5
Henry 13
James C. 93
James H. 1
Martha 15
Mary 30
Mary C. 46
Robert 44
Kinnian, James F. E. 21
Kinner, Elias H. 8
Kinser, Andrew A. 26
Elizabeth 38
James L. 53
John 31
Kinsor, Louisa 88
Kinzalow, Elmira 84
Kinzy, Henry M. C. 83
Kipps, Mary 13
Kirby, Calvin 39
George 58
John 76
Kirk, Daniel 13
Matthew S. 19
Kirklin, George 90
Kirkpatrick, Amelia 26
Caroline 27
Margaret Emaline 11
Mary A. 63
Kirksey, A. J. 80
John W. 15
Parthaney 5
Kiser, John 63
Kitchen, Harrison 95
Susan 76
William 4
Kitcher, Rebecca Ann 63
Kline, John L. 12
Knight, Mary A. 78
Knox, Elijah 39
Elizabeth 38
Henry H. 96
Jeremiah 53
John W. 35
Lidia Lucindy 51
Nathaniel 39
Samuel M. 40
Susanah 12
William 55
Wm. 95
Knoxx, Benjamin 36
Lacy, Esther 14
Lafferty, Mary A. E. 66
Lafforty, Eliza 39
Lamar, Aman 89
Mary 89
Sarah L. 90
Lamare, Rachel 58
Lambert, Cathrin 88
Z. T. 92
Lammons, Reuben 35
Lamor, Hannah 29
Land, James 94, 95
Landers, James 41
Luk 79
Luke 79
M. A. F. 96

Landers (cont.)
  Martha E. 97
Lane, Eldred 29
  John 4
  John F. 35, 96
  Patton 10
  Samuel 63
  Sarahann 34
  Sidney Ann 51
Langford, Gibson 29
  John W. 29
  Levil 3
  Robert 29
  William 61
Large, George 69
  James 62
  John W. 92
  Nancy Jane 69
Largent, McCamy 39
  Susan 33
  Susannah 58, 60
Largon, J. J. 57
Larrew, Keziah 2
Lasater, Wiley 40
Lasiter, Louiza J. 81
  Nancy A. 12
  Sarah Jane 31
Latham, Silas G. 78
Latimore, Samuel 3
Lattemore, Rachel 11
Lattimore, Orlenia 93
  Thomas 15
Lawson, Caldena 33
  Carrutt 76
  Charlotte 27
  David 73
  Elias 74
  Elizabeth 9
  James H. 84
  Jane 56
  Jeremiah 18
  Litty 55
  Louisa 28
  Louvicy 10
  Lucinda 2, 17
  Martha 56
  Mary Ann 43
  Nathan 10
  Nathaniel 72
  Nathanl 92
  Nelson 44
  Matilda 16
  Polly A. 32
  Sarah 55, 60
  Sarah M. 37
  Savanah 40
  Wm. L. 74
Lea, James (Lee) 29
  Major 5
  Prior 4
League, Joseph 45
Leamon, Sarah 94
Leaper, Drew 14
Leatherwood, John M. 90
Ledbetter, Lucus (see
    Ludbetter)
Lee, Edward 60
  Elizabeth 16, 35
  James (see Lea)
  John Sevier 11
  Pleasant N. 25
  Susan 25
  William 14
  Zilphia 36
Lemare, Mahaley 47
Lemmons, Houston 74, 74
  James 48
  Levi 4

Lemmons (cont.)
  Lien Anna 61
  Nancy 52
  P. M. 95
Lemon, G. W. 9
Lemons, F. J. 88
  Roberts 9
Lennox, Eliza Jane 42
Lenny, Rebecca 55
Lenoir, W. F. 22
Lenty, John R. 58
Levan, Joseph L. 18
Lewis, Burton 24
  Carroll C. 42
  David 83
  Emely 60
  George W. 68
  Isaac 68
  J. F. J. 89
  James 42, 56
  John 52, 62
  John A. 5
  Larkin 53
  Mary 51
  Oliver 65
  Patience 8
  Sarah 76
  Scyntha 32
  Susannah 18
  Thomas 59
Lide, Janett V. 29
Liece, S. G. (Rice) 91
Light, Mary 48
Lile, Elizabeth 40
  Martha Jane 46
Liles, Jamima 64
  John 88
  Martha 38
  Stephen 93
  Wm. 85
Lillard, Cintha Ann 62
  Mary L. 72
Liming, Chandler 20
Liner, E. C. 60
  James S. 27
  John W. 53
  Nancy E. 67
  Phebe J. 47
Linos, Clarrinda 44
Lipscomb, Margaret 18
Lirret, Rebecca 88
Little, Polly 59
Llarmer, Jefferson 35
Lockmiller, Jedson 92
Logan, Bloomfield 16
  Eglinetine 65
  Elizabeth 24
  Huldy 3
  Mary Ann 25
  Tebitha 96
  W. C. 92
  William 7
Lolleman, Caroline 35
Long, Albert D. 68
  Ann 36
  Casander 9
  Elizabeth 2, 30
  Elizabeth H. 12
  Isaac 46, 70
  J. A. 34
  James 46, 65
  Jane 37
  John H. 28
  John L. 8
  Joshua 86
  Levi 28
  Lidia 55
  Lourena 63

Long (cont.)
  Lusey 66
  Margaret 23
  Mary 10
  Moses 92
  Nancy 38
  Pleasant M. 30
  Rebecca 17
  Riley R. 77
  Robert 94
  Ruth 16
  T. M. 86
  William 67
  Wm. 78
  Wm. R. 48
  Wm. T. 78
Longforth, Henry 51
Lonley, James 2
Loomey, Theressa 53
Looper, Calvin 71
Lorgin, Lucinda 18
Lorison, William 3
Louder, George 37
Loughmer, Wm. H. 96
Loughmiller, Alfred 73
  Dorcus E. 61
  Elizabeth A. 58
  G. W. 72
  Geo. W. 61
  H. J. 73
  Hiram 18
  Mary Jane 77
Love, Elizabeth 17, 19
  John P. 76
  Mary 4
  Mary E. 91
Lovel, David 15
  John 17
Lover, Elizabeth 49
Low, Isaac 12
  Jacob 12
  Joshua 48
Lowden, Austin 36
  John 38
Lowe, Caroline 50
  Nathan 35, 70
Lower, Michael M. 48
Lowers, Katherine 15
Lowery, A. E. 91
  Harriet M. 84
  John D. 6
  John W. 84
  Matta 85
  P. C. 89
  R. A. 82
  T. J. 95
  Virginia M. 94, 95
  Willie 89
Lowry, A. A. 76
  A. M. 48
  Eliza J. 86
  Frances E. 67
  James H. 11
  James R. 72
  John D. 80
  Mary 3, 55
  Mary Jane 48
  Nancy J. 21
  Nancy L. 77
  P. 39
  Susan R. 80
  Thomas J. 30
Loyd, David P. 5
  Jane 26
  Mary 79
Luck, Abraham L. (Slack)
    65
Ludbetter, Lucus (Ledbetter)
    88

McCollum (cont.)
Margaret (see MCollum)
Sarah 77
McConnell, I. S. 5
Mary 37
McConnelly, Wm. (see MConnelly)
McCoy, Daniel 2
James 31
McCramy, Robert 67
McCrary, Martha 76
Nancy 50
Serelsey 85
McCray, Franky L. 47
McCroskey, D. P. 70
James S. 40
Sarah A. 86
McCrosky, Isaphena M. 61
McCuistian, Miles H. 90
McCuiston, Andrew J. 71
Miles H. 87
McCulley, Geo. M. 42
McCullum, Chas. 40
McCully, Elizabeth 12
George M. 91
McDaniel, Daniel 17
Mira 33
Nancy 49
Sarah C. 87
T. J. 82
W. J. 87
Wm. 64
McDeehan, Lydia (see McKeehan)
McDonald, Daniel 11
Lorency 7
Thomas M. 66
Virginia 56
William 3
McDonnell, Polly 4
McDougald, Katharine 7
McElden, W. W. 62
McElhaney, Ellen M. 64
Mary 64
McElhamy, Thomas N. 73
McEnturff, Thomas 57
McEwin, Robert N. 65
McGaughey, Margaret J. 87
McGaughey, Rebecca A. 77
McGeecie, Michael 36
McGehee, George W. 69
McGeho, Malinda 49
McGendey, Joseph 1
McGentry, John 26
McGhehan, Adaline 84
McGill, Walter M. 8
McGinley, John 25
McGinty, Elbert 68
John 72
Madison 63
Martha Katharine 51
McGoss, Lucindy 61
McGougal, Floyd 54
J. M. 60
McGrew, John H. 88
McGuire, Jackson 47
Letty 24
Mary 28
Nancy 57
Sarah 44
McInturf, John 87
McInturff, Mary Ann 55
Sarena Caroline 14
Susan C. 10
McKamy, Elizabeth J. 58
McKanbe, Alcary (McNabb) 60

McKeean, Rebecka 4
McKeehan, Ameline 64
Elbert S. 68
Elizabeth 64
George H. 63
James 69
Lydia (McDeehan) 25
Martha M. 77
McKehen, Amy A. 72
McKenzie, Charles 69
Christiam P. 62
Darcus 75
Elizabeth A. 57
Mary Jane 59
McKeown, William M. 68
McKnight, L. A. 81
McLester, William W. 25
McLin, William C. 12
McMahan, Mary 52
McMalenta, Mary L. 55
McMillan, Jane 75
John 31, 75
Joseph W. 62
Narcessa 3
R. A. 34
McMillaon, R. A. (McMillion) 78
McMillian, C. 92
McMillin, D. C. 29
J. W. 3
McMillion, R. A. (see McMillaon)
McMinn, Alzira 26
Chrisada 36
James 26
Nancy G. 12
McNabb, Alcary (see McKanbe)
Elizabeth 47, 76
Isaac H. 22
James 72
Mary 63
Matthew G. 43
Nathaniel 14
Nathanl 10
Rhoda T. 65
McNeilly, Isabella 78
McNelly, Robert 30
McNenny, John 10
McNutt, John A. 22
McPhail, John P. 89
Wm. D. 86
McPherson, Elizabeth 20, 64
McReynolds, Sarah A. 14
McRoy, Curtes 4
John 4
McSpadden, Jane 75
Mary E. 56
Saml 32
McVay, Joseph 2
McWhen, Sarah Ann 63
Meadows, James L. 55
Mechail, Elizabeth L. 8
Meigs, Theresa C. 5
Melins, Rebecca 45
Melton, Alfred 83
Armen(?) Jane 61
Calloway 35
Elisha 47, 51
Elizabeth 90
G. W. 72
Jesse 22
Mahala 42
Malinda 94, 95
Martha A. 81
Nathan 42
Rebecca 61

Melton (cont.)
Reuben 47
Robert 48
Sarah 44
Sarah C. 91
Stephen J. 70
Susannah 42
Thomas 59
William 54
Wright 72
Melvin, Elizabeth 2
Meredith, Quincy 79
Mesimores, Thomas 40
Metcalf, Amelia 25
E. A. 91
Thomas 9
Mezell, Samuel 73
Michael, Alexander 76
Frederick 44
Michaels, John 56
Middleton, H. D. 14
Rebecca 47
Miers, Marinda 9
Millard, Eliza S. 18
Miller, Armenia 29
Elisha 12
Elizabeth 32
Enoch 51
I. B. 39
Jackson 53
Jacob S. 30
Jemima 31
John 13, 22, 79
John F. 86
John G. 13
John W. 49
Katharine 37
Luke L. 43
Lydia E. 20
M. E. 63
Margaret 48
Mary 27
Mary A. 47, 86
Nancy 34, 63
Nancy C. 86
Paralee C. 35
Robert 24
Russell 58
Sarah Ann 78
Susan 43
Wm. W. 56
Millhight, Mary Jane 63
Million, Frances N. 76
George W. 19
Mills, Charles H. 56
Millsaps, Isabella 93
Lidia 62
Milton, Ailey 17
Edy 57
Mins, Margaret 64
Minsey, John M. 64
Minzes, Erwin S. 27
Mires, Margaret 4
Peggy Salina 11
Misemer, William B. 61
Mitchell, Currinda 92
Hazy 18
Julia A. 85
Laura A. 89
Lavesta 85
Salie H. 87
Mize, Daniel W. 82
Eell(?) 53
Henry Jackson 57
Henry W. 52
Rebecca Jane 81
Mizell, Eveline 35
James 34

Mizell (cont.)
Samuel 58
Mizer, John 18
Mizes, Isaac 7
Monger, John E. 25
Joseph 30
Monroe, Catherine 31
George 16, 78
James 63, 89
Lizer 62
Robert 3
Moon, Archibald R. 73
Elizabeth 69
Jacob 33
Lucy 33
Mary E. 74
Susannah 69
Moor, John P. 46
Moore, Allen 87
Caroline 11
Chas. 12
Chaw 16
Christen 31
George W. 27, 67
Henry 16, 85
James 85
Malissa 47
Mary 45, 77
Nancy 70
Narcissa 2
Nimrod 2
R. E. 64
Sarah 70
Sophia 44
Thomas P. 18
William 72
Wm. 85
Moose, Sarah B. 10
More, James 42
Moreland, James A. 52
Morgan, Chrokee A. 57
Delila 62
Eliza 68
George W. 52
Harry 38
Henry 56
John 54
John K. 55
Kaziah J. 24
Lydia 79
Mary 29
Mordecai H. 72
Rebecca 63
Saml. 4
Sarah E. 38
Silas 31
Wm. M. 71
Wm. R. 42
Wm. S. 82
Morris, Alfred W. 61
Eliza 9
Elizabeth 32
George W. 62
Isaac 43
John 4
Mariah J. 37
Martha 50
Martha J. 73
Melvina 29
Thomas 52
Morrison, S. A. 51
Morrow, H. J. 91
Mary J. 92, 95, 97
Sarah Ann 74
Morton, Joseph 2
Moss, B. H. 71
Clarissa 56
Hardy 85

Moss (cont.)
John R. 97
Rebecca 37
Sarah M. 97
Warren 32
Warren D. 61
William 49
Mouldin, James H. 9
Mulkey, Amanda 14
Mulvany, Mark 13
Murney, Stocia 69
Murphy, Celia 83
Jefferson D. 30
John 73
Robert 3
Murray, John H. 75
Mary 96
Murrell, C. G. 2
Emily L. 68
Murry, Darcus 87
Myers, Elizabeth C. 65
Elvira 28
James 48
John 22
Lithey L. 38
M. L. 36
Sydney Ann 75
Mynatt, Aalsay 73
Levista 72
Myrick, O. S. 33
Mysy, John 11
Nailo, Nancy M. 13
Nance, Jennett 39
Julian 33
Mary Ann 71
Payton T. 50
Naney, Matilda 45
Nanry, Sarah (Manry) 58
Napier, Nancy 2
Thomas N. 6
Nasom, Nancy 45
Nath, Mary M. C. 88
Nation, Elizabeth 50
Nations, Nancy 47
Rachel 41
William 44
Naves, John H. 18
Neal, Abraham B. 4
Katherine 19
Philip 89
Neel, Sarah E. 64
Neely, Wm. H. 64
Neil, John 81
John R. 49
Joseph 55
Neill, Elizabeth 77
Hamilton 75
Neils, C. E. 36
Nelson, Arthur 10
Henry 17
M. 77
Minerva 25
N. C. 77
Netherland, E. V. 94, 96
Virginia W. 69
Netherly, Julian W. 72
Newberry, Dorcus 17
Newcum, Eliza 89
Newkirk, Elizabeth Ann 41
Nancy 41
Newland, Mary 21
Sarah Ann 19, 20
Newman, Arthur 32
Clenton B. 44
Eliza 38
Eliza C. 63
Elizabeth 9
Emily C. 91

Newman (cont.)
Jacob P. 64
John 23, 80
John C. 75
Laura S. 24, 89
M. J. 34
Mary S. 12
Rebecca 28, 94, 94
Rebecca J. 87
Robert M. 35
Robert S. 68
Samuel 92
Sarah E. 78
Sarah F. 21
Sarah J. 75
Susannah 25
William H. 2
Newton, Arrena 33
Caroline 74
E. M. 37
Edward 94
G. W. 23
James A. 23
Jasper 64
Lucinda 13
Mahala 44
Malinda L. 60
Polly 46
Sarah 26
Thomas 9
William 20, 44
Nice, William G. 68
Nichols, Elizabeth 24
Thos. 49
Nickels, Elizabeth 62
Niel, David 28
Noel, Tebetha 14
Norman, Flemming S. 43
Nancy 28
North, Squire 32
Norvell, Martha J. 61
Norvill, C. L. 91
Norville, Eliza Jane 78
Novel, William 21
Norwell, Greenbery 48
Nunn, P. B. 70
ODaniel, William H. 72
Officer, James 2
Nancy 2
Ogle, Fany 23
Olden, Milly 38
Oliver, Elizabeth A. 31
Jas. M. 65
ONail, James 16
ONeal, Andrew 7
Laisens 11
Onich, Martin 30
Orick, Felix 89
Only, Martha 62
Mary E. 55
Orr, David G. 16
Delila 19
Nancy 2
Rachel 13
William 57
Orrick, Felix 67
Orten, Charles 38
John 76
Susan 30
Orton, Emeline 60
Mary 62
Overholser, Jacob 24
Owen, C. L. 69
James R. 71
James W. 26
Marshall C. 75
Martha 14
Mary 32, 69

Owen (cont.)
Mary J. 90
Thomas A. 55
W. C. 36
Owens, A. J. 87
Eliza 13
Elizabeth 9
Elizabeth S. 64
Harriet 33
Hayney 11
John 8
Martha 7
Nancy 69
Philip 9
S. E. 90
Owins, Haney 5
Pack, Andrew 5
Jeremiah 5
Timothy 8
Pain, Elizabeth E. 46
James 14
Pangle, Eli S. 35
Margaret 30, 30
Pangles, James 25
Paris, Elvey 66
Jerusha 77
John W. 74
Mary W. 60
Robert H. (Parris)
(Pharis) 57
Sarah 53
Stephen (Pharis) 23
Wm. 85
Parker, John I. 36
Louiza C. 88
Samuel H. 39
Parkeson, Daniel 25
Parkinson, Julia Ann 74
Parkison, James 17
Manuel 23
Polly 4
Parks, Elizabeth J. 69
Martha 76
Sarah A. 42
Parlinson, Nancy 43
Parrett, Thomas 38
Parris, Lucinda 26
Robert H. (see Paris)
William 41
Parryman, Elizabeth D.
10
Parshall, Elizabeth 52
J. G. 84
Parsons, Anna 57
George 35
Nancy 16
Thomas 14
Patrick, John 9
Patterson, Caroline 78
Elizabeth 52
Frederick 79
James E. 52
Polly 82
Samuel 80
Washington 9
Patton, Jane O. 60
John P. 34
Mary A. 69
Robert 96
Patty, Amanda E. 61
Edith 77
Elizabeth 15
George O. 24
I. R. 61
James M. 64
Josiah 51
Martha 6
Obed C. 18

Patty (cont.)
Owen West 51
R. J. 35
Sarah M. 71
Sarah N. 71
Susan J. 17
William H. 31
Paul, Mareda 67
Thomas T. 46
Payne, John J. 26
Madison 11
Mary 23
Uriah 33
Peace, Abigail A. 35
Peak, Buford 23
T. 15
Peake, Wm. C. 76
Pearce, Daniel 24
David 27, 58
David, Jr. 59
James 37
John L. 93
Louisa E. 59
Lucinda 85
Martha A. 95
Minerva 28
Nancy 4
Sarah 15
Sarah Jane 11
Pearman, Eliza 64
Henry 76
Mike 89
Susanah 80
Pearson, Eliza 16
Gazilda 70
Louisa 14
Mary J. 67
Nancy 43
Sherwood W. 4
Peck, Laura Jane 50
W. W. 73
William F. 32
Pendergast, Robert (see
Pendergrass)
Pendergrass, Robert
(Pendergast) 36
Penneon, McKarry 14
Pennington, David 14
F. M. 94, 95
J. O. 77
James 26
Nelson 39
Peoples, Caroline 39
Peper, G. M. 36
Perkins, James D. 67
Perrin, Lucinda 70
Perry, James 9
May 36
Pertileo, Emaline 11
Pesterfield, Elizabeth A.
69
Peters, Christian 4, 14,
32
Delila 12
Eliza 29
J. P. 96
Landon C. 21
Maryilla 34
N. I. 36
Phebe S. 12
Robert G. 15
Samuel A. 12
Susan 43
Petitt, Elijah 94
Elizabeth C. 52
Pettitt, Elijah 95
Pew, Rebecca 83
Pharis, Robert H. (see
Paris)

Pharis (cont.)
Stephen (see Paris)
Philips, Edward 92
Julian 28
Louesa 19
Thomas 70
Phillips, John C. 36
Martha 48
Thomas P. 50
Wm. 37
Philpot, William 41
Philpots, John 59
Pickens, Charles A. 17
Martha 14
Nancy 10
Pickins, Rebecca 4
Reese 4
Pickle, Lewis W. 77
Pierce, Amanda 85
Eliza J. 86
Ephraim 2
Joana 3
John 37
Josiah 22
Mary A. 84
Pike, Eliza M. 43
James W. 93
Mary 24
Pinda, John 80
Pitner, Eliza 5
Plank, James W. 30
Nancy 52
Plumlee, Daniel (see
Plumly)
Plumly, Daniel (Plumlee)
36
Poe, Daniel 10
Jane 36
John L. 63
Mariah 71
Stephenson 24
William 29, 58, 60
Poller, Uriah E. 83
Pope, Fielding 5
Porter, Ann A. 42
Eliza 73
Elizabeth Catharine 77
Harriet 57
John H. 3
Lusena J. 72
M. Ann 41
Mary D. 56
Narcissa 90
Robert W. 2
William S. S. 31
Power, Arlie E. 89
Wm. 91
Powers, David 21
G. H. 88
Malinda 93
Robert 48
Samuel 78
William 17
Prather, Fathamany 25
John A. 80
Wm. M. 76
Presley, Mary 85
Presly, Lucinda 33
Nancy 21
Presnell, Elias 4
Price, Edward 44
Jane 9
John 76
Martha 72
Prigmore, L. G. 32
Ruth K. 32
Prince, Catherine 41
Jackson 15

Prince (cont.)
James 35
Sandford 10
Printwood, John 36
Pritchard, Jas. 87
Proctor, Chas. A. 76
Proffat, B. A. 54
Proffet, Rebecca 19
Prophet, J. W. 68
Jane 60
Pry, John 79
Pugh, Elijah 23
Evaline 76
Jonathan F. 33
Josiah 50
Matheirsa 22
Nancy 57
Sarah 17
Purcell, William M. 52
Purdy, J. G. 94
Pusmon, A. 15
Queener, Elizabeth 15
George W. 11
James C. 19
Jnhn 31
Quinn, Morris O. 59
Rabay, Nancy A. 84
Rabourn, Joseph 4
Sarah 86
Raburn, Lucinda 68
Wm. 77
Ragan, William S. 69
Rains, Amanda 67
Ramsey, Lewis 25
Wm. B. A. 4
Ramsy, Edward 3
Ramy, Elizabeth 67
Randell, Jane 11
Randolph, G. C. 89
Gilbert 9
Gilmore 16
Harriet E. 88
Hezekiah 14
Malissa 45
Maranda 21
Robert 31
Sarah 3
Wm. 96
Ranins, John 24
Raper, John S. 30
Rather, Arminda 78
Ratledge, George L.
(Rutledge) 85
James 81
Jas. (Rutledge) 90
Ray, F. S. 76
Melvina 81
William 10
Rayborn, John 92
Rayburn, Elizabeth A. 28
Henry 59
James J. 54
Rawlings, Elijah 42
Reabourn, Eliza J. 90
Read, John H. 23
Mary 42
Reagan, Sarah E. 27
Reatherford, Adaline 85
Margaret 23
Silday M. 92
Reavely, Francis 88
Rector, Caroline 65
Coraline 65
Elijah 38
Maximillan 39
William W. 20, 20
Redfearn, Emiline 17
Reece, Frances M. 56

Reed, Elizabeth 33
James 46
Jane 36
Joseph 73
Loretta 96
Martha 54, 81
Mary 58
Nancy 1
Simeon 65
Reeding, Joseph 38
Reese, Sarah 43
Regan, Frances E. 74
Reggins, Hily 36
Reid, Ann 5
John 36
John S. 46
Reinhardt, Ephraim 5
Reneau, Louisa 32
Susan 31
William (see Reno)
Winney 78
Renfro, Nancy 33
Renfrow, Elizabeth 79
Reno, William (Reneau) 45
Rentfrel, Langden C. 43
Rentfro, Manda M. 8
Thomas 50
Wm. 81
Renue, Louisa C. 89
Reynolds, Charles L. 74
Eliza Ann 42
Elizabeth 42
Emaline 14
H. C. 35
Hannah 23
Humphrey 4
I. M. 41
James M. 80
John 76
Joseph C. 66
Lucy J. 82
M. G. 53
Molly 90
Montraville 39
Nancy Eveline 51
Pelina 35
Pleasant M. 31
Rebecca 66
Robert 42
Reyton, Benton 61
Rhea, James H. 21
Mary 46
Nancy 33
Rhoades, S. S. (see
Rhohdes)
Rhodes, William A. 50
Rhohdes, S. S. (Rhoades)
80
Rhom, Mahala 68
Rice, C. W. 32
Elizabeth 8
Henry 74
Jesse C. 95
M. W. 80
Martha 87
Mary Jane 70
Nancy P. 55
Orville 90
Ovrille 90
Rebecca Ann 92
S. G. (see Liece)
S. W. 91
Susan 43
W. L. 97
William J. 26
William L. 28
Richard, Adaline 84
Richards, Cinthia Malissa
50

Richards (cont.)
Eliza 62
Jane 20
Richardson, Jane M. 53
Tabitha Ann 52
Thomas L. 5
Richey, Silas H. 59
William 61
Rickey, William W. 64
Riddle, Anne 18
Benj. 44
Emeline 49
James 42
John M. 85
Martha 45
Miles H. 88
Pleasant 66
Sally C. 34
Samuel C. 21
Rider, Caroline 83
Rigg, Sarah 41
Riggins, Thomas 22
Riggs, Amanda J. 67
B. A. 90
Martha E. 88
Martin 87
Nanny 44
Rhoda 4
S. P. 41
Rily, Sarah Katharine 45
Rinker, Wm. 82
Ripley, Thomas C. 3
Ritchardson, Robert 2
Ritchey, Robert 84
Ritchie, John J. 46
Rivers, Mary Ann 47
Milley 42
Pleasant M. 27
Robbinett, John F. 65
Robert, Edmun D. 9
Roberts, Benjamin 27
Caroline 23
Catharine 22
David F. 75
E. W. 75
Edmond 52
Edmund 5
Elizabeth 2
Elizabeth H. 44
Hugh 66
James F. 78
Joel 49
Joseph 44
Lois 80
Margaret M. 91
Mary 20
Mary E. 79
Matthews 95
Peter 30
Sarahan 52
Sidney A. 39
Syphey 6
Tenesse 5
Teplecy 7
Thomas C. 34
William 33
William S. 26
Wm. E. 70
Robertson, Catherine 42
Glapha Ann 30
Joseph 61
Milton 56
Robeson, Edward W. 31
Emeline 34
Hiram 33
Jane 27, 35
Joseph 25
Margaret(?) 49

Robeson (cont.)
Mary Ann 30, 40
Nancy 19
Robinett, Hugh 83
May C. 95
Robinson, Mary 96
Nancy A. 47
Robison, Dempsey 51
Jane 48, 49
Mary C. 13
Synthy 10
Wm. S. 81
Roddair, N. J. 78
Rodden, Elizabeth 47
James M. 88
Sarah Emeline 65
Rodes, John 52
Roe, Easter 32
Susannah 59
Rogers, Andrew L. 57
E. E. 24
Eliza J. P. 72
Elizabeth 78
Henry 94
Hugh 36
James W. 21
Lawson W. 5
Leona A. 82
M. E. 84
Mary D. 94
Mildred 61
Nancy 30, 54
Sarah A. 82
Thos. 40
William S. 56
Roland, Abraham 7
Katherine 10
Rolin, Isaac 45
Rolling, Andrew 56
Rollings, Martha J. 21
Rollins, Mary 90
Romack, James 4
Romerus, Jane 24
Romine, Jonathan 8
Ronack, Margaret 52
Rose, Caroline 77
David 19, 20
Louisa 77
Samuel 83
William 74
Ross, Elizabeth 40
Rothrons, Jane 34
Rothwell, Lucy Ellen 77
M. C. 49
W. H. 22
Walter 27
Rowan, Francis M. 51
Keziah 39
M. M. 84
Rowland, Isaac 84
J. T. 67
Philip 86
Rowles, M. L. 24
Rowly, John A. 50
Royston, S. W. 52
Rucker, James 7
James C. 56
James H. 89
Jas. M. 75
Jesse 35
Mary C. 55
Milly 5
Nancy C. 58
Polly 22
Rachael M. 45
Robert 85
Samuel B. 81
Sarah C. 75

Rucker (cont.)
Silas N. 95
Rudd, Elijah 21
Herrod 23
Isaiah 14
Jas. B. 87
John 66
Mahala 57
Martha 29
Nancy 9
Pamelia 13
Parker 38
Sarah Jane 47
Sophrona 34
Wm. H. 75
Ruder, S. K. 20
Rue, Caroline 88
John 92
Rumedy, Sarah 44
Runnion, Nancy E. 88
Rush, Malinda 5
Syrus 5
Rusner, John 17
Russel, Lucinda 25
Russell, James S. 26
John 89
L. C. 89
Rutherford, A. H. 34
Alphy 46
Elizabeth A. 8
Fanny E. 61
James 6, 31
James M. 29
Joseph R. 59
Larkin B. 72
Lidia Ann 40
Mary J. 45
Randle 58
Robert A. 77
Sarah 16
William 15
William P. 58
Wm. 41
Wm. J. 39
Rutledge, George L. (see
Ratledge)
Jas. (see Ratledge)
Ryan, Samuel D. 55
Salle, Charity 13
Sallee, Amanda A. 79
Caroline 57
Eliza 45
Margaret 79
Sample, T. B. 83
Samples, John 51
Sampley, Wm. B. 83
Sampson, Josiah 94, 96
Samuel 9
Samson, Sarah Ann 13
Sanders, Arden 40
Clemmons 39
Elender J. 47
Elizabeth 11, 39
James 79
Thompson 5
Sane, Daniel 16
Sanndry, Mary Irene 50
Sarlin, John 28
Sattefield, Eliza 10
Saunders, Catherine 54
Says, Elizabeth 31
Scarborough, M. J.(?) 63
Wm. 31
Scarbrough, John H. 90
Wm. 78
Scheck, S. Fenley 67
Schell, E. W. (see Shell)
James (see Shell)

Scivils, Polly Ann 93
Scoggins, D. F. 41
Jackson (see Scroggins)
Scott, George W. 56
Joseph 13
Robert 3
Thomas C. 67
Scroggins, Jackson
(Scoggins) 53
Scruggs, Thomas 51
Seay, Jane 29
Nancy 2
Woodson 2
Secrest, Nancy Malinda 59
Seertman, Jane 64
Sehorn, Elizabeth 25
William 24
Seller, Harriet L. 95
Sellers, Harreitt L. 94
Harriett L. 94
J. W. 45
James M. 45
Joseph H. 91
Martha M. 57
Sarah I. 44
Selph, John A. 55
Senter, James P. 89
Luzireen 34
Polly 3
Susan 83
Sewel, Eliza 8
Sewell, George S. 84
Marcus E. L. 43
Oston 88
Sewells, Sipy T. 4
Sexton, James R. 2
Seybert, John 6
Shamblain, Sarah 83
Shamble, Catharine 2
Shamblin, Jane 74
William 3
Shapman, Jacob 1
Sharits, Mary 82
Mary J. 89
Sarah A. 82
Sharp, Addison 56
Eliza E. 29
Elizabeth 58
Jacob 47
Joseph 62
Robert 12
Robert P. 19
Samuel T. 46
Turner 70
Shaw, Mary Ann 70
Sheets, William 37
Shell, Benjamin 47
Charles 87
E. W. (Schell) 54
James (Schell) 21, 73
McKamy 63
Sarah 79
Shelton, Anna 8
Catharine 86
David T. 30
Elizabeth 61, 70
J. D. 16
Jackson 19
James W. 34
Jane 46
John E. 70
Larkin 81
Lucinda 22
Malinda 13
Mary 6
Nancy 90
Samuel 6
Sterling 22

Shelton (cont.)
Thomas 23
William 74
Shepheard, Betsey 1
Sherel, Ezekiel 90
Sherman, Thomas J. 69
Sherrell, Elizabeth 26
Ezekiel 74
Isaac 30
John B. 41
Sherrill, James 51
Sherrle, Benjamin C. 17
Shields, Banner 1
John 47
Margaret 3
Rebecca Jane 3
Rebeckah Jane 67
William 16
Shile, Vera 19
Shiphugh, Adam 13
Shipleigh, Adam 15
Shipley, Alexander 34
David F. 58
E. W. 91
Eliza 74
Elizabeth 41
John C. 83
M. J. 34
Martin J. 80
Martin V. 44
Mary 75
R. W. 86
Robert L. 46
Sterline 60
Thomas 46
William 32
Shoemaker, Calvin 70
John W. 86
Nancy 71
Noah 82
Reuhanna 19
William 58
Wm. 92, 95, 97
Shoerelt, Nancy Ann 65
Shook, Ann 47
Eliza 84
Elizabeth 54
Hetty 59
Lucy 86
Margaret 67
Mary 41
Mary Ann 88
Peter 33
Sarah 11
William, Jr. 49
Shulton, Rhoda 24
Shults, Elizabeth A. 28
Humphrey 57
Sarah S. 96
Shultz, Mary Ann 60
Shumake, Mary Ann 71
Shutz, Henry 53
Simons, Mary 85
Simpson, Henry M. 38, 70
Margaret 78
Wm. H. 76
Wm. M. 91
Sims, G. W. 33
John W. 74
Sisk, James 30
Sivels, A. 63
Jeptha 5
Polly 44
Sively, Abigale 55
Sivils, Mary Ann 29, 66
Sivley, Abigale 46
Slack, Abraham L. (see Luck)

Slacnere, Elizabeth 15
Slager, Christopher 9
Slater, Henry 42
Slaughter, Jacob W. 5
John 5
Melissa E. 68
Rebecca 5
Sliger, A. J. 96
Adam 55
Asa 83
Christopher 77
Francis M. 78
James E. 28
Joseph 36
Mary 69
Wyatt 83
Sloop, Caroline 52
Juletts 35
Malorina 58
Slover, W. H. 24
Small, Albert G. 51
James A. 21
Nelson 69
Wilson 29
Smallen, Solomon M. 17
Smart, A. J. 37
Archibald F. 30
Isaac 63
Nancy 16
William 18
Smedley, Elizabeth E. 3
John L. 94
Smider, A. R. (Snider) 47
Smith, A. 54
Arby H. 22
Asa 5
B. W. 32
Bluford 42
Boling 4
C. 54
C. J. 39
Dorcas C. 20
E. S. 73
Eli 17
Elijah 16
Eliza 31, 48, 90
Elizabeth 48
Elizabeth D. 42
Elizabeth Jane 47
Emeline 48
Hannah E. 94, 96
Harriet A. Delea 90
Hesekiah 65
Hugh 3
Israel C. 69
J. N. 75
James 2, 5
James A. 83
Jane L. 20
Jas. 65
Jas. D. 86
Jas. T. 36, 89
Jesse W. 73
John 22
John B. 59
John W. 13
Johnson 40
Jonathan D. 9
Jonathan T. 41
Joseph 2, 19, 33
Joseph H. 67
Julian 39
Laura P. 27
Leah 61
Letice W. 19
M. A. 96
Malinda 17

Smith (cont.)
Manerva 96
Margaret 21, 43
Margaret Ann 78
Marshall 76
Martha 9
Martha C. E. 92
Mary 39
Mary A. 23
Mary Ann 21
Mary B. 14
Mary Elizabeth 57
Mary M. 91
Mary M. M. 76
Mary T. 79
Matilda C. 71
Morris M. 31
Nancy 22
Nancy B. 30
Nancy Jane 59
Nancy M. 45
Nat. D. 11
Newton 48
Rachel 15
Russell H. 5
Salina J. 80
Samuel A. 41
Sarah 4, 19
Sarah A. 35
Sarah E. 81
Susan E. 93
Tennessee 95
Thomas H. 80
William H. 50
William P. 87
Willis 1
Wm. 49, 63
Wm. A. 47
Smithers, Thos. 86
Snider, A. R. (see Smider)
Andrew J. 77
M. C. 74
Peter 72
Robert M. 73
Snoddy, Geo. 75
Isbell 10
Mary J. 22
Nancy 75
Sarah C. 48
William 35
Snodgrass, Eleanor 31
Elizabeth 12
Thomas 11
Snow, Dolly 3
Southan, Aaron 28
Southard, Elizabeth 24
Emeline 31
Jackabena 30
James M. 68
John 24
William 12, 26
Sowell, Mary 72
Sower, Zany 26
Sparks, Celia D. 27
Elmira 19
John 30, 86
Lee 54
Spear, John 20
Spearman, Mary 49
Sarah 67, 67
Spearmon, Susan 66
Spencer, John 2
Spradlin, Mortimer 10
Spradling, Amanda 28
Richard, Sr. 31
Spriggs, Ezekiel 60
Stacecy, Sarrah E (Stacey) 92

117

Stacey, Sarrah E. (see
  Stacecy)
Stainer, Polly 55
Stallion, Matthew 35
Standefer, Elizabeth 70
Standifer, Jackson 61
  Martha J. 76
Staner, Peter 53
Stanfield, James 23
  Thomas 5
Stanner, Coonrod 3
Stansberry, Elizabeth 86
  Esther J. 35
  J. N. 79
  Jane 66
  L. L. 92
  Louisa 74
  Martha A. 89
  Mary Elizabeth 52
  Sarah Ann 56
Stansfield, Israel 80
Stanton, Abigail S. 82
  E. C. G. 35
  I. R. 92
Staples, Luzany F. 90
  W. H. 79
Starnes, Jacob K. 39
Starr, Nancy 3
Station, Martha 53
Stead, John 4
  Lucinda 31
Steed, Bettie 95
  Henry 14, 61
  Justus C. 31
  Mary 69
  Matilda 80
  Nancy L. 26
  Nancy M. 61
  P. C. 51
Stephen, David
  (Stephens) 2
  Sampson 7
Stephens, Allen 47
  G. W. 86
  George 72
  J. N. 80
  J. T. 92
  Margaret A. 26
  N. B. 78
  Polly 17
  Wm. A. 84
Stephenson, Andrew 84
  Anna 9
  Arminda 91
  D. D. 66
  James M. 66
  Martha 6
  Rachel 19
  Robert A. 71
  S. B. 71
  Susanah 7
  Synthia 58
  T. M. 91
  William 48
Sterns, Mary C. 43
Stewart, Mary 54
  Samuel 20
St. John, Catherine 23
  Mary E. 72
  Rebeckah O. 69
Stone, Carline 40
  Sarah 22
  William 27
  William G. 59
Stout, Abraham 1
  Alfred P. 43
  Ann 68
  Robert L. 57

Stowe, Solomon L., Jr.
  40
Strain, Martha J. 76
Stratton, E. 37
Stroud, Merrit B. 19
Strullin, Riley 86
Strutten, Dacus E. 88
Stuart, Margaret 62
  Richard 62
Stubblefield, Mary Ann 65
  Wm. H. 75
Stubbs, James M. 15
Stublefield, P. B. 64
Studdard, Elizabeth 67
  Hugh 17
  Nancy 78
  Thomas 61
Studdart, Elizabeth 75
Suddard, William 48
Sugart, Mary J. 91
Sullins, Mary L. 10
  Rebecca L. 55
Suntan, Mary M. 45
Suthard, M. M. 36
Sutton, John 5
Swaffer, Elizabeth M. 80
  Julia 66
Swafford, John 87
  Larkin F. 82
  Nancy 81
  S. 32
  Sarah J. 71
Swaford, Lucinda 65
Swagerty, Jackson 91
Swanford, Charity 12
  Polly 9
Swawford, James 11
Sweeney, Martin M. 77
Sweeny, John D. 33
  Jonathan H. 48
Swenney, Mary Ann F. 42
Swinboro, Zechiaria 20
Swinford, Elijah 60
  Isaac 33
  James 64
  Levi 58
  Mariah 57
  Sidney 81
Swinney, N. F. 81
Taber, Patience 2
Tabor, Polly 1
Taff, Frances A. 86
Tagris, Jell 38
Tallant, Lydia 70
Tally, Margaret 11
Tate, John 4
  Sarah 3
Taylor, Elizabeth 4
  James B. 37
  Stephen 53
  Susan 62
Teague, David 60
  Franklin C. 60
  John W. 96
Templeton, Caroline 39
  Dear Jane 41
  Emily 39
  Eve 89
  George 66
  Martha A. 48
  Matilda 3
  William B. 67
Tennell, John W. 8
Tenny, Isaac 20
Terry, Isabella 57
  Mary 30
  Sarah Ann 31
Tetters, Isaiah 18

Tewell, J. A. 86
Thalch, Eliza (see Thatch)
Thatch, Eliza (Thalch) 62
Thomas, Angeline 82
  Anna 10
  Caroline 75
  Joana 10
  John L. 53
  Louisa 54
  Maryann 47
  Nancy C. 56
  Samuel 35
  Samuel W. 33
Thomasson, Alfred 4
  John 2
Thompson, Amy 45
  Bryant 48
  C. S. 94
  Charles 22
  Elizabeth Ann 17
  H. M. 94, 95
  Isaac R. 30
  J. M. 95
  James 1, 6, 91
  James S. 3
  Jemimah 57
  John 50, 61
  John A. 3, 78
  L. C. 66
  Louisa 62
  M. A. E. 74
  Mary 22, 27
  Mary Ann 68
  Mathew 78
  Matthew 65
  Nancy 92
  R. R. 81
  Rachel 21, 56
  Rebecca 83
  Samuel H. 59
  Sarah 59, 60
  Sarah J. 84
  Thos. J. 78
  Uriah 33
  William 35, 46
  Wm. Z. 18
Thornhill, Rachel M. 85
Thornton, Mariah 53
  Mary 17
  Mildred A. 27
  Sarah A. 21
  Virginia F. 63
Thurman, Nancy 94
  Peter 74
Tinney, Isaac 45
Tinsley, Lucinda 2
Tipton, William B. 63
Tira, Juliann 89
Tompkins, Libbie J. 95
Tomson, Elizabeth 89
Toomey, Daniel A. 31
  T. L. 89
Torbalt, Rachel 1
Torbet, John O. 13
Torbett, E. S. 40
  Mary Ann 61
Tortner, William 16
Townsend, Lotty 37
  Thomas 41
  William C. 10
Townsley, Annalize 10
Trew, Eliza 19
  George W. 58
  John M. 27
  Mary Ann 27
  Warren 14
Tribbue, Jacob 51
Trim, Emeline C. 14

Weatherly (cont.)
William 13
Weathers, George 3
Weathery, Patsy 85
Weaver, Alfred G. 12
George W. 74
Weavers, Polly 3
Webb, H. 82
Hiram 59˚
John 33
Katherine 16
Wm. 82
Weddows, Jabez 25
Weeks, David 44
Hiram 46
Weir, David 62
John 71
Welch, Serbrenny Vandary
65
Welcher, Benjamin F. 27
Wellem, Berryman 65
Wells, Arvetzena 83
Benjamin 25
Diabah 70
Jane 52
Julia Amanda 52
Mary J. 90
Robt. H. 96
Sarah F. 86
Wengewood, Jane 32
Wesham, Sarah 54
Wessengton(?), Mary 6
West, Archibald 66
E. S. 75
Elizabeth 50
Francis M. 76
Hannah (Mrs.) 31
James H. 45
Margaret Jane 49
Mary 16
Mary Jane 85
Polly 21
Thos. P. 97
Wetherly, Eveline 73
Whaley, C. W. 42
Ira 82
Joseph L. 42
Malinda 24
Sarah 88
Thomas F. 54
Wheeler, Margaret 74
Saml. 5
Sarah 58
Wheselle, P. K. 81
Whit(?), Jas. T. 87
White, Daniel 36
Edmund 77
Elisha 16
Elizabeth 11, 91
James M. 30
Jesse 17
John 42, 79
John H. 81
Lucinda 21
Mary 37
Nancessa 31
Thos. R. 89
William 39
Wm. 49
Whitlock, Wm. 90
Whitsell, Lucy 90
Whitten, George 81
Marinda 71
Polly 72
Wiate, H. J. 35
Widows, Isaac 57
Wight, Mariah 39
Wiginton, John 9

Wiles, Alexander 4
Wilkens, Charley T. 63
Wilkerson, Lawson H. 24
Wilkinson, Elias 24
Willett, Thomas G. 4
Willhite, Cintha P. 84
Joseph 22
Williams, Amy 93
Armena 50
Colvin 26
E. W. 66
Elijah 89
Elisha 66
Frederick S. 5
Granville 83
Henry 20, 24
J. H. 87
James 2, 44
Jane 73
John E. 48
Madison 29
Martha J. 74
Mary E. 79
Noah 39
Sarah 88
Thomas 21
W. H. 54
Willing, Sarah 45
Willis, John 68
Sarah 20
William T. 62
William V. 13
Willson, James G. 48
Wilson, Armstead F. 65
Catherine J. 32
Clarissa 68
David A. 43
David M. 82
Dealtha R. 73
Dicy 26
Effee N. 82
Emaline 28
Frances Jane 50
Franklin 25
George W. 65
Isaac M. 63
J. F. 84
Jackson C. 50
James 32
James E. 72
James N. 28
James W. 2
Jane 58
John 2
John E. T. 53
Josephine 61
Joshua B. 63
Lemgra 48
Margaret A. 60
Margaret E. 84
Martha 13, 20
Martha C. 32
Martha J. 66
Mary 14, 28, 88
Mary Ann 74
Mary T. 49
Nancy 36
Nancy A. 87
Patrick W. 58
R. J. 89
Raphael 88
Saphrona Adaline 51
Sarah 55, 67
Wilbern 62
Wm. 39
Wimberly, Jacob 27
Wingo, Jane C. 80
Winsant, James 41

Winsch, John Karl 44
Winston, Holoway T. 86
Winters, Nancy A. 86
Wiseman, Dorcas 3
Witt, James H. 5
Margaret A. 95
Martha 97
Mary 19
Rufus 49
Rutherford 5
Sarah J. 79
Silas 77
Witte, Wm. C. 79
Wolf, Amanda C. 55
Arrena 79
Charles 80
Mary 91
Wolff, Elizabeth 47
Joseph 27
Wolffe, Martha 76
Womack, Daniel 41
Gemima 62
Jacob 54
Mary 60
Narcissa 84
Polly Ann 50
Prudence 30
Sarah 84
William 73
Wommack, Jemima 80
Mary 75
Nancy A. 83
Wood, John 20
John H. 92
Matilda 15
Woodall, Matilda 35
Wooddall, William 43
Woodey, John 90
Woods, Andrew 83
Clement 8
Elizabeth J. 86
Johnson 23
Keziah 33
Matilda 9
Woodward, A. 10
Woody, Elizabeth Ann 38
Sarah 89
Woolsey, John 94
Wooten, John R. 10
Wordon, Eliza 33
Workman, John M. 40
Martha Ann 40
Samuel 79
Sarah E. 32
Worley, John H. 63
Matilda 23
William 11
Worsay, Sarah 26
Worthy, Thomas 49, 52
Wray, Sarah 29
Wright, Elizabeth 23
Hannah E. 47
Isaac G. 20
James C. 17
John H. 51
John M. 42
Nancy 68
Robert 19
Thomas B. 61
Willis 44
Wm. R. 33
Wyatt, Catharine 63
William 24
Wyrick, Katharine 50
William 33
Yadle, Joseph 82
Yancy, Winny 26
Yearwood, J. M. 96

Yearwood (cont.)
  J. N. 94
  James M. 80
  Martha J. 63
  Nancy 8
  Sarah D. 39
Yokum, F. L. 22
York, John J. 30
  Uriah L. 90
Young, Bedience 51
  Charlotte 13, 16
  Jane 49
  Jeremiah 46
  John 57

Young (cont.)
  John H. 39
  Margaret 46
  Martha C. 50
  Mary Jane 50
  Nancy 51
  Nancy A. 19
  Thomas T. 37
  William F. 46
  Wm. 81
Yount, Catharine 70
  Daniel 1
  John 49

Yount (cont.)
  Louisa Jane 62
  Mary M. C. 78
Zargles, Michael 7
Zegler, Joseph A. 40
Zeigler, Benj. T. 11
  C. M. 75
  Catharine 77
  Jacob 92, 97
  Joram R. 70
  Martha 95
  Tubeller 66
Zeyler, Lucinda A. 10

ADDENDA

Jack, Caroline 70   Jack, Francis B. 95   Neil, William R. 30
  Emeline 71

www.ingramcontent.com/pod-product-compliance
Lightning Source LLC
Chambersburg PA
CBHW070926270326
41927CB00011B/2742